W9-AZY-557

CHRISTIANS WILL GO THROUGH THE TRIBULATION
And how to prepare for it

PRESENTED TO: _____

ON: _____

MESSAGE: _____

_____

_____

_____

_____

_____

_____

_____

_____

PRESENTED BY: _____

"About the Time of the End,
a body of men will be raised up
who will turn their attention to the Prophecies,
and insist upon their literal interpretation,
in the midst of much clamor and opposition."

—Sir Isaac Newton

CHRISTIANS WILL GO THROUGH THE TRIBULATION

And how to prepare for it.

by Jim McKeever

Omega Publications
P.O. Box 4130
Medford, Oregon 97501

CHRISTIANS WILL GO THROUGH THE TRIBULATION
And how to prepare for it

Copyright © 1978 by James M. McKeever

Omega Publications
P.O. Box 4130
Medford, Oregon 97501

Printed in the United States of America
First printing — May, 1978
Second printing — December, 1978
Revised third printing — June, 1979
Fourth printing — November, 1979
Fifth printing — March, 1980
Revised sixth printing — August, 1980

Library of Congress Catalog Card Number 78-55091

ISBN 0-931608-01-5 (Hardbound)
ISBN 0-931608-02-3 (Softbound)

"*I have been in countries where the saints are already suffering terrible persecution. In China the Christians were told, 'Don't worry, before the tribulation comes, you will be translated—raptured.' Then came a terrible persecution. Millions of Christians were tortured to death. Later I heard a Bishop from China say, sadly, 'We have failed. We should have made the people strong for persecution rather than telling them Jesus would come first.'*

"*Turning to me he said, 'You still have time. Tell the people how to be strong in times of persecution, how to stand when the tribulation comes—to stand and not faint.'*

"*I feel I have a divine mandate to go and tell the people of this world that it is possible to be strong in the Lord Jesus Christ. We are in training for the tribulation. . . .*

"*Since I have gone already through prison for Jesus sake, and since I met that bishop from China, now every time I read a good Bible text I think 'Hey, I can use that in the time of tribulation.' Then I write it down and learn it by heart.*"

—*Corrie ten Boom*

This book is dedicated first and foremost to the
glory of God.

On the human level, this book is dedicated to
my precious and wonderful wife, Jeani.

TABLE OF CONTENTS

DETAILED OUTLINE

AND INDEX

ACKNOWLEDGEMENTS

There are so many people that I am grateful to for their contributions to my spiritual growth and insights, some of which are reflected in this book. I can never possibly name them all, but am particularly indebted to Dr. Bill Bright, Dr. W. A. Criswell, Dr. Billy Graham, Jerry Hassell and the late Dawson Trotman. I appreciate very much the efforts of Dr. Carlton Booth, Ric Durfield, Ed Gruman, Jack Gustafson, R. E. Mc-Master, Gerald Oliver, Bob Owen, Gary Vanlandingham and Stacy Wood, who reviewed all or parts of this manuscript and gave me invaluable feedback.

I would also like to thank all of the publishers and authors who have given us permission to quote from their books. We have not stated this with each of the many references, but their quotes are used with permission, since they are copyright material. There is not a book mentioned in this volume that I would hesitate to recommend purchasing and reading. We have tried to give enough information — the publisher and frequently the publisher's address as well — so that the books can be ordered directly or from your local book store. I am especially appreciative of The Lockman Foundation, copyright holders of the *New American Standard Bible,* for their permission to quote extensively from this excellent translation.

More than anyone else, however, my wife Jeani is responsible for the existence of this book. Not only did she perform the usual loving functions of a writer's wife, such as providing gentle encouragement and inspiration, but she also served efficiently as editor, proofreader, contributor of ideas, critic and best friend. I praise the Lord for her and her invaluable contribution to this volume. I cannot imagine a more perfect collaborator. I salute her with my whole heart.

Jim McKeever
P.O. Box 4130
Medford, Oregon 97501

INTRODUCTION

I have always disliked long introductions to books, so I will try to make this one as brief as possible.

First and foremost, I must clearly state that this book is written to those individuals who know for sure that Jesus Christ is their Savior. It doesn't matter if they are Catholic, Protestant, or of some other faith, as long as they acknowledge that Jesus Christ is the Son of God and that the way to Heaven is through Him.

If you are not absolutely certain that you have received Christ as your personal Savior, I would like to ask you to stop now and read Appendix A on page 321, which discusses how to become a Christian. The things that we will be discussing in this volume will have very little meaning for you unless you have first made this all important step of accepting Christ as your Savior and Master.

Most Christians have only heard about a pre-Tribulation Rapture. Most of them probably believe in it because they have not heard a viable alternative presented intelligently. This volume is designed to briefly present the case for the post-Tribulation Rapture so that Christians who find themselves in this position will have an opportunity to examine an alternative.

For the readers of this volume who do (or will) then embrace the view that Christians will go through the Tribulation, this book also gives very practical suggestions on how to prepare for the catastrophes that Christians will be experiencing during the Tribulation. I deal with both physical preparation and the even more important spiritual preparation. I also discuss how to obtain the supernatural power needed in order to go through the great Tribulation victoriously.

In previous times of trial, God did not remove his people from the trial, but allowed them to go through it and gave them victory over the circumstances. The Old Testament records many such episodes—Daniel in the lion's den, the three Hebrew men in the fiery furnace, and the children of Israel during the plagues that hit Pharoah and Egypt. In each case God did not take His people out of the situation, but gave them victory as they went through it; they were unharmed by the trial that they were in. It is very possible that in a similar way God will have Christians go through the Tribulation in a victorious and unscathed manner.

In a nutshell, the purpose of this book is:

1. To alert Christians of the likelihood that they are going through the Tribulation.

2. To give practical suggestions as to *how* to prepare for that experience.

May the Lord bless you as you read this volume.

Jim McKeever

PART 1

THE CRUCIAL QUESTION

". . . they received the word with great eagerness,
examining the Scriptures daily,
to see whether these things were so.
Many of them therefore believed . . ."

—Luke

1

THE RAPTURE OF BELIEVERS —

When will it happen?

Recently I was the speaker at a typical meeting of Evangelical Christians. There were men, women, and youths who knew Jesus Christ as their personal Savior and loved Him. They knew the Word of God fairly well. I read to these precious people the following verses from Matthew 24 (unless otherwise noted, I will be quoting from the *New American Standard Bible,* copyright by The Lockman Foundation, quotations used by permission):

40 "Then there shall be two men in the field; one will be taken, and one will be left.

41 "Two women *will* be grinding at the mill; one will be taken, and one will be left.

As you can see, these verses deal with two people doing everyday things; one of them is taken away or caught up, and the other is left. I asked this group of born-again Christians to raise their hands if they thought this Scripture was talking about the Rapture, and that the people taken away were the Christians, and the ones left behind were the non-Christians.

How many hands do you think were raised? None, a few, many? It was 100 percent; every single hand was raised!

Since you, dear reader, and I will be getting to know each other quite well throughout these coming pages, I might also

ask you the same question. Do you think this passage is referring to the Rapture of the believers and their being caught up in
the air to meet the Lord? You need not raise your hand, of
course. You might simply say an internal "yes" or "no."

Where Will They Be Taken?

I then had this group of Bible-believing people turn to
Luke 17 and we read the following verses:

> **34** "I tell you, on that night there will be two men in one bed;
> one will be taken, and the other will be left.
> **35** "There will be two women grinding at the same place; one will
> be taken, and the other will be left.
> **36** ["Two men will be in the field; one will be taken and the other
> will be left."]
> **37** And answering they said to Him, "Where, Lord?" And He said
> to them, "Where the body *is*, there also will the vultures be gathered."

I also had someone in the group read verse 37 out of *The
Living Bible* (copyright 1971 by Tyndale House Publishers,
Wheaton, Illinois), and here is what he read:

> **37** "Lord, where will they be taken?" the disciples asked. Jesus
> replied, "Where the body is, the vultures gather!"

This is the passage from Matthew, as recorded in the Gospel
of Luke. However, after stating that in each of these cases one
person would be taken away and the other left, Luke records
the fact that the disciples then asked Jesus where the people
that are taken would go. Christ's reply was that they would be
taken to the place where there are corpses and carcasses—where
the vultures gather. (The *King James Version* and the *Revised
Standard Version* incorrectly translate "vultures" as "eagles.")
These people are going to be taken to the land of the dead. That
means that this could not be talking about Christians being
caught up in the air to meet Jesus, and yet I have seen this
taught by Christian leaders, and believed by many Christians,
as a Scripture dealing with the Rapture. What many of these
Christians do not realize is that numerous leading proponents
of the pre-Tribulation Rapture (the Rapture occurring before

the Tribulation) do not believe that this passage deals with the Rapture.

Dr. John F. Walvoord, president of Dallas Theological Seminary, deals with the subject in his book, *The Blessed Hope and the Tribulation* (published by Zondervan Publishing House, Grand Rapids, Michigan 49506). On pages 89 and 90 he says:

"An argument advanced by Alexander Reese and adopted by Gundry is that the references in Matthew 24:40, 41 should be interpreted as referring to the Rapture. These verses state, 'Then shall two be in the field; the one shall be taken, and the other left. Two women shall be grinding at the mill; the one shall be taken and the other left.' . . .

"Claiming that those taken in verses 40 and 41 are taken away in the Rapture, Gundry in discussing the parallel passage in Luke 17:34-37 ignores verse 37. There two are pictured in the same bed, with one taken and the other left. Two are grinding together, and one is taken and the other left. Two are in the field, one is taken and the other left. Then, in verse 37, the question is asked, 'Where, Lord?' The answer is very dramatic: 'And He said unto them, Wherever the body is, there will the eagles be gathered together.' It should be very clear that the ones taken are put to death and their bodies are consumed by the vultures. If the ones taken are killed, then verses 40, 41 of Matthew 24 speak of precisely the same kind of judgment as occurred in the flood where the ones taken were taken in judgment. Matthew 24 is just the reverse of the Rapture, not the Rapture itself."

As can be seen in this quote, Dr. Walvoord—a well known proponent of the pre-Tribulation Rapture theory—clearly believes that this passage in Matthew 24, which deals with some people being taken and others being left, does not refer to the Rapture.

Perhaps at this point you are a little confused as to what you really do and should believe. There are possibly many such misconceptions that are held by Christians today. I will try to help clear up some of them before the end of this book.

WHAT IS THE RAPTURE OF THE CHURCH?

You might say to me: "Slow down, Jim. You've started off in high gear and I'm way back at the corner stop sign. I'm not even sure that I'm clear on what the 'Rapture' is. What is it and where is it found in the Bible?"

If you are in that position, please forgive me; we'll go back and start at the beginning. The word "Rapture" is not found in the Bible. It is a term that has been coined by theologians to label an event that will take place in the future when Christians (those who have received Jesus Christ as their Savior) will be caught up in the air to meet Christ. The Christians who have died will be caught up first, followed by the ones who are still alive.

The Scripture that best describes this event is in 1 Thessalonians 4 where Paul writes:

> **16 For the Lord Himself will descend from heaven with a shout, with the voice of *the* archangel, and with the trumpet of God; and the dead in Christ shall rise first.**
>
> **17 Then we who are alive and remain shall be caught up together with them in the clouds to meet the Lord in the air, and thus we shall always be with the Lord.**

I definitely feel that this event will occur, and as prophesied here in 1 Thessalonians. However, a key and very critical question comes as to *WHEN* it will occur. We will see later why this question is so crucial.

Many Evangelical leaders, teachers, and writers today teach that this Rapture will occur at the beginning of the seven-year Tribulation period, and in fact will be the event with which the Tribulation starts. I've read many books, by such men, which depict the world going about its everyday affairs with the Rapture suddenly occurring. Since Christian pilots, bus and automobile drivers would all immediately disappear, there would be airplane crashes and freeway pileups. This, compounded by the disappearance of Christians in many critical situations—such as Christian surgeons in the middle of operations—would create a totally disastrous situation.

These Christian brothers teach that once the Rapture has occurred, and all of the Christians have been removed from the earth, then the great Tribulation will begin. I would like to suggest that the *timing* of the Rapture is still very much in question. Many outstanding Christian leaders today believe that it will occur at the end of the Tribulation and others believe that it will occur during the middle of the Tribulation.

WHY THE QUESTION OF "WHEN" IS SO CRUCIAL

The answer that you come up with as to *WHEN* the Rapture will occur is so important that it will affect almost every decision you make: where you live, what skills you develop, what vocation you enter, how hard you pursue God, how righteously you live, and so on.

In Revelation we see that during the Tribulation there will be famine to such a degree that 100 percent of a man's salary will have to be used to purchase food. If a Christian believed that he might well experience this, there are certain preparations that he might make. However, if he believed that he were not going to experience it, he would likely make no preparation whatsoever.

Revelation also says that Christians will not be able to buy and sell in the world's economic system. This means that they will have to live in a self-supporting manner. They will need to have skills or goods that they can barter for items needed by them and their loved ones. If a Christian felt that a day were coming when he could no longer buy and sell, again there would be many preparations that he would make (possibly moving to a farm, for example). If he felt that he were not going to experience this, he would be making no preparation.

It is predicted in Revelation that during the Tribulation there will be a tremendous persecution of Christians. If a Christian suspected strongly that he would be subject to that kind of persecution, there would certainly be much that he would do in preparation.

Do you begin to see why the question of *WHEN* the Rapture will occur is so important? It could affect your entire life! What you decide to believe concerning this question could determine how you respond to God regarding some very practical things that He may be leading you to do.

The most popular theory around today is that the Rapture will occur just before the Tribulation begins. I would encourage those who teach this theory to reexamine their position. If in the end they are found to be wrong, they may have lulled other Christians to sleep by telling them that they need not worry nor prepare, because they would not experience the Tribulation. Obviously this is a nice theory to teach. Christians will gladly receive it. Anyone would rather anticipate being joyously with Jesus instead of on the earth while it is experiencing one gigantic catastrophe after another. If you are one of these Christian leaders or one of their followers, I would beg you to examine this question *FOR YOURSELF.* Do not rely on what others (including myself) say. Use an open Bible and have an open heart, and God will show you the truth.

Not a Theological Debate

This book is not meant to present an airtight theological argument. I will leave that for the scholars and professors of theology. I'm also not attempting to teach anyone anything. Only the Holy Spirit of God can teach a Christian in a way such that the teaching becomes integrated into his heart and life. I feel that the Holy Spirit has led me to write this book to share what God has shown me concerning these things.

I would ask you to pause right now and pray. Ask God to give you an open heart and to teach you by the Holy Spirit. Ask Him to make real to your heart anything contained in this book that is truth, and to shield you from anything that is not truth.

I'm confident that, if you have an open heart, the Lord will lead you into His truths. On the other hand, if you think that you have all of the answers, that you know all about the Rapture, the Tribulation and prophecy, and your mind is closed, then God can not teach you. The first requisites for growth as a Christian are a heart and mind open to the Spirit of God.

A PERPLEXED NEW CHRISTIAN

I received Christ as my personal Savior in 1952, about halfway through college. I was attending Southern Methodist University (SMU) in Dallas, Texas. Many of the Christians that I met, as a baby Christian, wanted to tell me what I should believe about a whole host of subjects, including the Rapture and the Tribulation. I told them all to go away for I wanted to read the source document first. I hibernated with the Bible and read it all the way through. After this I asked these people what they believed. They began to tell me, and at times I had a great deal of difficulty reconciling what they were telling me with what the Bible said.

One of the things that particularly disturbed me was this Rapture business. They had Christ coming back halfway to the earth, stopping in the air, Christians going up to meet him, and then all of them going back to heaven. This was at the beginning of the Tribulation. Christ would then be coming back in power and glory at the end of the Tribulation to defeat all of the armies of the world and the Antichrist. When they would talk about the "Second Coming of Christ" I never knew which one they were talking about. Were these two actually a "Second" and a " Third Coming" of Christ? Instead, perhaps we should count the Rapture as one and a half and the appearance at the end of the Tribulation as number two. As you can probably tell, I was somewhat befuddled.

Another thing that perplexed me was Matthew 24. There I read:

> 1 And Jesus came out from the temple and was going away when His disciples came up to point out the temple buildings to Him.
> 2 And He answered and said to them, "Do you not see all these things? Truly I say to you, not one stone here shall be left upon another, which will not be torn down."
> 3 And as He was sitting on the Mount of Olives, the disciples came to Him privately, saying, "Tell us, when will these things be, and what *will* be the sign of Your coming, and of the end of the age?"

The disciples asked Jesus a straightforward question about His return and the end of the world. In my mind, there was no reason that He should do anything but tell them what was going to happen in a chronological sequence. It seemed that He began to do this, for I read on:

> 7 "For nation will rise against nation, and kingdom against kingdom, and in various places there will be famines and earthquakes.
> 8 "But all these things are *merely* the beginning of birth pangs.
> 9 "Then they will deliver you up to tribulation, and will kill you, and you will be hated by all nations on account of My name.

10 "And at that time many will fall away and will betray one another and hate one another.

11 "And many false prophets will arise, and will mislead many.

We see that there will be wars, earthquakes, famines, and persecution and that these are just the beginning of the sorrows to come. I read further in Matthew 24 about what Jesus said was going to occur next:

16 then let those who are in Judea flee to the mountains;

17 let him who is on the housetop not go down to get the things out that are in his house;

18 and let him who is in the field not turn back to get his cloak.

19 "But woe to those who are with child and to those who nurse babes in those days!

20 "But pray that your flight may not be in the winter, or on a Sabbath;

21 for then there will be a great tribulation, such as has not occurred since the beginning of the world until now, nor ever shall.

22 "And unless those days had been cut short, no life would have been saved; but for the sake of the elect those days shall be cut short.

Here we see the beginning of the Tribulation, to the extent that Jesus said the people would flee to the mountains. He continued by telling about the end of the Tribulation:

29 "But immediately after the tribulation of those days THE SUN WILL BE DARKENED, AND THE MOON WILL NOT GIVE ITS LIGHT, AND THE STARS WILL FALL from the sky, and the POWERS OF THE HEAVENS WILL BE SHAKEN,

30 and then the sign of the Son of Man will appear in the sky, and then all the tribes of the earth will mourn, and they will see the SON OF MAN COMING ON THE CLOUDS OF THE SKY with power and great glory.

31 "And He will send forth His angels WITH A GREAT TRUMPET and THEY WILL GATHER TOGETHER His elect FROM THE FOUR WINDS, FROM ONE END OF THE SKY TO THE OTHER.

As we can see, here Jesus will be coming in power and glory, there will be the sound of a great trumpet and His angels will gather together the Christians (the elect) from all over the earth. But back in verse 29 He said this would occur *immediately after* the Tribulation.

At that point, early in my life with Christ, I felt that verses 40 and 41 were talking about the Rapture:

40 "Then there shall be two men in the field; one will be taken, and one will be left.
41 "Two women *will* **be grinding at the mill; one will be taken, and one will be left.**

If these verses or even verse 31 was talking about the Rapture, then the whole chronology of the chapter was all messed up. I would have needed to cut out these verses and put them before verse 21. I knew in my heart that this wasn't correct, because I believed that Christ had told it in chronological order. All I could do was remain perplexed.

Another point of confusion for me was the fact that I did not see the Rapture of the Church, at the beginning of the Tribulation, in the book of Revelation. The book of Revelation deals with this whole period. In my mind, if an event as gigantically important as the Rapture of the Church occurred at the beginning of the Tribulation, it would have to be included in the book of Revelation. Some people tried to tell me that John being caught up into heaven was symbolic of the Rapture of the Church, but I had a hard time swallowing that.

In any case, because I was quite a new Christian and did not have an answer for all these perplexities, I embraced the belief in a pre-Tribulation Rapture for the first several years of my Christian life. I did this not because I was comfortable with it, but because it was the only semi-logical scheme of things that had been presented to me.

HOW GOD CHANGED MY THINKING

During the first ten years of my Christian life, many times I prayed asking God what the truth was concerning these things. I was open and honest with Him; I confessed that I wasn't comfortable with the Rapture at the beginning of the Tribulation, but didn't really know what else to believe. I prayed this prayer consistently through those first ten years.

Finally, God brought me to a man who was an engineer, had a logical mind, and was a very dedicated Christian. I asked him how he reconciled all of the difficulties about the Rapture that I outlined to him. When the Bible talked about the Second Coming of Christ, I asked him how he knew which one it was referring to. I shared with him the difficulties I had with Matthew 24 being out of sequence and so forth.

God led him to say one sentence to me. He said, "Jim, go back and reread all the Scriptures, considering it *AN EVENT* rather than *TWO EVENTS.*" After talking with him I could hardly wait to get home to my Bible. With great enthusiasm, I reread the portions in Matthew, Luke, and Thessalonians that deal with the end times, and reread the entire book of Revelation. Considering the Second Coming of Christ and the Rapture as *A SINGLE EVENT* made everything fall into place; the confusion was gone! My heart shouted a gigantic *PRAISE THE LORD!* After ten years of searching He had given me the answer. It became obvious to me that night that this *SINGLE EVENT* had to occur at the *end* of the Tribulation. Even though God was to later show me a much more solid Biblical basis for believing this, at that time I received by faith what He said to me by His Spirit.

Formerly, I had believed that Christ would come down from heaven partway to the earth and stop in the sky, without touching the earth. The dead Christians would rise first to meet Him in the air, followed by the Christians who were still alive. These Christians would return to heaven with Christ, and remain there while the earth experienced seven years of tribulation. At the end of the seven years, Christ, accompanied by the sound of a trumpet, would return to the earth in power and glory with his heavenly army, and would defeat the armies of the world in the Battle of Armageddon. Christ would then set up reign on the earth for one thousand years.

After God revealed to me that there was only *ONE* second return of Christ, rather than two, I began to realize that the Tribulation would begin without the tremendous fanfare of the Rapture of Christian believers. In fact, I do not believe that once we are in the Tribulation we will be able to look back and pinpoint the day on which it started. I believe the beginning will be gradual. Things will progressively worsen. At the end of the seven years, I now believe that Christ will start toward earth in power and glory, followed by His heavenly army. As He breaks down through the clouds, the trumpet will sound and the dead Christians will rise into the air, followed by the Christians still living. Immediately all of these Christians will be transformed and become part of his heavenly army. The Christians thus will return to the earth at that time, with Christ, to participate in the defeat of the armies of the world and the Antichrist. After this last great battle, Armageddon, the Millennial reign of Christ will begin.

MEETING THE LORD IN THE AIR

This concept of the Christians going up to meet the Lord in the air, and then reversing their direction to come back to the earth with Him, may be new to some people. In my research, however, I discovered that this is exactly what the word "meet" means, as is used in 1 Thessalonians 4:17 (where it says we will "meet" the Lord in the air). The Greek word for "meet" used here is "apantesis." This Greek word is only used in three places in the New Testament. Arthur D. Katterjohn, Associate Professor at Wheaton College, very beautifully affirms this on page 45 of his book, *The Tribulation People* (copyright 1975 by Creation House, Carol Stream, Illinois):

"Another pretribulation distinctive is associated with the word 'meet.' It teaches that when we have met the Lord in the air, He will reverse direction, lead us back to heaven, and there we will pass the seven-year period in which tribulation racks the earth. Does the word 'meet' mean to change direction and return along the path just traveled? It is used only three times in Scripture: Matthew 25:6, Acts 28:15, and here. (1 Thessalonians 4:17)

"In the first instance, Jesus uses the word to describe the meeting of the five virgins and the bridegroom in the parable we already have discussed. Notice that the bridegroom comes, meets the virgins, and continues on to the wedding feast. He does not change direction; his destination is forward and so he proceeds. The meeting is called 'the hour wherein the Son of man comes,' joining this parable with the second coming and the consummation of the age.

"In Acts 28, the second instance, Paul is traveling toward Rome. Christian brothers were alerted to his arrival, and came as far as the Three Taverns to meet him. From that point, the delegation accompanied Paul to the Imperial city, much encouraged by the exchange of fellowship. Paul approaches, is met, and continues on.

"If the word 'meet' in 1 Thessalonians 4:17 has essentially the same meaning as in the other two occurrences, then we get a picture of Christ descending to the earth, being met by His people in the air, and continuing down to set right the heresies of the tribulation. The saints, and not Christ, reverse direction. The Captain of the hosts does not retreat on His way to victory. He continues on."

It is interesting to note that, in my early days as a Christian, maybe 10 percent of the people believed Christians would go through the Tribulation and about 90 percent believed they would be "Raptured out" before the Tribulation, and not experience it. Today, as I travel all over the world, I would say that the percentages have changed; about 60 percent of the people now believe that Christians will go through the Tribulation, and only about 40 percent believe that they will be "Raptured out" beforehand. The change in this belief is due purely to the Holy Spirit's teaching in individual hearts. I know of no widely-known teachers or well-known books that advocate this point of view. I've found it in the Orient, Latin America, Europe —everywhere I go there is definitely a move towards Christians believing that they will go through the Tribulation.

However, this is not a reason for you to change your belief. The Holy Spirit of God must show you personally. Perhaps He will use some of the Scriptures in the next chapter to help in this process. I know you will continue to pray and be open to whatever the Holy Spirit has to say to you.

2

IS THERE A BIBLICAL BASIS

FOR BELIEVING THAT . . .

Christians will go through

the Tribulation?

Before turning to the Scriptures to examine a Biblical basis for believing that Christians will go through the Tribulation, and that the Rapture will occur at the end of it, we need to examine the definitions of two words. These words are "first" and "last."

FIRST—According to the dictionary, the word "first" means "preceding all others in time." In other words, there are no others before it, or it wouldn't be the first.

LAST—The word "last," according to the dictionary, means "following all others." There are none after it, or it wouldn't be the last.

I in no way want to insult your intelligence by belaboring these simple definitions, but they are very important to the concepts that we will be discussing in this chapter. So, as we proceed, let us remember that if something is the "first" there could not have been anything before it, and if something is the "last" there could not be anything else after it.

Now let us turn our attention, prayerfully, to St. Paul's first letter to the church at Corinth. From 1 Corinthians 15 we read:

> **50** Now I say this, brethren, that flesh and blood cannot inherit the kingdom of God; nor does the perishable inherit the imperishable.
>
> **51** Behold, I tell you a mystery; we shall not all sleep, but we shall all be changed,
>
> **52** in a moment, in the twinkling of an eye, at the last trumpet; for the trumpet will sound, and the dead will be raised imperishable, and we shall all be changed.

Verse 51 tells us that we will not all sleep (die), but that we will all be changed, and verse 52 amplifies on this by saying that this change will take place in a split second—in the twinkling of an eye. It also states that the dead will be raised at that time. The important part of the Rapture is not the catching up into the air, but that we will be changed, from physical bodies in the physical realm to resurrected bodies in a higher realm.

A significant thing is that verse 52 tells us *WHEN* all of this will occur, and that is "at the *LAST* trumpet."

Remembering the definition of "last," this means that there will not be any more trumpets after the one referred to here. The trumpet that causes the dead to rise and us to be changed in the twinkling of an eye *will be* the *LAST* trumpet. It would then seem reasonable to turn to the book of Revelation to find out something about this "last" trumpet.

THE FINAL SEVEN TRUMPETS

Before considering the final seven trumpets, we need to look at Chapter 5 of Revelation which talks about a scroll sealed with seven seals. We see that there was great sadness because no one was worthy to open the seals of this scroll. Finally, the Lamb of God took the scroll to open the seven seals and there was tremendous rejoicing in heaven.

In order to understand a little about this scroll and the seals, we should examine the use of scrolls in the first century. It was very common for someone to write a letter on a scroll to high officials and such. The writer would roll up the scroll so that the letter was covered and seal it at that point. He would then write a note to perhaps the high official's secretary, instructing that person to hold it for his return, track him down, or whatever. The writer would then roll the scroll past that note and place a second seal there. He might also write a note to the door keeper, telling him to promptly deliver the scroll to the secretary, and then roll up the remainder and seal it again. When the scroll was delivered, whoever was authorized or "worthy" to open the first seal would break it open, unroll the scroll just to the second seal and read what instructions there were. In this case, it would be to give the scroll unopened beyond that point to the high official's secretary. The secretary would open the second seal, unroll it to the third seal and read his instructions. Presumably he was then to give the rest of the scroll, with the third seal intact, to the high official.

The door keeper would not have dared to open the second seal because he was not "worthy" in position or rank to legitimately do this. It is because of this that there was sadness in heaven; no one was worthy to open any of the seals that secured the scroll containing the events of the end of this age. Only Jesus Christ, the Lamb of God, was worthy to break these open.

Chapter 6 of Revelation deals with the opening of the first six seals. I believe we can envisage, without detracting from the Holy Scriptures, that after one seal was opened the scroll was unrolled to the second seal and the things contained there were executed on the earth. When the second seal was opened and the scroll was unrolled to the third seal, the things written in that portion were accomplished on the earth. These first six seals are dealt with in a matter of a few verses each, although the consequences on the earth are tremendous and extremely significant. Later in this book we will be looking more closely at what occurred during the breaking of these seals.

However, the seventh seal is in a category all of its own. It is very complex and several chapters in Revelation are devoted to it. In Revelation 8 we read:

> 1 And when He broke the seventh seal, there was silence in heaven for about half an hour.
>
> 2 And I saw the seven angels who stand before God; and seven trumpets were given to them.
>
> 3 And another angel came and stood at the altar, holding a golden censer; and much incense was given to him, that he might add it to the prayers of all the saints upon the golden altar which was before the throne.
>
> 4 And the smoke of the incense, with the prayers of the saints, went up before God out of the angel's hand.
>
> 5 And the angel took the censer; and he filled it with the fire of the altar and threw it to the earth; and there followed peals of thunder and sounds and flashes of lightning and an earthquake.
>
> 6 And the seven angels who had the seven trumpets prepared themselves to sound them.

Here we see that the seventh seal actually is composed of seven trumpets. The angels now are getting ready to blow these seven trumpets in sequence. Reading on in Revelation 8, we see the results of the first trumpet:

> 7 And the first sounded, and there came hail and fire, mixed with blood, and they were thrown to the earth; and a third of the earth was burnt up, and a third of the trees were burnt up, and all the green grass was burnt up.

(We might ask ourselves if this is the *LAST* trumpet. The answer is obviously "no" because there are six more yet to come.) We then read about the second trumpet:

> 8 And the second angel sounded, and *something* like a great mountain burning with fire was thrown into the sea; and a third of the sea became blood;
>
> 9 and a third of the creatures, which were in the sea and had life, died; and a third of the ships were destroyed.

(Again, trusting not to insult your intelligence, we have to realize that *this* couldn't be the last trumpet since there are yet five to come.) The third trumpet's impact is seen as we continue to read:

> 10 And the third angel sounded, and a great star fell from heaven, burning like a torch, and it fell on a third of the rivers and on the springs of waters;
>
> 11 and the name of the star is called Wormwood; and a third of the waters became wormwood; and many men died from the waters, because they were made bitter.

After this trumpet there are four more to follow. The results of the fourth trumpet sounding are found in Revelation 8: 12-13, the fifth in Revelation 9:1-12, and the sixth in Revelation 9:13-21. (We will cover these in detail in Chapter 4.) Then only one trumpet remains.

THE SEVENTH AND LAST TRUMPET

The trumpets appear to be getting progressively more and more important. The first four trumpets each had just one or two verses dedicated to them, while the descriptions of the fifth and sixth trumpets took a half a chapter each. The seventh trumpet has at least two chapters devoted to it. We find the introduction to this final trumpet in Revelation 10:

> 1 And I saw another strong angel coming down out of heaven, clothed with a cloud; and the rainbow was upon his head, and his face was like the sun, and his feet like pillars of fire;
>
> 2 and he had in his hand a little book which was open. And he placed his right foot on the sea and his left on the land;
>
> 3 and he cried out with a loud voice, as when a lion roars; and when he had cried out, the seven peals of thunder uttered their voices.
>
> 4 And when the seven peals of thunder had spoken, I was about to write; and I heard a voice from heaven saying, "Seal up the things which the seven peals of thunder have spoken, and do not write them."
>
> 5 And the angel whom I saw standing on the sea and on the land LIFTED UP HIS RIGHT HAND TO HEAVEN,
>
> 6 AND SWORE BY HIM WHO LIVES FOREVER AND EVER, WHO CREATED HEAVEN AND THE THINGS IN IT, AND THE EARTH AND THE THINGS IN IT, AND THE SEA AND THE THINGS IN IT, that there shall be delay no longer,

7 but in the days of the voice of the seventh angel, when he is about to sound, then the mystery of God is finished, as He preached to His servants the prophets.

The peals of thunder in verses 3 and 4 are not part of the seventh trumpet, because the angel is still *preparing* to sound. Similarly, the things that transpire from Revelation 10:8 through 11:14 are not part of it; the seventh trumpet has not yet sounded.

When the other six trumpets sounded, disastrous things occurred on the earth: a hail of fire and blood burnt up a third of the trees, a great burning mountain was thrown into the sea, a third of mankind was killed by plagues and battles, and so on. When the seventh trumpet is sounded something quite different happens. We read in Revelation 11:

15 And the seventh angel sounded; and there arose loud voices in heaven, saying,

"The kingdom of the world has become *the kingdom* of our Lord, and of His Christ; and He will reign forever and ever."

16 And the twenty-four elders, who sit on their thrones before God, fell on their faces and worshiped God,

17 saying,

"We give Thee thanks, O Lord God, the Almighty, who art and who wast, because Thou hast taken Thy great power and hast begun to reign.

18 "And the nations were enraged, and Thy wrath came, and the time *came* for the dead to be judged, and *the time* to give their reward to Thy bond-servants the prophets and to the saints and to those who fear Thy name, the small and the great, and to destroy those who destroy the earth."

19 And the temple of God which is in heaven was opened; and the ark of His covenant appeared in His temple, and there were flashes of lightning and sounds and peals of thunder and an earthquake and a great hailstorm.

After reading these verses carefully, if someone asked you what happened when the seventh trumpet blew, what would you answer? You may want to reread the verses before you give your answer. What actually *did* happen? Express it in your own words.

After reading this passage, it seems we can conclude that several things happened:

1. Christ began to reign.

2. The time for the dead to be judged was at hand.

3. The time to give rewards to the Christians was at hand.

4. The wicked people who wanted to destroy the earth would now be destroyed.

5. The Ark of the Covenant appeared in the temple.

We find these identical things as we read Revelation 19 and the first six verses of Chapter 20. To resolve this, we have three choices:

1. Revelation 12:1 through 20:6 is an amplification of the events that occurred in Revelation 11:15-19. Thus, John repeated the events, similar to the two accounts of the creation of man in Genesis.

2. The book of Revelation is not completely sequential. Thus, we would have the events of Revelation 12:1 through 20:6 occurring in parallel with the events of Revelation 6:1 through 11:19.

3. The book of Revelation is sequential and these events occurred once in the middle of the seven years of Tribulation and again at the end of the Tribulation. (The logical conclusion of this view would be that the Rapture occurs in the middle of the Tribulation.)

It really does not matter to me which one you believe; wise men of God have held each of these views. The position for which there is no basis is that the Rapture will occur before the Tribulation. It *cannot* occur until the *LAST* trumpet.

I do not believe that the events of the book of Revelation are sequential. Of the three choices listed above, I am most comfortable with number one—that is, the events of Revelation 12:1 through 20:6 are a detailed amplification of the seventh trumpet of Revelation 11:15-19. We see this repetitious construction throughout the Bible. The best known example is the two separate and distinct accounts of the creation of man. Obviously there were not two different creations of man—one on the sixth day and the other after the seventh day. The second account simply retells the story, giving more detail. The first account is in Genesis 1:

> 27 And God created man in His own image, in the image of God He created him; male and female He created them.
>
> 28 And God blessed them; and God said to them, "Be fruitful and multiply, and fill the earth, and subdue it; and rule over the fish of the sea and over the birds of the sky, and over every living thing that moves on the earth."

The second account we read in Genesis 2:

> 3 Then God blessed the seventh day and sanctified it, because in it He rested from all His work which God had created and made.
>
> 4 This is the account of the heavens and the earth when they were created, in the day that the LORD God made earth and heaven.
>
> 5 Now no shrub of the field was yet in the earth, and no plant of the field had yet sprouted, for the LORD God had not sent rain upon the earth; and there was no man to cultivate the ground.
>
> 6 But a mist used to rise from the earth and water the whole surface of the ground.
>
> 7 Then the LORD God formed man of dust from the ground, and breathed into his nostrils the breath of life; and man became a living being. . . .
>
> 20 And the man gave names to all the cattle, and to the birds of the sky, and to every beast of the field, but for Adam there was not found a helper suitable for him.
>
> 21 So the LORD God caused a deep sleep to fall upon the man, and he slept; then He took one of his ribs, and closed up the flesh at that place.
>
> 22 And the LORD God fashioned into a woman the rib which He had taken from the man, and brought her to the man.
>
> 23 And the man said,
>> "This is now bone of my bones,
>> And flesh of my flesh;
>> She shall be called Woman,
>> Because she was taken out of Man."
>
> 24 For this cause a man shall leave his father and his mother, and shall cleave to his wife; and they shall become one flesh.

25 And the man and his wife were both naked and were not ashamed.

In verse 2 of Genesis 2 we see God resting on the seventh day. Then in verse 6 we see God creating man, and later, in verse 20, we see Him creating woman. If we view this as purely sequential, we would have to conclude that God created another man and woman sometime after the seventh day. Here, obviously, the writer is simply coming back to expand upon this event.

This is what the Spirit of God is telling me occurs in Revelation. The activities of Chapters 12-20 are a detailed expansion of the synopsis contained in Revelation 11:15-19. However, if someone prefers one of the other resolutions, I have no argument. Every man should believe as God shows him.

Let's come back to the main issue. We have seen that the seventh trumpet has been sounded, and that it is the *LAST;* there are no more trumpets recorded in the Scriptures after this one. At the last trumpet comes the beginning of Christ's reign and the judgment of the living and the dead. If I believed that this last trumpet sounded in the middle of the Tribulation, I would believe in a mid-Tribulation Rapture. However, based on the thoughts above, I believe that it will sound at the end of the Tribulation. This places the Rapture at the end of the Tribulation.

MORE PROOF—THE SHOUT AND THE MYSTERY

The Rapture at the end of the Tribulation may be such a new thought to some that additional evidence is desirable. One evidence is the shout (loud voices) that usually accompanies a significant trumpet blast in the Scriptures. When Jericho was conquered, we read that the seventh trumpet was accompanied by a great shout of the people. We find this recorded in Joshua 6:

20 So the people shouted, and *priests* blew the trumpets; and it came about, when the people heard the sound of the trumpet, that the people shouted with a great shout and the wall fell down flat, so that the people went up into the city, and every man straight ahead, and they took the city.

21 And they utterly destroyed everything in the city, both man and woman, young and old, and ox and sheep and donkey, with the edge of the sword.

In 1 Thessalonians 4:16, which we have already quoted, we see the Lord descending, at His Second Coming, with a shout and with the trumpet of God.

It is exciting to discover that the seventh and last trumpet in Revelation was also accompanied by loud voices (shouts). You can reexamine this in Revelation 11:15 and also Revelation 14:14-20.

Another factor is the "mystery," spoken of in 1 Corinthians 15:

51 Behold, I tell you a mystery; we shall not all sleep, but we shall all be changed,

The mystery that Paul refers to here is the changing that takes place at the Rapture. This mystery will be finished when the Rapture occurs. Right? If we are correctly interpreting the Scriptures, this should occur at the seventh trumpet. It is beautifully tied together in Revelation 10:

7 but in the days of the voice of the seventh angel, when he is about to sound, then the mystery of God is finished, as He preached to His servants the prophets.

THE FIRST RESURRECTION

I would like to repeat the Scriptures from 1 Thessalonians 4 that we dealt with earlier:

15 For this we say to you by the word of the Lord, that we who are alive, and remain until the coming of the Lord, shall not precede those who have fallen asleep.
16 For the Lord Himself will descend from heaven with a shout, with the voice of *the* archangel, and with the trumpet of God; and the dead in Christ shall rise first.
17 Then we who are alive and remain shall be caught up together with them in the clouds to meet the Lord in the air, and thus we shall always be with the Lord.

As we discussed earlier, the dead in Christ shall rise and be caught up in the air to meet Him *before* the Christians who remain alive are caught up. Thus, we have a resurrection recorded as part of the Rapture.

It would be impossible for this resurrection (as part of the Rapture) to take place at the beginning of the Tribulation, because we read in Revelation 20:

> 1 And I saw an angel coming down from heaven, having the key of the abyss and a great chain in his hand.
>
> 2 And he laid hold of the dragon, the serpent of old, who is the devil and Satan, and bound him for a thousand years,
>
> 3 and threw him into the abyss, and shut *it* and sealed it over him, so that he should not deceive the nations any longer, until the thousand years were completed, after these things he must be released for a short time.
>
> 4 And I saw thrones, and they sat upon them, and judgment was given to them. And I *saw* the souls of those who had been beheaded because of the word of God, and those who had not worshiped the beast or his image, and had not received the mark upon their forehead and upon their hand; and they came to life and reigned with Christ for a thousand years.
>
> 5 The rest of the dead did not come to life until the thousand years were completed. This is the first resurrection.
>
> 6 Blessed and holy is the one who has a part in the first resurrection; over these the second death has no power, but they will be priests of God and of Christ and will reign with Him for a thousand years.

In verse 4 we see that some Christians come to life and reign with Christ for a thousand years. Verse 5 tells us that this is the *FIRST* resurrection. There could not be a resurrection at the beginning of the Tribulation, or this one spoken of in Revelation 20 would not be the *first*.

If a Christian will put out of his mind all of his preconceived ideas about a Rapture occurring at the beginning of the Tribulation, and will look objectively at what the Scriptures have to say, I believe he will conclude that the Rapture will occur at the *end* of the Tribulation. 1 Corinthians 15 tells us that we will be changed in the twinkling of an eye, and that the dead will be raised at the "last trumpet." In Revelation, at the *LAST* trumpet we see the beginning of Christ's reign and the

FIRST resurrection. Nothing could be simpler. There are no complications, if you accept the fact that the Rapture occurs at the end of the Tribulation. If the Spirit of God enables you to accept this, you may still wonder how a God of love could allow His children to experience the terrible things that are going to occur during the Tribulation. Let's take a look at that question, for it is a very legitimate one.

TRIBULATION BUT NOT WRATH

Even though the Christians may experience the Tribulation, they will never experience the wrath of God.

All the way through the Scriptures we are told that Christians *will* experience tribulation. For example, Jesus has this to say to us in John 16:

> 33 "These things I have spoken to you, that in Me you may have peace. In the world you have tribulation, but take courage; I have overcome the world."

Here He clearly informs us that we are going to have tribulation, but tells us to have courage, for He will give us victory over the world.

The apostle Paul said that we would enter the kingdom of God through tribulations. We find this in Acts 14:

> 21 And after they had preached the gospel to that city and had made many disciples, they returned to Lystra and to Iconium and to Antioch,
> 22 strengthening the souls of the disciples, encouraging them to continue in the faith, and *saying,* "Through many tribulations we must enter the kingdom of God."

In Chapter 5 of his letter to the Romans, Paul amplifies on the subject of tribulation:

> 3 And not only this, but we also exult in our tribulations, knowing that tribulation brings about perseverance;
> 4 and perseverance, proven character; and proven character, hope;
> 5 and hope does not disappoint, because the love of God has been poured out within our hearts through the Holy Spirit who was given to us.

Paul expands further on tribulations in a very precious way in Romans 8:

> 35 Who shall separate us from the love of Christ? Shall tribulation, or distress, or persecution, or famine, or nakedness, or peril, or sword?
>
> 36 Just as it is written,
>> "FOR THY SAKE WE ARE BEING PUT TO DEATH ALL DAY LONG;
>> WE WERE CONSIDERED AS SHEEP TO BE SLAUGHTERED."
>
> 37 But in all these things we overwhelmingly conquer through Him who loved us.
>
> 38 For I am convinced that neither death, nor life, nor angels, nor principalities, nor things present, nor things to come, nor powers,
>
> 39 nor height, nor depth, nor any other created thing, shall be able to separate us from the love of God, which is in Christ Jesus our Lord.

It is wonderful that all of the terrible things that we will experience during the Tribulation will not separate us from the love of Christ!

We have seen that Christians are expected to go through tribulation. However, this does not mean that we will experience the wrath of God. Paul, in Romans 5, tells us that we will not:

> 9 Much more then, having now been justified by His blood, we shall be saved from the wrath of God through Him.

By negative implication, we see the same thing in John 3:

> 36 "He who believes in the Son has eternal life; but he who does not obey the Son shall not see life, but the wrath of God abides on him."

It says that those who believe in the Son have eternal life, but those who do not obey Him, not only will not have life, but the wrath of God abides on them. The implication is that those who believe in the Son will not experience the wrath of God.

The wrath of God will be poured out against the world. We can rejoice because we are not part of the world. Revelation 7:2-3 tells us that God will seal the foreheads of His bondservants to protect them. Remember, God did not remove the children of Israel from Egypt during the plagues. If they obeyed

Him, He protected them from the disasters being poured out upon the earth. Similarly, we can go through the Tribulation victoriously by following and obeying God.

Spiritual Interpretation

Up until now, we have been interpreting the book of Revelation in a purely physical way. For many years this was the only way that I considered interpreting it. More and more I see that there is a parallel spiritual interpretation. For example, we read that Christians should not take the mark of the beast on their foreheads or on their right hands. I do believe that there will be a physical mark, as we will discuss later, that people will have to take in order to buy and sell. To obtain the mark they will have to renounce Christ.

A spiritual interpretation would identify the mark on the forehead as being symbolic of the things that we think, and the mark on the right hand symbolic of the things that we do. As we *THINK* and *DO* as the world does, we—through a process— take on the mark of the beast.

As God has begun to reveal that there *is* a spiritual interpretation, I believe that some Christians have gone overboard in the other direction; they believe and teach only the spiritual interpretation and no longer support a physical interpretation. I believe that the events of Revelation will occur both physically and spiritually, as we have seen in the example of the mark of the beast. If Christians know they will be experiencing the Tribulation, there may be certain physical preparations to be made, but also—in the spiritual realm—they would do well to be careful of how they think and act, lest they be squeezed into the mold of the world. I must include this verse from Romans 12:

> 2 **And do not be conformed to this world, but be transformed by the renewing of your mind, that you may prove what the will of God is, that which is good and acceptable and perfect.**

Paul admonishes us to have our minds renewed and to do the will of God.

I would love to dig into the precious spiritual interpretations of some of these truths. However, that is not within the purpose or the scope of what God has laid on my heart for this book. I would encourage you to read the book of Revelation, asking God to show you the spiritual interpretations, which are equally as valid as physical interpretations. Even though I will be interpreting the book of Revelation physically, this does not mean that I am doing it in the natural. All interpretations must be done in the Spirit.

THIS AGE AND THE AGE TO COME

There are a number of Greek words translated as "age" in the New Testament. The one we are interested in here is the Greek word "aion." Sometimes, in the *King James Version,* this word is incorrectly translated as "world." Thus, sometimes that version talks of the "end of the world," when it should be talking about the "end of the age." This Greek word for age in the Scriptures refers to a large number of years, usually of indefinite length. Let's look at a Scripture which refers to the age that we are presently in and one that is still in the future. We find this in Matthew 12:

> 32 "And whoever shall speak a word against the Son of Man, it shall be forgiven him; but whoever shall speak against the Holy Spirit, it shall not be forgiven him, either in this age, or in the *age* to come.

In Hebrews 6, we read again about the future age, which shows that there is at least one yet to come:

> 4 For in the case of those who have once been enlightened and tasted of the heavenly gift and have been made partakers of the Holy Spirit,
>
> 5 and have tasted the good word of God and the powers of the age to come, . . .

Christ, wanting to reassure his disciples when He gave them the great commission, let them know that He would be with them throughout this present age. We find this in Matthew 28:

> 19 "Go therefore and make disciples of all the nations, baptizing them in the name of the Father and the Son and the Holy Spirit,

20 teaching them to observe all that I commanded you; and lo, I am with you always, even to the end of the age."

It is natural to assume something special is going to occur to mark the end of this present age, because each previous age ended with a significant event. For example, the last age ended with the death and resurrection of Christ. What do you think might occur on the *last day* of our present age? We find part of the answer in John 6:

39 "And this is the will of Him who sent Me, that of all that He has given Me I lose nothing, but raise it up on the last day.

40 "For this is the will of My Father, that every one who beholds the Son, and believes in Him, may have eternal life; and I Myself will raise him up on the last day." . . .

44 "No one can come to Me, unless the Father who sent Me draws him; and I will raise him up on the last day. . . .

54 "He who eats My flesh and drinks My blood has eternal life; and I will raise him up on the last day.

We see that the resurrection of the Christians is going to occur on the last day of this present age. This is consistent with the things that we have been discussing, since the Tribulation is the last seven years of our present age. But what about the judgment of the non-Christians? That should occur at the same time, shouldn't it? Let's turn to John 12 for the answer:

48 "He who rejects Me, and does not receive My sayings, has one who judges him; the word I spoke is what will judge him at the last day.

Here we notice that those who have not received Jesus Christ will receive judgment on the last day of the present age.

Certainly everyone would agree that the *next* age is the one thousand year period (the Millennium) during which Jesus Christ will reign on the earth. There is no evidence that there will be a seven-year "gap" between ages; none of the other ages have such a "mini-age" between them. Thus, the things said to occur on the last day, will occur at the end of this age, which will be the last day of the Tribulation.

The following diagram depicts the ages as I see them:

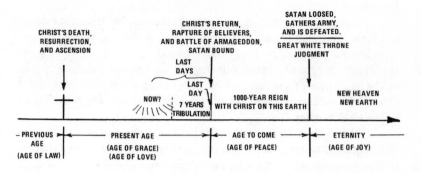

Figure 2.1

As can be seen, each age ends with a dramatic and significant series of events.

Not a Theological Argument

The information contained in this chapter is in no way meant to be a complete theological argument. Rather, it is a sharing of some of the major things that God has shown me with regard to the reason that we should believe the Rapture will occur at the end of the Tribulation. To delve into all of the reasons why we should believe this would require a separate book.

Such a book has been written; it is *The Church and the Tribulation,* by Robert H. Gundry (published by Zondervan Publishing House, Grand Rapids, Michigan 49506). I would highly recommend it, even though it is somewhat scholarly in approach. In introducing the issue, Gundry says (pages 9 and 10):

"The issue which we are approaching has to do with the possibility of Jesus' return to evacuate the Church from the earth before a future period of intense tribulation. If we favor the possibility of such a pretribulational rapture, it becomes incumbent to stand in constant readiness for the event. However, if Jesus will return solely after the tribulation, that readiness should include mental and moral preparation for prior experience of the tribulation itself. The exhortation to 'endure to the end' and the special warning about the leading astray of, 'if possible, even the elect' (Matt. 24:12, 13, 24) highlight the danger of dismay and loss of faith on the part of whatever saints do find themselves in the last great time of testing.

"Ten to twenty years ago this issue peaked on the American evangelical scene, and then abated. But recent events in the Middle East have revived interest in biblical prophecy concerning the future. It therefore seems appropriate to reconsider the chronology of the rapture—the more so since in the last spate of publications on the topic posttribulationism gained neither the volume of press nor the exegetical backing which were given to pretribulationism. . . .

"The present thesis is threefold: (a) direct, unquestioned statements of Scripture that Jesus Christ will return after the tribulation and that the first resurrection will occur after the tribulation, coupled with the absence of statements placing similar events before the tribulation, make it natural to place the rapture of the Church after the tribulation; (2) the theological and exegetical grounds for pretribulationism rest on insufficient evidence, *non sequitur* reasoning, and faulty exegesis; (3) positive indications of a posttribulational rapture arise out of a proper exegesis of relevant Scripture passages and derive support from the history of the doctrine. . . .

"It is hoped that the following pages will contribute to an understanding and appreciation of the posttribulational position and that it will do so in a manner characterized by 'the wisdom from above . . . first pure, then peaceable, gentle, reasonable, full of mercy and good fruits, unwavering, without hypocrisy' (James 3:17)."

I would hope, as Dr. Gundry, that my book, as well as his, will contribute to an understanding of the post-Tribulational position. I have found that so many Christians, have never had an intelligent presentation of anything other than the pre-Tribulational position.

I have done a thorough study of all of the different Rapture positions: pre-Tribulational, mid-Tribulational and post-Tribulational. I have read all of Dr. Walvoord's books, including *The Rapture Question* and *The Blessed Hope and the Tribulation.* I know Hal Lindsey and I have read each of his books. In addition to reading these and most of the books written on the subject, I have had personal conversations with many of the leaders of the pre-Tribulational point of view. (Appendix B deals with the three Scriptures that could possibly imply a pre-Tribulation Rapture.) After examining all of this and going to the Scriptures with an open heart, the Lord has lead me to believe that the Rapture will occur at the end of the Tribulation.

Another book that deals with the post-Tribulation position is *The Blessed Hope,* by George Ladd (published by Wm. B. Eerdmans Publishing Company, 255 Jefferson Avenue S.E., Grand Rapids, Michigan 49502). In this book, Ladd points out that a pre-Tribulation Rapture was not a belief of the early church fathers, but became popular in the nineteenth century, through the Plymouth Brethren. After dealing with the historical background of the "blessed hope" of our early church fathers, and the rise of the theory of a pre-Tribulation Rapture, he presents (beginning in Chapter 3) solid Biblical evidence that the long-held post-Tribulation Rapture position is the Scriptural one.

On page 162 of this concluding chapter we read the following:

"We have now concluded our study both of the Biblical teaching about the Blessed Hope and of the history of pretribulationism, and have come to the following conclusions. The idea of a pretribulation rapture was not seen in the Scriptures by the early church fathers. They were futurists and premillennialists but not pretribulationists. This of itself indicates that pretribulationism and premillennialism are not identical and that the Blessed Hope is not the hope of a rapture before the Tribulation. Pretribulationism was an unknown teaching until the rise of the Plymouth Brethren among whom the doctrine originated. From this source, it has come to America where, although warmly received by some, it has been rejected by other devout students of the Word, or has been at first accepted and later rejected by others. This very fact should suggest caution in making pretribulationism an essential element in prophetic interpretation.

"The vocabulary of the Blessed Hope knows nothing of two aspects of Christ's coming, one secret and one glorious. On the contrary, the terminology points to a single indivisible return of Christ. Scripture says nothing about a secret coming of the Lord.

"The Scriptures which predict the Great Tribulation, the Rapture and the Resurrection nowhere place the Rapture and the Resurrection of the saints at the beginning of the Tribulation. Nor does Scripture know anything of two phases of the first resurrection—that of the saints and that of the tribulation martyrs—separated by a seven-year period of tribulation. On the contrary, the one passage which is most specific as to chronology places the resurrection of both martyrs and saints after the Tribulation."

Another outstanding book which beautifully presents the Biblical position of a post-Tribulation Rapture is *The Tribulation People,* by Arthur Katterjohn, mentioned in Chapter 1. On pages 10 and 11, Katterjohn says:

"And so we dream. Popular gospel songs declare the theme of Jesus' surprise reentry, and evangelical films scare children into hasty professions of faith by threatening that some night soon mommy or dad may be snatched away forever into heavenly glory—'I wish we'd all been ready!'

"Contrary to the hope of many devout and godly believers, the Bible may suggest that history is on a crash course to the most concentrated and worldwide trouble of all time, with God's people on the center of the burner. Evil men will find easy power as convulsing nations beg for stability and capitulate social ideals to leaders who promise normalcy in exchange for limitless authority. Then one leader will emerge, a man more perverse than history's lowest infidel, demented enough to demand that nations worship him, ruthlessly jealous of any higher thing. . . .

"Could the Bible teach that Jesus will return at the end of the tribulation, and that believers living before His return will be faced with the most devastating persecution ever endured by the saints of any period? The question gains its serious importance from the possibility that we may be those tribulation people."

From an entirely different point of view, there is a book well worth reading, entitled *The Incredible Cover-Up,* which gives additional reasons for believing in a post-Tribulation Rapture. This book is by Dave MacPherson, who for eighteen years has been a news reporter, covering train disasters, plane crashes, forest fires, floods, and so on. In this book he combines the contents of two of his former books: *The Unbelievable Pre-Trib Origin* and *The Late Great Pre-Trib Rapture.* He recently turned his attention to finding out where this pre-Tribulation Rapture theory came from. He visited England, and Scotland and searched the libraries. His conclusions were that it began in approximately 1830, based on some visions and prophecies of a woman named Margaret Macdonald. Later, Edward Irving and John Darby popularized the pre-Tribulation Rapture belief through the Plymouth Brethren. Dave MacPherson went back to Margaret Macdonald's handwritten statement of her visions, and discovered that her utterance in no way claimed that the church would escape the attacks of the Antichrist. On page 93 of *The Incredible Cover-Up* (published by Logos International, Plainfield, N. J. 07060), he says:

"We have seen that a young Scottish lassie named Margaret Macdonald had a private revelation in Port Glasgow, Scotland, in the early part of 1830 that a select group of Christians would be caught up to meet Christ in the air *before* the days of Antichrist. An eye-and-ear witness, Robert Norton M.D., preserved her handwritten account of her pre-trib rapture revelation in two of his books, and said it was the *first* time anyone ever split the second coming into two distinct parts, or stages. His writings, along with much other Catholic Apostolic Church literature, have been hidden many decades from the mainstream of evangelical thought and only recently have surfaced.

"Margaret's views were well-known to those who visited her home, among them John Darby of the Brethren. Within a few months her distinctive prophetic outlook was mirrored in the September, 1830, issue of *The Morning Watch* and the early Brethren assembly at Plymouth, England. Early disciples of the pre-trib interpretation often called it a new doctrine. Setting dates for Christ's return was a common practice at that time."

If you are interested in reading her vision, which I do not think implies a pre-Tribulation Rapture, it is contained in its entirety in MacPherson's book.

All of the books mentioned in this chapter have excellent bibliographies listing additional books for use in a more detailed study.

Conclusion

Nowhere do the Scriptures say that the Rapture will precede the Tribulation. There appears to be ample evidence that a Rapture at the end of the Tribulation is both Biblical and representative of the historic position of the church on this subject. You may not agree with this, or with some of the things that I have said thus far. I am not asking you to agree. I am asking that you get alone with God and, with an open heart and mind, ask Him to show you if Christians are going through the Tribulation, rather than be "Raptured out" beforehand. Regardless of *what* you have believed, or how *strongly* you have believed it, do open your mind and heart to whatever God has to say. This is a prerequisite to His leading you.

However, what a person believes concerning the Rapture should not be the basis of our fellowship, or a test of the orthodoxy of his belief. Our fellowship is around the *person* of Jesus Christ and the blessed hope of His coming again.

I wish that the Rapture were going to occur at the beginning of the Tribulation, and that my fellow believers and I would not have to experience the terrible things that are coming. However, since I believe, as do growing scores of Christians, that the believers *will* go through the Tribulation, my family and I are making both physical and spiritual preparations for it. My precious brothers who believe in a pre-Tribulation Rapture are making no preparations.

If I have correctly heard God's warnings, as Joseph did, and prepare for the seven bad years ahead, I believe that my life during the Tribulation will be easier and more fruitful than that of my brothers who do not prepare.

If the proponents of a pre-Tribulation Rapture are wrong, and you believe them, where do *you* stand? You could wind up going through the Tribulation unprepared. If the supporters of a post-Tribulation Rapture are wrong, and you believe them, where do you stand? You might have made some provisions—such as storing some food—that will be left behind in the event of a pre-Tribulation Rapture for your non-Christian friends and relatives to utilize during the Tribulation. (They will need all the help they can get!)

I believe that God has told me that we Christians will not be Raptured out before the Tribulation, but will go through it. The Holy Spirit seems to be saying to *PREPARE*. This brings us logically to the question of how near these events might be. If they are hundreds or thousands of years away, preparation at this time would be wasteful and useless. If the events are close at hand, urgent preparation would be essential.

3

ARE WE LIVING IN THE END TIMES?

Before we can intelligently discuss whether or not we are living in the end times, we must understand what is meant by the "end times." This is a fairly loose term, probably with many definitions, but most often used in Christian circles to indicate the period of time immediately preceding and including the Tribulation. This is the way we will be using the term in this book. Some people might incorrectly interpret it as the time of the end of the world.

Since the phrase "end times" is not found in the Scriptures, if one must use this term, I would prefer that he say the "end times of this present age." (See Chapter 2 for a discussion of the ages.) If we were to use a more Biblical term—one found in the Scriptures—we would talk about the "last days" or, more precisely, the "last days of this present age." This would be the period of time preceding the last *day* of this age, much as the last minutes of a football game precede the last minute of the game.

WHAT WILL HAPPEN DURING THE
LAST DAYS OF THIS PRESENT AGE?

We have some clues from various places in the Scriptures as to what will occur. One of these is found in Acts 2, where Peter quotes from the prophet Joel:

15 "For these men are not drunk, as you suppose, for it is *only* the third hour of the day;
16 but this is what was spoken of through the prophet Joel:

17   'AND IT SHALL BE IN THE LAST DAYS,' GOD SAYS,
       'THAT I WILL POUR FORTH OF MY SPIRIT UPON ALL
           MANKIND;
       AND YOUR SONS AND YOUR DAUGHTERS SHALL
           PROPHESY,
       AND YOUR YOUNG MEN SHALL SEE VISIONS,
       AND YOUR OLD MEN SHALL DREAM DREAMS;
18   EVEN UPON MY BONDSLAVES, BOTH MEN AND
           WOMEN,
       I WILL IN THOSE DAYS POUR FORTH OF MY SPIRIT
       And they shall prophesy.
19   'AND I WILL GRANT WONDERS IN THE SKY ABOVE,
       AND SIGNS ON THE EARTH BENEATH
       BLOOD, AND FIRE, AND VAPOR OF SMOKE.
20   'THE SUN SHALL BE TURNED INTO DARKNESS,
       AND THE MOON INTO BLOOD,
       BEFORE THE GREAT AND GLORIOUS DAY OF THE
           LORD SHALL COME.
21   'AND IT SHALL BE, THAT EVERY ONE WHO CALLS
           ON THE NAME OF THE LORD SHALL BE SAVED.'

We see here that the Holy Spirit will be poured out on
Christians during the last days. The young will prophesy and
have visions, and God will speak to the old men in dreams. I believe that this is being fulfilled. The gifts of prophecy and visions
have been poured out by the Holy Spirit upon true believers in
Christ of all denominations. I have personal knowledge that
God is speaking to the old men in dreams.

The signs in the sky that are discussed in verses 19 and 20
I believe will be part of the Tribulation, for these are almost the
exact words used by John in describing some of the coming
catastrophes. All this will precede the great and glorious day of
the Lord's return.

Peter gives further insight into this, in writing to the Christians who were scattered throughout the world:

3 Know this first of all, that in the last days mockers will come
with *their* mocking, following after their own lusts,

4 and saying, "Where is the promise of His coming? For *ever*
since the fathers fell asleep, all continues just as it was from the beginning of creation" (2 Peter 3).

We see that there will be mockers making fun of Christianity and of God. They will probably even claim something ridiculous like "God is dead."

Paul, in writing to his spiritual son Timothy, gives us a different viewpoint on the difficult times that will be coming in the "last days." He depicts mankind as becoming very self-centered, unholy and treacherous. He says that men will love pleasure more than they love God, even though they might have a form of "religion." We find this in 2 Timothy 3:

1 But realize this, that in the last days difficult times will come.

2 For men will be lovers of self, lovers of money, boastful, arrogant, revilers, disobedient to parents, ungrateful, unholy,

3 unloving, irreconcilable, malicious gossips, without self-control, brutal, haters of good,

4 treacherous, reckless, conceited, lovers of pleasure rather than lovers of God;

5 holding to a form of godliness, although they have denied its power; and avoid such men as these.

6 For among them are those who enter into households and captivate weak women weighed down with sins, led on by various impulses,

7 always learning and never able to come to the knowledge of the truth.

As we look at this passage of Scripture, we get some additional hints as to what the last days will be like. I believe that we are seeing this occurring now. Surely men are lovers of self, lovers of money, disobedient to parents, and lovers of pleasure rather than lovers of God. You will have to decide for yourself whether or not you think that our present time qualifies as meeting the criteria laid down in these verses. I know that with God as your guide you will be able to discern whether or not it applies to today.

A GROWING WORLDWIDE AWARENESS

As an international consulting economist, I travel all over the world to speak at monetary conferences. Everywhere I go— Japan, Korea, Hong Kong, Philippines, Indonesia, Europe, Latin

America, Canada, and the United States—the feeling is stronger and stronger among Christians that we are indeed living in the last days of this present age (the end times). Assuming that this prompting is of the Holy Spirit, and I have no reason to doubt that it is, it appears that God is speaking to the hearts of Christians, independent of one another, telling us to ready ourselves, for we are living during the time of the end of this age. This worldwide feeling that we are living in the end times is shared by pre-, mid- and post-Tribulationists alike and it is something that no human being or organization could achieve.

If you go to a local Christian bookstore to find out what our Christian writers have to say, these are some of the titles that you will find on the shelves:

The End of This Present World
The Tribulation People
There's A New World Coming
Armageddon
End of the Days
Goodbye World
How to Recognize the Antichrist
The Terminal Generation
The Antichrist is Alive Today
Those Who Remain
The Late Great Planet Earth
World War III and the Destiny of America
Get All Excited—Jesus is Coming Soon
The Soon to be Revealed Antichrist
The End of the Days

The titles themselves tell you a great deal about what these Christian leaders and authors are sensing in the Spirit. Almost every one of them either states or implies in his writing that he feels Jesus is coming soon, and that we are living in the end times. (Some of them feel that the Rapture will occur at the beginning of the Tribulation, but that is all right. Our concern here is awareness of Christian laymen, leaders, and writers that we are likely living in the last days of this present age.)

It would be interesting to note what a couple of these authors have to say. Dr. Charles R. Taylor, on page 11 of his book, *Those Who Remain* (published by Today in Bible Prophecy, Inc.), says:

"The many documentations in this book give solid evidence that the *rapture of the Church* and God's judgment on Earth are both very, very near.

"The Lord has given us many prophecies about the *signs of the times* and His return. Now, those prophecies are coming to pass, and His return is not only imminent: It is at the very doors."

Dr. Taylor feels very strongly that we are living in the end times, and that the Antichrist is alive today. He even goes into detail as to who he believes to be the two most likely candidates for the Antichrist. He calculates a Bible generation to be thirty-five years. (Others say forty years.) He feels that with the re-establishment of Israel as a nation in 1948, the final "generation" may have begun.

The title of Hal Lindsey's book, *The Terminal Generation* (published by Fleming H. Revell Company), lets you know immediately that he feels this is the last or terminal generation of the present age. On page 65 of this book, he has this to say:

"More and more people are becoming interested in Bible prophecy, not just as a whim, but as a verification of events in the world today. Scientists, psychologists, sociologists, and educators who might not believe in the Bible as the source of truth, are making the same predictions as those of the ancient prophets!

"We have seen significant changes on the world scene, even in the past five years: Arab power; Israel's deteriorating position; alignment of the Third World with the Arabs; an avalanche of crime and lawlessness; China's attempt to unify Asian countries behind it; famine, earthquakes, weapons of war; move toward one-worldism; decline of morality; increase in the occult.

"As an individual looks for a way to cope with life—as he searches for hope in what appears to be a hopeless world—many are helpless. In this state, there are many false hopes and false prophets waiting to occupy the void in empty lives.

"How discerning we must be! As Jesus has warned, 'For false Christs and false prophets will arise and will show great signs and wonders, so as to mislead, if possible, even the elect' (Matthew 24:24).

"How alert we should be! When I see all these events coming together simultaneously I feel like shouting, 'Wake up, World, Jesus is almost here!'"

Both Dr. Taylor and Hal Lindsey feel that the nation of Israel is God's time clock. By reading correctly what is happening to Israel, we can discern God's timetable for the last days. According to these men, the clock started its final countdown in 1948 when Israel became a nation again. In conversations I have had with Hal Lindsey, I have heard him say that there is absolutely no doubt that we are living in the last generation, and that we will see Christ come back. I have had to disagree with him on this. We can claim that the Spirit is saying that we are living in the last generation, and that there is a high probability Christ will be coming back in our time, but there is no way we can be *absolutely* sure. We will look at Matthew 24 to see why I say this. However, let me hasten to add that, in looking at the Scriptures and the evidence in events of the world around us, it does appear as though the history of this present age is racing to a climax.

EVIDENCE OF THE LAST DAYS

The first evidence that I would like to examine is the nation of Israel. On May 14, 1948 David Ben-Gurion read the Declaration of Independence announcing the establishment of the nation of Israel. God had foretold that Israel would be restored. In 1948 that prophecy was fulfilled. After the nation of Israel was established, the Israelis captured the city of old Jerusalem, with all the sacred sites, fulfilling another prophecy. I could be wrong, but I believe that they will never let go of Jerusalem. There has also been a lot of debate and discussion about the rebuilding of the temple in Jerusalem. Only God knows whether or not this is something that they will do in the physical sense. The nation of Israel is certainly in a position to do it, if they wanted to.

Many years ago it was difficult to understand why some of the final battles of this age would be fought in the Middle East. There was nothing over there but sand, desert and a few palm trees. But now one of the reasons is apparent to all: *OIL*. It is very clear how important and crucial that area is, since the vast majority of the world's oil reserves are in the Middle East.

Figure 3.1 is a graph of the projected oil production of the world. This projection is based on the work of M. King Hubbert of the U. S. Geological Survey and was published in the *Scientific American.* The projected curve assumes some additional major discoveries, such as the Alaskan North Slope.

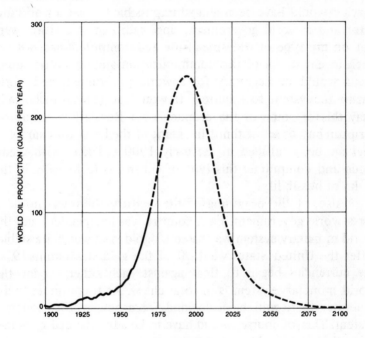

Figure 3.1

As can be seen from this chart, world oil production will peak at about the year 1995, and by 2015 it will be only 50 percent of what it was at the peak. Thus, if there is going to be a major battle in the Mideast over oil, it certainly will occur somewhere between now and the beginning years of the next century.

An additional important factor for a major conflict in the Mideast is the rising to world power of both Russia and China. Ezekiel 38 talks about the mighty army out of the outermost parts of the North (Gog). Russia appears to meet all of the criteria very nicely. Similarly, Revelation 16 talks about the kings of the East and the armies that poured across the dried up Euphrates, which could well mean China. In fact it even refers to this army from the East, in an indirect manner, as the "dragon." We see both Russia and China arming heavily militarily; certainly they would be able to engage in such conflicts.

Another thing that we see in the end times is the rise of a world government and a world dictator. At the turn of the century, it would have been almost impossible to have a world dictator and a world government, since radio and television were not in any type of widespread use and computers had not yet been invented. All of this communication and computer equipment would be necessary for a world government and world economic system to function. It would have been technically difficult for some of the prophecies in Revelation—where no man can buy or sell without the mark of the beast for example—to have been fulfilled in the early 1900's. Today with credit cards and computers, this type of control is technically in the realm of possibility.

Also, at the beginning of the century there was no need for a world government. Each country was independent and the world monetary system was based on gold, and was quite stable. After the United States went off of the gold standard in 1972, the currencies began to float against each other. Today the world monetary system is in total chaos. As it continues to degenerate, there will be a demand for a new world economic system. This, of course, would have to be administered by something akin to a world government.

Another way to view this is that in the United States from every side there is a cry for a redistribution of wealth. The poor want it, many ministers want it, and the senators and congressmen evidently want it also. This redistribution is working because U. S. citizens, both rich and poor, are under the authority of the federal government. The government can then take from the rich (and middle class) and give to the poor.

In a similar way, there is a worldwide cry for redistribution of wealth from the richer nations to the poorer nations. We see this in the Arab oil cartel. The Arabs are saying that they want a bigger slice of the world's pie. Many other of the developing nations are saying the same thing, and are borrowing money from the richer nations that they never intend to repay. If these poorer nations are to get wealth, it has to come from the richer nations. There are three basic ways that this transfer of wealth can occur:

1. The richer nations can voluntarily give to the poorer nations.

2. There can be war, wherein the poorer nations take from the richer nations.

3. There can be a world government, which will have authority over all of the national governments. This world government will then have the power to take from the richer nations and give to the poorer nations.

I believe that the ultimate resolution of this problem will be the third option—a world government. There is pressure for this from almost every direction.

Along with the world government, we see in the Scriptures that in the end times there will be a world church. Again, at the beginning of this century a world church would have seemed almost ridiculous. Today the World Council of Churches and the Catholics are moving progressively closer to one. Within a few years we could see a world church.

I could go on and on with the evidences of the events occurring today that match with the prophecies. Yet I hesitate to do so, because in my lifetime I have seen Hitler, Mussolini, Stalin and even Henry Kissinger labeled as the Antichrist. It is a bit dangerous to try to take a contemporary individual, nation or event and tack it solidly to a piece of prophecy. However, some of the worldwide movements—such as one toward a world government, a world church, and a world economic system— and the importance of Israel and the Middle East, are things that have never occurred before in the history of the world, and could well be some of the events of the last days.

THE END OF THE AGE—WHEN?

You may have some questions. The disciples did. I would like to go back to a couple of Scriptures that we discussed earlier. In this first one, the disciples came to Jesus and asked Him perhaps the very questions that you have on your heart.

> 3 And as He was sitting on the Mount of Olives, the disciples came to Him privately, saying, "Tell us, when will these things be, and what *will be* the sign of Your coming, and of the end of the age?" (Matthew 24).

You can see here that they asked Him plainly what the sign of His coming and of the end of the age would be. The rest of Chapter 24 is His answer to that question. We covered most of this in Chapter 1, but I would suggest that you take your own Bible and read Christ's answer.

In answering them, Christ had this to say as to *when* these events would take place:

> 29 "But immediately after the tribulation of those days THE SUN WILL BE DARKENED, AND THE MOON WILL NOT GIVE ITS LIGHT, AND THE STARS WILL FALL from the sky, and the POWERS OF THE HEAVENS WILL BE SHAKEN,
>
> 30 and then the sign of the Son of Man will appear in the sky, and then all the tribes of the earth will mourn, and they will see the SON OF MAN COMING ON THE CLOUDS OF THE SKY with power and great glory.
>
> 31 "And He will send forth His angels WITH A GREAT TRUMPET and THEY WILL GATHER TOGETHER His elect FROM THE FOUR WINDS, FROM ONE END OF THE SKY TO THE OTHER.
>
> 32 "Now learn the parable from the fig tree: when its branch has already become tender, and puts forth its leaves, you know that summer is near;
>
> 33 even so you too, when you see all these things recognize that He is near, *right* at the door.
>
> 34 "Truly I say to you, this generation will not pass away until all these things take place.
>
> 35 "Heaven and earth will pass away, but My words shall not pass away.
>
> 36 "But of that day and hour no one knows, not even the angels of heaven, nor the Son, but the Father alone (Matthew 24).

He said that no one, not even Himself or angels, knows the day and the hour when the end of the age will occur. I have to say this very loudly and clearly: *WE CANNOT KNOW WHEN IT WILL OCCUR.* But, looking at the evidence and the way the

Holy Spirit is warning those who believe in Jesus, I would have to conclude that there is a high probability that we are living in the last days of this present age, and could well see the return of Christ.

We cannot know for certain when the Lord's return will be, but as Christians we have a responsibility to have a general idea of when it might be. I think that this is pointed out very beautifully in 1 Thessalonians 5:

1 Now as to the times and the epochs, brethren you have no need of anything to be written to you.

2 For you yourselves know full well that the day of the Lord will come just like a thief in the night.

3 While they are saying, "Peace and safety!" then destruction will come upon them suddenly like birth pangs upon a woman with child; and they shall not escape.

4 But you, brethren, are not in darkness, that the day should overtake you like a thief;

5 for you are all sons of light and sons of day. We are not of night nor of darkness;

6 so then let us not sleep as others do, but let us be alert and sober.

I particularly would like to call your attention to verse 4 of the passage above. It states that, as brothers in Christ, we are not in the darkness, and that the day should not overtake us like a thief—as it will the rest of the world. I do not believe this means that we will know exactly when it will occur, but that, by the prophecies in the Scripture and the witness of the Holy Spirit to our hearts, we should have a good idea of the times and the seasons in which we live. Verse 6 admonishes us to be in a state of readiness for the Lord's return.

Let me restate what we have just covered. For non-Christians, the Lord's coming will be like that of a thief in the night; it will catch them totally unaware. But as Christians, we should not be overtaken as by a thief. We should not be surprised by the return of Christ!

WE SHOULD WATCH AND PRAY

We have just seen that we cannot know when the end of this age will occur. We saw earlier that on the last day of this age the Son of God will come. In spite of the uncertainty concerning the timing, we are commanded in the Scriptures to be ready:

40 "You too, be ready; for the Son of Man is coming at an hour that you do not expect" (Luke 12).

In Matthew 24 we have the answer that Christ gave in response to the disciples' question of what the signs of the end of the age and of His coming would be. Chapter 1 of this book divulged that no place in Matthew 24 is a pre-Tribulation Rapture referred to. Towards the end of that chapter, Christ said to His disciples:

42 "Therefore be on the alert, for you do not know which day your Lord is coming.

We are to be on the alert *BECAUSE* we do not know when the Lord is coming back. He obviously was not talking about being prepared for a pre-Tribulation Rapture, since He has not discussed one. He must be telling us to be alert and ready for His return at the end of the Tribulation.

I think that one of the best summaries of what we are talking about is found in Mark 13:

32 "But of that day or hour no one knows, not even the angels in heaven, nor the Son, but the Father *alone.*

33 "Take heed, keep on the alert; for you do not know when the *appointed* time is.

34 *"It is* like a man, away on a journey, *who* upon leaving his house and putting his slaves in charge, *assigning* to each one his task, also commanded the doorkeeper to stay on the alert.

35 "Therefore, be on the alert—for you do not know when the master of the house is coming, whether in the evening, at midnight, at cockcrowing, or in the morning—

36 lest he come suddenly and find you asleep.

37 "And what I say to you I say to all, 'Be on the alert!'"

Summary and Conclusion

Thus far we have seen that there is Biblical evidence for a Rapture, but that the Rapture will most probably take place at the end of the Tribulation—in fact on the *last day* of the Tribulation, which is also the last day of this present age.

We have further seen that we cannot know when this will occur, but that we are commanded in the Scriptures to be on the alert, and to be ready for it. Since the Tribulation will likely begin in a gradual way, rather than on a specific day, we cannot say that the Lord's coming is seven years after a certain event. Thus, Christ's words that He will come like a thief in the night are certainly true. His return, to end the Tribulation, is what has been referred to throughout the centuries as the "blessed hope" of Christians. We talk a great deal about faith and love, but most of us forget the third member of that trinity—*HOPE.* Perhaps this is because we have life so easy. However, in the rougher times that are ahead, *hope* will become a very important aspect to the Christian.

We then saw that, although we cannot know *when* His return will be, the Holy Spirit appears to be moving worldwide, showing believers that we are in the end times and warning us to prepare. If this is indeed a work of the Holy Spirit, He could be saying to the Christians (the Body of Christ) that we are to get ready spiritually and physically for the Tribulation which we will experience.

Let us now take a very brief overview of some of the catastrophies that the Bible says we will experience during the Tribulation.

4

SOME CATASTROPHES
WE WILL FACE

There are many things that I would rather write about than the catastrophes which will occur on the earth during the period of the great Tribulation—catastrophes that we all, Christians included, might experience. Before outlining some of the events that will occur, let us first examine the length of the Tribulation. Most people automatically think of the "seven years" of tribulation. If you were to ask them where they got the idea that it was seven years, they would probably say that they heard it in a sermon or read it in a book. They would tend to be ignorant as to the Biblical basis for it.

It is interesting that there is not complete agreement among Biblical scholars, as to the length of the Tribulation. Some feel that it will be three and a half years, others feel that it will be ten and a half years, while the majority feel that it will be seven years. The first clue we have as to the length of time is found in Revelation 11:

> 3 "And I will grant *authority* to my two witnesses, and they will prophesy for twelve hundred and sixty days, clothed in sackcloth."

We see that the two witnesses will prophesy for twelve hundred and sixty days, which is almost three and a half years. (Actually it is three and a half years of thirty-day months.) The next clue we have is in Revelation 12:

> 6 And the woman fled into the wilderness where she had a place prepared by God, so that there she might be nourished for one thousand two hundred and sixty days.

Here we see the woman fleeing to the wilderness for one thousand two hundred and sixty days. This again is a three and

a half year period. The last one that we will look at is in
Revelation 13:

**5 And there was given to him a mouth speaking arrogant words
and blasphemies; and authority to act for forty-two months was
given to him.**

The beast will be in authority for forty-two months. This
is exactly three and a half years.

There are those who feel that each of these is referring to
the same three and a half year period, and that this would coin-
cide with "a time, times and a half time"—which most scholars
feel is three and a half years—spoken of by Daniel (Daniel 7 and
12). Other Biblical scholars would say that each of the three
periods of three and a half years is separate and, therefore, the
whole Tribulation lasts for ten and a half years.

The vast majority feel that the first three and a half years
spoken of in Revelation 11 take us to the middle of the Tribulation and then the second two references, in Chapter 12 and 13,
are referring to the same three and a half year period. Thus,
these people come out with the seven-year duration.

Personally, I am inclined to believe that the Tribulation
will probably last seven years, although I have no argument at
all with someone who believes otherwise. All I know is that it
will be long enough for God to achieve all the things that He
wants to accomplish.

In this chapter we will look at an overview of the events
of the Tribulation. Later we will examine particular catastrophes
in greater depth. Therefore, bear with us since we must, of
necessity, be very brief in this chapter.

WHY HAVE THE TRIBULATION?

Before we get into the events on the Tribulation, I think
that it is important to understand why the Tribulation is going
to occur. Most Christians have never even thought about this.
Let us first assume something. If Jesus Christ started to reign
for a thousand years on earth tomorrow, what is the first thing
that would have to occur? He would have to destroy all that is
evil. Houses of prostitution, dope peddlers, criminals, and all

that is evil would have to go. Since He would be the government, there would be no need for national, state or local governments, so all of those buildings would need to be destroyed.
The earth that has been so corrupted would have to be plowed
up and made new. Some of the inhospitable parts of the earth
would need to be made productive. Do you get the picture?
There would have to be a time of destruction of evil, eradica-
tion of institutions and organizations that we know today, and
a plowing up of the earth. This would be a messy way to start
His peaceful, joyous reign of a thousand years.

A major purpose of the Tribulation, then is to destroy all
of the evil and unrighteousness on the earth, to tear down the
world government institutions, armies and police forces, and to
physically plow up the earth in preparation for it to become a
garden once again. After this purging and purifying of the earth,
nature will be set free; the wolves and the sheep will be able to
live in harmony with each other, and Christ will reign over a
revised planet earth.

Evidently God wants Christians here on the earth during
this process of purification of the earth. This must mean that
He wants to use us in the process. I find that really exciting!
I am going to witness God purifying the earth, and possibly be
used as one of His tools to that end! Not only do I believe that
I will be here to go through it; I am really looking forward to it.

Now let us look at how this purifying process (the great
Tribulation) begins.

GOSPEL TO ALL NATIONS (SEAL ONE)

In an earlier chapter, we discussed the Lamb being the only
One worthy to break the seals from the scroll, and that as He
broke each seal and unrolled the scroll to the next seal, the
events written on that portion of the scroll would occur on the
earth. We see the first seal being broken in Revelation 6:

1 And I saw when the Lamb broke one of the seven seals, and I
heard one of the four living creatures saying as with a voice of
thunder, "Come."
2 And I looked, and behold, a white horse, and he who sat on it
had a bow; and a crown was given to him; and he went out conquering, and to conquer.

I believe that the white horse and its rider represent Christians going forth to win souls for Christ (conquer for Christ). The crown signifies the authority that Christ gives to all believers representing Him, their Master, here on the earth. As Christ was talking about the end of the age, He said this in Mark 13:

7   "And when you hear of wars and rumors of wars, do not be frightened; *those things* must take place; but *that is* not yet the end.

8   "For nation will arise against nation, and kingdom against kingdom; there will be earthquakes in various places; there will *also* be famines. These things are *merely* the beginning of birth pangs.

9   "But be on your guard; for they will deliver you up to *the* courts, and you will be flogged in *the* synagogues, and you will stand before governors and kings for My sake, as a testimony to them.

10   "And the gospel must first be preached to all the nations.

11   "And when they arrest you and deliver you up, do not be anxious beforehand about what you are to say, but say whatever is given you in that hour; for it is not you who speak, but *it is* the Holy Spirit.

12   "And brother will deliver up brother to death, and a father *his* child; and children will rise up against parents and cause them to be put to death.

13   "And you will be hated by all on account of My name, but it is the one who has endured to the end who will be saved. . . ."

Here we see many of the things listed that are also found in the six seals. There are famines, persecution of Christians, earthquakes and wars. Verse 10 says, "And the gospel must first be preached to all the nations." Since this is earmarked with all of the events found in the first six seals, it too should be represented in the seals. I believe that it is represented here in the first seal by the white horse that went out to conquer. This is a symbolic picture of the gospel going out to all nations. Since the Tribulation starts with this seal, it will be very difficult to know exactly when it has begun.

WORLD WAR III (SEAL TWO)

The second seal tells of a coming war. This war is not the Battle of Armageddon. It is World War III, which will precede the Battle of Armageddon by about seven years. Further in Revelation 6 we read:

> 3 And when He broke the second seal, I heard the second living creature saying, "Come."
> 4 And another, a red horse, went out; and to him who sat on it, it was granted to take peace from the earth, and that *men* should slay one another; and a great sword was given to him.

When the second seal is broken, a rider on a red horse takes peace "from the earth," and thus we know that it will be a worldwide war. According to most of the prophetic writers, it will be a nuclear war. As a result of World War III, evidently much of the world's food will be destroyed, because the next major thing to occur in the Tribulation is . . .

WORLD FAMINE (SEAL THREE)

The world's food supply today is very delicately balanced. As the population continues to grow geometrically, the food supply is not keeping up with it. One year's loss of crops is all that it would take to create significant food shortages. Revelation 6 tells of one that is coming:

> 5 And when He broke the third seal, I heard the third living creature saying, "Come." And I looked, and behold, a black horse; and he who sat on it had a pair of scales in his hand.
> 6 And I heard as it were a voice in the center of the four living creatures saying, "A quart of wheat for a denarius, and three quarts of barley for a denarius; and do not harm the oil and the wine."

We can see in verse 6 that a quart of wheat cost a denarius, which was equivalent to about 18 cents in silver. Back in the time this was written, that was a day's wage, and therefore what this passage is saying is that a man would have to work all day to earn a quart of wheat, or three quarts of a less desirable grain. This means that 100 percent of a working man's wages would have to be used to buy food. This would leave nothing to pay the rent, buy clothes, and so forth. Can you imagine the economic and social calamities that would occur today if 100 percent of a man's wage had to go to buy food? Place that kind of famine, starvation and upheaval after a nuclear war, and you can begin to see the horrors of what might be ahead.

It is also interesting to note in verse 6 that the oil and wine will not be so escalated in price. These tend to be luxury items.

Evidently the wealthy will fare much better than the average working person.

KILLING WITH SWORD, FAMINE, PESTILENCE AND WILD BEAST (SEAL FOUR)

When the next seal is broken and the events occur (Revelation 6:7, 8), we see the inhabitants of one-fourth of the earth killed. They are killed by various things—some die by the sword (more war), and some die of starvation (more famine). These two things we have already seen.

During this seal we see two additional causes of death. The first is pestilence. The dictionary defines this as a devastating epidemic disease. This epidemic might be casued by the radiation from a nuclear war, or it could be caused by all of the dead bodies around. There are approximately 4 billion people living on the planet today. If 25 percent of these died, there would be 1 billion bodies to bury. It would take many months to bury that many people. The disease created by these corpses could be the pestilence that sweeps the earth. Even more likely, this plague could come from biological (germ) warfare. The U. S. has supposedly stopped producing supplies for chemical or biological warfare. However, the Russians are still producing these in vast quantities, and continue to develop new ones. No matter what the cause, the Word of God says that this epidemic disease, in spite of our modern medical miracles, will kill vast numbers of people. It will make Bangladesh look like a Sunday school picnic.

The other thing that occurs when this seal is broken is that people are killed by the "wild beasts of the earth." These may indeed be the grizzly bears, lions, tigers, and so on. However, I would like to propose an alternative to that. As a result of the famine, people will not have enough food to feed their dogs and cats. Since most people love their pets, they would not kill them. What would they do with them then? They would likely turn them loose to fend for themselves. I have seen a "pet" dog on Catalina Island get hungry and begin to kill wild goats. Once a tame dog gets the taste of blood, he is extremely dangerous. In this particular case on Catalina, the animal had to be disposed of.

We could see packs of dogs and cats, wild with hunger, running through the cities and neighborhoods attacking anything that moved. This could be a very real and grave danger. Whether the killing be by animals that we normally think of as wild beasts or by our domesticated pets gone wild, or by both, the Scriptures clearly say that many people will die because of attacks by animals.

PERSECUTION OF CHRISTIANS (SEAL FIVE)

When the fifth seal is broken, we see Christians who have not only been persecuted, but killed because they maintained their testimony. Revelation 6 relates this:

9 And when He broke the fifth seal, I saw underneath the altar the souls of those who had been slain because of the word of God, and because of the testimony which they had maintained;

10 and they cried out with a loud voice, saying, "How long, O Lord, holy and true, wilt Thou refrain from judging and avenging our blood on those who dwell on the earth?"

11 And there was given to each of them a white robe; and they were told that they should rest for a little while longer, until *the number of* their fellow servants and their brethren who were to be killed even as they had been, should be completed also.

These Christians, who were martyred because they would not deny Christ, are crying to the Lord, urging Him to avenge their deaths. The Lord tells them to wait awhile longer, for the judgment will not take place until even more Christians have been martyred.

EARTH UPHEAVAL (SEAL SIX)

The events of this seal involve the planet earth itself. There will be an earthquake of such gigantic proportion that it really should not be called a quake, but an earth upheaval. This is described in Revelation 6:

12 And I looked when He broke the sixth seal, and there was a great earthquake; and the sun became black as sackcloth *made* of hair, and the whole moon became like blood;

13 and the stars of the sky fell to the earth, as a fig tree casts its unripe figs when shaken by a great wind.

14 And the sky was split apart like a scroll when it is rolled up; and every mountain and island were moved out of their places.

15   And the kings of earth and the great men and the commanders and the rich and the strong and every slave and free man, hid themselves in the caves and among the rocks of the mountains;

16   and they said to the mountains and to the rocks, "Fall on us and hide us from the presence of Him who sits on the throne, and from the wrath of the Lamb;

17   for the great day of their wrath has come; and who is able to stand?"

In verse 14 we see that the earth upheaval John saw in his vision was of such a colossal magnitude that every mountain and island were moved out of their places. This type of cataclysm would leave very few structures standing on the earth, including single story dwellings. The soot thrown into the air, from torn fissures and volcanos that would be created, would be of such volume that the sun would become as black as sackcloth, and the moon like blood.

Because there were no structures left, even the kings and the great men hid themselves in caves and among the rocks in the mountains. One of the reasons for being in the mountains would be to escape the tremendous tidal waves that would be created by this earth upheaval. It would be possible to see tidal waves of 1,000 feet, or higher, which could destroy much of the coastal areas of the continents.

Before any other catastrophic events are poured down on the earth, there is a pause in Revelation 7 while the servants of God are sealed on their foreheads. The angels who were going to harm the earth, the sea, and the trees could not go forth until God's bond servants had been sealed. This seal will protect them from the wrath of God to follow.

SEVEN TRUMPETS (SEAL SEVEN)

The seventh seal is actually subdivided into seven parts, each represented by the sounding of a trumpet. As part of the catastrophies of these trumpets, we see hail and fire raining down on the earth, a burning mountain being cast into the sea, waters becoming bad, the sky being darkened, a plague of locust-like creatures that hurt men, and 200 million horsemen (soldiers) that kill one-third of mankind. But let us examine these trumpets one at a time.

Hail and Fire (Trumpet One)

In Revelation 8, we learn that the seventh seal consists of seven trumpets, and that the first trumpet sounds as follows:

1 And when He broke the seventh seal, there was silence in heaven for about half an hour.

2 And I saw the seven angels who stand before God; and seven trumpets were given to them. . . .

6 And the seven angels who had the seven trumpets prepared themselves to sound them.

7 And the first sounded, and there came hail and fire, mixed with blood, and they were thrown to the earth; and a third of the earth was burnt up, and a third of the trees were burnt up, and all the green grass was burnt up.

Here we see a mixture of hail, fire, and blood that was poured down on the earth and burned up a third of the trees and all of the grass (grass would include wheat and other grains). Many of the plagues in Revelation bring to mind the plagues that God created through Moses, in order to get the children of Israel out of Egypt. Exodus 9 recounts one which is similar to this event in Revelation:

22 Now the Lord said to Moses, "Stretch out your hand toward the sky, that hail may fall on all the land of Egypt, on man and on beast and on every plant of the field, throughout the land of Egypt."

23 And Moses stretched out his staff toward the sky, and the Lord sent thunder and hail, and fire ran down to the earth. And the Lord rained hail on the land of Egypt.

24 So there was hail, and fire flashing continually in the midst of the hail, very severe, such as had not been in all the land of Egypt since it became a nation.

25 And the hail struck all that was in the field through all the land of Egypt, both man and beast, the hail also struck every plant of the field and shattered every tree of the field.

God frequently uses natural phenomenon to achieve the miraculous. It is possible that the rain of hail and fire, both in Revelation and in Exodus, was created by rocks and particles in the tail of a comet. Such rocks would have a large static electrical charge. If a comet passes close enough to the earth, the gravitational force of the earth will cause some of the rocks and particles from the tail of the comet to be pulled down. These particles, charged with static electricity, would discharge this electricity when they hit the earth. Thus, you would have a rain of hail mixed with fire. The discharge of static electricity could easily ignite grass and even some trees.

If not from a comet, the rain of hail and fire could consist of "rocks" from space that became very hot because of their entry into the earth's atmosphere. However it occurs, 33 percent of the earth will be burnt up by the fiery hail.

Burning Mountain Cast into Sea (Trumpet Two)

In Revelation 8 we see this recorded:

8 And the second angel sounded, and *something* **like a great mountain burning with fire was thrown into the sea; and a third of the sea became blood;**

9 and a third of the creatures, which were in the sea and had life, died; and a third of the ships were destroyed.

If a comet, such as we were discussing—which could be a hundred miles or more in diameter—were to land in the Atlantic Ocean, it would certainly kill the creatures in that ocean and destroy any ships that were there. Thus, it is easy to see how a third of the creatures in the sea and a third of the ships could be destroyed.

Some scientists estimate that if a meteor the size that caused the great meteor crater in Arizona were to hit the Atlantic, it would create a tidal wave that would cover the Appalachians. When this giant burning mountain falls into the sea there will be tremendous destruction even on the land, because of the tidal waves.

Some prophetic scholars view the occurrences of the first and second trumpets as the results of a nuclear explosion in the ocean. Even though I don't agree with them, this is perfectly fine. A nuclear blast would rain hail mixed with fire and would destroy the life in the sea. It really doesn't matter exactly *what* God uses. What we are looking at here is the end result—the destruction that will occur on the earth.

Waters Made Bitter (Trumpet Three)

There was something that John described as a star falling which made a third of the rivers and springs on the earth so bitter that people died just because they drank the water. It doesn't matter what falls from the skies—a man-made rocket, a meteor, or some supernatural creation of God; the fact remains that the water is going to be contaminated, and that many people will die because of it. Revelation 8 gives the following account of this:

> 10 And the third angel sounded, and a great star fell from heaven, burning like a torch, and it fell on a third of the rivers and on the springs of waters;
> 11 and the name of the star is called Wormwood; and a third of the waters became wormwood; and many men died from the waters, because they were made bitter.

Darkening of the Sky (Trumpet Four)

Possibly the dust and dirt particles from the tail of the aforementioned comet (or the residual from a tremendous nuclear blast, or volcanic dust and soot) would contaminate the atmosphere to the point where our daylight would only be a third as long as it normally is. Perhaps the sun would only be able to shine through when it was close to overhead. (This would obviously make the famine and food situation even worse. Crops must have sunlight in order to grow.) We read of a darkening of the sky when the fourth trumpet is sounded:

> 12 And the fourth angel sounded, and a third of the sun and a third of the moon and a third of the stars were smitten, so that a third of them might be darkened and the day might not shine for a third of it, and the night in the same way.
> 13 And I looked, and I heard an eagle flying in midheaven, saying with a loud voice, "Woe, woe, woe, to those who dwell on the earth, because of the remaining blasts of the trumpet of the three angels who are about to sound!" (Revelation 8).

Five Months of Torment (Trumpet Five)

As the fifth angel sounded there was a further darkening of the sky, because of the smoke that went up when the bottomless pit was opened. Out of the pit came forth some creatures that John described as being like locusts but having something like the sting of scorpions in their tails. These creatures were not allowed to hurt any green thing or any tree, but only men who did not have the seal of God on their foreheads. They were not permitted to kill anyone—only to torment them. Let's see how the Word of God records it:

1 And the fifth angel sounded, and I saw a star from heaven which had fallen to the earth; and the key of the bottomless pit was given to him.

2 And he opened the bottomless pit; and smoke went up out of the pit, like the smoke of a great furnace; and the sun and the air were darkened by the smoke of the pit.

3 And out of the smoke came forth locusts upon the earth; and power was given them, as the scorpions of the earth have power.

4 And they were told that they should not hurt the grass of the earth, nor any green thing, nor any tree, but only the men who do not have the seal of God on their foreheads.

5 And they were not permitted to kill anyone, but to torment for five months; and their torment was like the torment of a scorpion when it stings a man.

6 And in those days men will seek death and will not find it; and they will long to die and death flees from them.

7 And the appearance of the locusts was like horses prepared for battle; and on their heads, as it were, crowns like gold, and their faces were like the faces of men.

8 And they had hair like the hair of women, and their teeth were like *the teeth* of lions.

9 And they had breastplates like breastplates of iron; and the sound of their wings was like the sound of chariots, of many horses rushing to battle.

10 And they have tails like scorpions, and stings; and in their tails is their power to hurt men for five months.

11 They have as king over them, the angel of the abyss; his name in Hebrew is Abaddon, and in the Greek he has the name Apollyon.

12 The first woe is past; behold, two woes are still coming after these things (Revelation 9).

I do not know if the "locust-scorpions" will be natural creatures as we know them—such as killer bees—creatures created by God specifically for this task, or human beings in an airborne attack. Remember that it doesn't matter *what* tool God uses; what we see here is that there will be five months of agonizing torment for those who do not know Christ.

A Third of Humanity Killed (Trumpet Six)

At the sixth trumpet, a third of humanity was killed by plagues and 200 million armed horsemen. We are not sure if this was a third of the people still alive at this point (remember, 25 percent have already been killed), or a third of the people alive at the beginning of the Tribulation. Either way, at least an additional 1 billion people will die here. It is recorded thusly:

13 And the sixth angel sounded, and I heard a voice from the four horns of the golden altar which is before God,

14 one saying to the sixth angel who had the trumpet, "Release the four angels who are bound at the great river Euphrates."

15 And the four angels, who had been prepared for the hour and day and month and year, were released, so that they might kill a third of mankind.

16 And the number of armies of the horsemen was two hundred million; I heard the number of them.

17 And this is how I saw in the vision the horses and those who sat on them: *the riders* had breastplates *the color* of fire and of hyacinth and of brimstone; and the heads of the horses are like the heads of lions; and out of their mouths proceed fire and smoke and brimstone.

18 A third of mankind was killed by these three plagues, by the fire and the smoke and the brimstone, which proceeded out of their mouths.

19 For the power of the horses is in their mouths and in their tails; for their tails are like serpents and have heads; and with them they do harm.

20 And the rest of mankind, who were not killed by these plagues, did not repent of THE WORKS OF THEIR HANDS, so as not to worship DEMONS, AND THE IDOLS OF GOLD AND OF SILVER AND OF BRASS AND OF STONE AND OF WOOD, WHICH CAN NEITHER SEE NOR HEAR NOR WALK;

21 and they did not repent of their murders nor of their sorceries nor of their immorality nor of their thefts (Revelation 9).

With all of the damage, destruction and death that had occurred upon the earth, the people left alive still did not repent; they continued to worship demons and idols.

THE TRIBULATION IS HALF OVER
(THREE AND A HALF YEARS HAVE ELAPSED)

We see the halfway point of the Tribulation in Revelation 11, which points out that for forty-two months (three and a half years) Jerusalem was tread underfoot by the nations of the world. Also during this three and a half year period (twelve hundred and sixty days), two witnesses were witnessing for Christ. Some people believe the two witnesses to be two individuals. I believe that it is likely that they will be two companies of people. The best that I can discern from the Lord is that these companies will be the Jews and Gentiles who know Jesus Christ as their Savior, who are actively witnessing for Him, and *doing miracles.* (We observe that people cannot harm the two witnesses. Fire comes out of their mouth to kill their attackers, and they have the power to prevent rain, to turn water into blood, and to smite the earth.) The day of mighty miracles by Christians is coming. Let's read of these exciting events in Revelation 11:

 1 And there was given me a measuring rod like a staff; and someone said, "Rise and measure the temple of God, and the altar, and those who worship in it.

 2 "And leave out the court which is outside the temple, and do not measure it, for it has been given to the nations; and they will tread under foot the holy city for forty-two months.

 3 "And I will grant *authority* to my witnesses, and they will prophesy for twelve hundred and sixty days, clothed in sackcloth."

 4 These are the two olive trees and the two lampstands that stand before the Lord of the earth.

 5 And if any one desires to harm them, fire proceeds out of their mouth and devours their enemies; and if any one would desire to harm them, in this manner he must be killed.

 6 These have the power to shut up the sky, in order that rain may not fall during the days of their prophesying; and they have power over the waters to turn them into blood, and to smite the earth with every plague, as often as they desire.

 7 And when they have finished their testimony, the beast that comes up out of the abyss will make war with them, and overcome them and kill them.

8 And their dead bodies *will lie* in the street of the great city which mystically is called Sodom and Egypt, where also their Lord was crucified.

9 And those from the peoples and tribes and tongues and nations *will* look at their dead bodies for three days and a half, and will not permit their dead bodies to be laid in a tomb.

10 And those who dwell on the earth *will* rejoice over them and make merry; and they will send gifts to one another, because these two prophets tormented those who dwell on the earth.

11 And after the three days and a half the breath of life from God came into them, and they stood on their feet; and great fear fell upon those who were beholding them.

12 And they heard a loud voice from heaven saying to them, "Come up here." And they went up into heaven in the cloud, and their enemies beheld them.

In verse 7 we see that when the beast (Antichrist) comes up out of the abyss, he will be able to kill the two witnesses. But, like Christ, they will arise in three and a half days. All will behold them in their resurrected state, as they go into heaven in the cloud. (Some feel that this is the Rapture and that it is in the middle of the Tribulation. However, the event of the beast arising has not yet occurred; this happens in Revelation 13. The death, resurrection and ascension of the two witnesses must therefore take place later in time, certainly after the last trump and Revelation 13.)

THE LAST TRUMPET (TRUMPET SEVEN)

We have dealt with this trumpet earlier, but would like to repeat the Scriptures concerning it here:

15 And the seventh angel sounded; and there arose loud voices in heaven, saying,

"The kingdom of the world has become *the kingdom* of our Lord, and of His Christ; and He will reign forever and ever."

16 And the twenty-four elders, who sit on their thrones before God, fell on their faces and worshiped God,

17 saying,

"We give Thee thanks, O Lord God, the Almighty, who art and who wast, because Thou has taken Thy great power and hast begun to reign.

18 "And the nations were enraged, and Thy wrath came, and the time *came* for the dead to be judged, and *the time* to give their reward to Thy bond-servants the prophets and to the saints and to those who fear Thy name, the small and the great, and to destroy those who destroy the earth."

19 And the temple of God which is in heaven was opened; and the ark of His covenant appeared in His temple, and there were flashes of lightning and sounds and peals of thunder and an earthquake and a great hailstorm (Revelation 11).

Here we see Christ beginning to reign, rewarding the saints and judging the dead. I believe that Revelation 12 through 19 is an amplification of this seventh trumpet, which is blown at the end of the Tribulation. Among other things, we will find in these chapters: the rising of the Antichrist, the mark of the beast, the seven bowls of wrath, and the fall of the great city Babylon. We will look at a few of the more significant events of this last half of the Tribulation.

War in Heaven—Satan Cast Down to Earth

When I talk about Satan being cast down in a future sense, many people might say: "Wait a minute. I thought that Satan was cast down a long time ago." Let us first see what Revelation 12 has to say about this:

7 And there was war in heaven, Michael and his angels waging war with the dragon. And the dragon and his angels waged war,

8 and they were not strong enough, and there was no longer a place found for them in heaven.

9 And the great dragon was thrown down, the serpent of old who is called the devil and Satan, who deceives the whole world; he was thrown down to the earth, and his angels were thrown down with him.

10 And I heard a loud voice in heaven, saying,

"Now the salvation, and the power, and the kingdom of our God and the authority of His Christ have come, for the accuser of our brethren has been thrown down, who accuses them before our God day and night.

11 "And they overcame him because of the blood of the Lamb and because of the word of their testimony, and they did not love their life even to death.

12 "For this reason, rejoice, O heavens and you who dwell in them. Woe to the earth and the sea; because the devil has come down to you, having great wrath, knowing that he has *only* a short time."

In the Old and New Testament, Satan has access both to the earth and the throne of God. We see him on the earth tempting Eve, and later, Christ. We also see him before God, as he asks for permission to try Job. Here in Revelation it says that he accuses the Christians before God. It also says that there will be a future war in heaven, and that Satan will be defeated and cast out. After that point Satan will no longer have access to the throne of God.

In verse 12 we see that Satan will know that he only has a *short time* left. He will need to quickly find a person(s) to control, and then he will begin his terrible persecution of believers in Christ.

Hal Lindsey, on page 175 of his book, *There's A New World Coming* (published by Vision House Publishers), had this to say in commenting on these verses:

"Satan is what I call a diehard! Here he is with his boys, making one last attempt to take over heaven. But God has a champion in the person of His archangel, Michael, and even though Jude 9 tells us of a prior dispute between Michael and Satan in which Michael handles him with kid gloves, we don't see any of that in this scene.

"Satan and his angels are instead booted out of heaven *to* the earth, and from that point on he is never allowed to come before God again with accusations against God's children or for any other reason.

"Since this conflict takes place at the middle of the Tribulation, I hate to think of the fury that Satan will unleash on the earth when he no longer has access to the heavenlies where he and his cohorts have resided since their original fall from heaven's good graces!

"For the last three and one-half years of the Tribulation, Satan will have a field day with those still left on earth, both believers and unbelievers. Since he can no longer accuse Christians before the Father, he'll no doubt seek to accuse and torment everyone on earth who has believed in Christ."

Satan Takes Over Two Men—The Two Beasts

Satan (the dragon) proceeds to take out his fury upon the earth:

17 And the dragon was enraged with the woman, and went off to make war with the rest of her offspring, who keep the commandments of God and hold to the testimony of Jesus (Revelation 12).

1 And he stood on the sand of the seashore.

And I saw a beast coming up out of the sea, having ten horns and seven heads, and on his horns *were* ten diadems, and on his heads *were* blasphemous names.

2 And the beast which I saw was like a leopard, and his feet were *like those* of a bear, and his mouth like the mouth of a lion. And the dragon gave him his power and his throne and great authority.

3 And I *saw* one of his heads as if it had been slain, and his fatal wound was healed. And the whole earth was amazed *and followed* after the beast;

4 and they worshipped the dragon, because he gave his authority to the beast; and they worshipped the beast, saying,

"Who is like the beast, and who is able to wage war with him?"

5 And there was given to him a mouth speaking arrogant words and blasphemies; and authority to act for forty-two months was given to him.

6 And he opened his mouth in blasphemies against God, to blaspheme His name and His tabernacle, *that is,* those who dwell in heaven.

7 And it was given to him to make war with the saints and to overcome them; and authority over every tribe and people and tongue and nation was given to him.

8 And all who dwell on the earth will worship him, *every one* whose name has not been written from the foundation of the world in the book of life of the Lamb who has been slain (Revelation 13).

Here we see the first man that Satan completely controls. Satan gives him great power and authority. The details of this symbolic image are explained in Revelation 17:7-17. There the angel explains to John that the waters mean the multitudes of the nations. The ten diadems (crowns) show that this beast will be a king or a world dictator. He will restore peace because no one will be able to war against him. Not only will he be a king-dictator, but—like Caesar—he will be worshipped as God. In this book, we will call this beast the "dictator-beast."

In the latter half of Revelation 13, we behold another beast coming up out of the land (earth). This beast does not have any crowns, and therefore is not in the political arena. Instead, he is in the religious arena. We will call him the "prophet-beast." He performs great signs and causes everyone to worship the dictator-beast:

> 11 And I saw another beast coming up out of the earth; and he had two horns like a lamb, and he spoke as a dragon.
>
> 12 And he exercises all the authority of the first beast in his presence. And he makes the earth and those who dwell in it to worship the first beast, whose fatal wound was healed.
>
> 13 And he performs great signs, so that he even makes fire come down out of heaven to the earth in the presence of men.
>
> 14 And he deceives those who dwell on the earth because of the signs which it was given him to perform in the presence of the beast, telling those who dwell on the earth to make an image to the beast who had the wound of the sword and has come to life.
>
> 15 And there was given to him to give breath to the image of the beast, that the image of the beast might even speak and cause as many as do not worship the image of the beast to be killed (Revelation 13).

We learn that anyone who does not worship the image of the dictator-beast will be killed by the prophet-beast. These two, along with Satan, make an unholy trinity, which is mentioned in Revelation 16:

> 13 And I saw *coming* out of the mouth of the dragon and out of the mouth of the beast and out of the mouth of the false prophet, three unclean spirits like frogs;
>
> 14 for they are spirits of demons, performing signs, which go out to the kings of the whole world, to gather them together for the war of the great day of God, the Almighty.
>
> 15 (Behold, I am coming like a thief. Blessed is the one who stays awake and keeps his garments, lest he walk about naked and men see his shame.)
>
> 16 And they gathered them together to the place which in Hebrew is called Har-Magedon.

Here we see all three in conjunction: the dragon (Satan), the beast and the false prophet. They are gathering nations to war against God.

The Mark of the Beast

The prophet-beast causes everyone to worship the dictator-beast, and the idol or image of the dictator-beast. Anyone who does not worship this image is to be killed. This means that Christians who refuse to worship the beast will all be under a death sentence. The prophet-beast also causes all inhabitants of the earth to receive the mark of the beast (dictator-beast) on their right hand or forehead. He insures that no one can buy or sell without this mark. At that point there will be a worldwide religious system—wherein everyone must worship the beast—and a world economic system, controlled by the world religious system, so that no one will be able to buy or sell without the mark of the beast. The Word of God relates this as follows:

> 16 And he causes all, the small and the great, and the rich and the poor, and the free men and the slaves, to be given a mark on their right hand, or on their forehead,
>
> 17 and *he provides* that no one should be able to buy or to sell, except the one who has the mark, *either* the name of the beast or the number of his name.
>
> 18 Here is wisdom. Let him who has understanding calculate the number of the beast, for the number is that of a man; and his number is six hundred and sixty-six (Revelation 13).

The Bible warns that there are dire consequences to receiving the mark of the beast and to worshiping the image (which is probably a prerequisite to receiving the mark of the beast). These terrible consequences are found in Revelation 14:

> 9 And another angel, a third one, followed them, saying with a loud voice, "If any one worships the beast and his image, and receives a mark on his forehead or upon his hand,
>
> 10 he also will drink of the wine of the wrath of God, which is mixed in full strength in the cup of His anger; and he will be tormented with fire and brimstone in the presence of the holy angels and in the presence of the Lamb.
>
> 11 "And the smoke of their torment goes up forever and ever; and they have no rest day and night, those who worship the beast and his image, and whoever receives the mark of his name."

12 Here is the perseverance of the saints who keep the commandments of God and their faith in Jesus.

13 And I heard a voice from heaven, saying, "Write, 'Blessed are
the dead who die in the Lord from now on!'" "Yes," says the Spirit,
"that they may rest from their labors, for their deeds follow with
them."

We learn that anyone who receives the mark of the beast
will receive the full wrath of God, and will be tormented day
and night forever.

Pause for a moment, Christian, and try to imagine what it
would be like if you were not able to buy or sell anything. You
could not go to the grocery store to buy food, you could not
buy water and electricity, you could not pay your rent, or buy
clothes. You would also be under death condemnation, according to what we have been reading. You would be a wanted person. What would you do? Where would you go? This should be
very much a matter of prayer, because it is likely that we will
experience this situation. We will have much more to say about
it in Chapter 9.

The Sun Scorches Men with Fire and Fierce Heat

In Revelation 16 there are seven bowls of the wrath of God
poured out into the earth. These I will let you read for yourself.
Many of them are repeats of some of these catastrophes we have
already discussed. However, there are two new ones that I would
like to mention briefly. One is from the fourth bowl:

8 And the fourth *angel* poured out his bowl upon the sun; and
it was given to it to scorch men with fire.

9 And men were scorched with fierce heat; and they blasphemed
the name of God who has the power over these plagues; and they
did not repent, so as to give Him glory (Revelation 16).

We see the sun scorching men with fierce heat. This could
result from the sun expanding the amount of heat it puts out,
the earth being knocked closer to the sun because of the impact
with a comet, a dissipation of the earth's atmosphere, or freak
weather conditions. These are just some of the possibilities.
Whatever the cause, this time of fierce heat is coming.

Earth Upheaval and 100 Pound Hailstones

As the seventh angel poured out his bowl, the following things occurred on the earth:

> 17 And the seventh *angel* poured out his bowl upon the air; and a loud voice came out of the temple from the throne, saying, "It is done."
>
> 18 And there were flashes of lightning and sounds and peals of thunder; and there was a great earthquake, such as there had not been since man came to be upon the earth, so great an earthquake *was it, and* so mighty.
>
> 19 And the great city was split into three parts, and the cities of the nations fell. And Babylon the great was remembered before God, to give her the cup of the wine of His fierce wrath.
>
> 20 And every island fled away, and the mountains were not found.
>
> 21 And huge hailstones, about one hundred pounds each, came down from heaven upon men; and men blasphemed God because of the plague of the hail, because its plague was extremely severe (Revelation 16).

In an earlier geologic upheaval we saw that every mountain and every island were moved out of their places. Here in verse 20, we see that every island and every mountain fled away and were not even to be found. *They were gone.* It is impossible to imagine the ramifications of such an earth upheaval.

In addition to this, there were 100-pound hailstones coming down. If these were to hit a man or a beast, he would be killed immediately. This kind of hail would demolish most homes. Again, it is difficult for us to conceive the damage that such a hail would do to crops, highways and even life as we know it today.

THE BATTLE OF ARMAGEDDON
(HAR-MAGEDON)

The Tribulation ends with the Battle at Armageddon (called Har-magedon in Hebrew)—a valley in Israel. We saw in Revelation 16:16 that the unholy trinity had gathered together the armies of the world in that place to battle God. Now we read of the battle itself:

> 19 And I saw the beast and the kings of the earth and their armies, assembled to make war against Him who sat upon the horse, and against His army.
>
> 20 And the beast was seized, and with him the false prophet who performed the signs in his presence, by which he deceived those who had received the mark of the beast and those who worshiped his image; these two were thrown alive into the lake of fire which burns with brimstone.
>
> 21 And the rest were killed with the sword which came from the mouth of Him who sat upon the horse, and all the birds were filled with their flesh (Revelation 19).
>
> 1 And I saw an angel coming down from heaven, having the key of the abyss and a great chain in his hand.
>
> 2 And he laid hold of the dragon, the serpent of old, who is the devil and Satan, and bound him for a thousand years,
>
> 3 and threw him into the abyss, and shut *it* and sealed *it* over him, so that he should not deceive the nations any longer, until the thousand years were completed; after these things he must be released for a short time.
>
> 4 And I saw thrones, and they sat upon them, and judgment was given to them. And I *saw* the souls of those who had been beheaded because of the testimony of Jesus and because of the word of God, and those who had not worshiped the beast or his image, and had not received the mark upon their forehead and upon their hand; and they came to life and reigned with Christ for a thousand years.
>
> 5 The rest of the dead did not come to life until the thousand years were completed. This is the first resurrection (Revelation 20).

The Battle of Armageddon is over, the catastrophes have ceased, and there will be a time of peace on the earth for one thousand years. Praise the Lord!

Do not Fear—God is in Control

In spite of all the catastrophes, Christians should not have any fear. God still loves them and is going to take care of them. *He* is the One in charge of the Tribulation—not Satan.

David Wilkerson, on page 121 of his book *The Vision* (published by Spire Books), in which he describes the calamities coming to the earth that God has shown him in a vision, ends with this admonition to Christians:

"Prepared Christians—wake up! Everything is under control and God is at work. He is saving, healing, baptising, and getting His house in order. To fear is to blaspheme. We are commanded to encourage ourselves in the Lord and to begin to sing and rejoice as we see the final hour approach. Do I hear someone ask, 'But how can I rejoice when I see this old sin-cursed world falling apart?' My answer is the Bible answer:

> For we know that the whole creation
> groaneth and travaileth in pain . . . waiting
> the redemption. (Romans 8:22, 23)

"A woman in labor may scream because of pain, yet in her heart she rejoices because of the fact of new birth.

"The kingdom of God is coming. The kingdom of Satan is falling. So the Christian can, with confidence, say: 'God has everything under control!'"

Do We Need to Prepare?

If God has everything under control, does a Christian need to make any preparation? Can't we just relax and know that God will take care of us? . . . These are very important questions and will be dealt with in the next chapter.

5

GOD WARNS

AND HIS SERVANTS PREPARE

In my travels, as I discuss the coming catastrophes with Christians, I frequently get this reaction: "Well, I don't have to worry. God loves me and He will take care of me whatever happens." That statement is so true that it is impossible to argue with it. However, there are some things that God *does* expect of us. For example, in the Old Testament if God warned one of His servants that a disaster was impending, then God *EXPECTED* that servant to make whatever preparations He told him to make. Let us take a couple of specific examples from the Scriptures.

WARNING OF FOOD SHORTAGES

Most of us, from the time we were children in Sunday school, have heard the story of pharaoh's dream and the interpretation that God gave to Joseph. Let's read this interpretation, as recorded in Genesis 41:

29 "Behold, seven years of great abundance are coming in all the land of Egypt;

30 and after them seven years of famine will come, and all the abundance will be forgotten in the land of Egypt; and the famine will ravage the land.

31 "So the abundance will be unknown in the land because of that subsequent famine; for it *will be* very severe.

32 "Now as for the repeating of the dream to Pharaoh twice, *it means* that the matter is determined by God, and God will quickly bring it about.

33 "And now let Pharaoh look for a man discerning and wise, and set him over the land of Egypt.

34 "Let Pharaoh take action to appoint overseers in charge of the land, and let him exact a fifth *of the produce* of the land of Egypt in the seven years of abundance.

35 "Then let them gather all the food of these good years that are coming, and store up the grain for food in the cities under Pharaoh's authority, and let them guard *it*.

36 "And let the food become as a reserve for the land for the seven years of famine which will occur in the land of Egypt, so that the land may not perish during the famine."

37 Now the proposal seemed good to Pharaoh and to all his servants.

38 Then Pharaoh said to his servants, "Can we find a man like this, in whom is a divine spirit?"

39 So Pharaoh said to Joseph, "Since God has informed you of all this, there is no one so discerning and wise as you are.

40 "You shall be over my house, and according to your command all my people shall do homage; only in the throne I will be greater than you." . . .

47 And during the seven years of plenty the land brought forth abundantly.

48 So he gathered all the food of *these* seven years which occurred in the land of Egypt, and placed the food in the cities; he placed in every city the food from its own surrounding fields.

49 Thus Joseph stored up grain in great abundance like the sand of the sea, until he stopped measuring *it*, for it was beyond measure. . . .

53 When the seven years of plenty which had been in the land of Egypt came to an end,

54 and the seven years of famine began to come, just as Joseph had said, then there was famine in all the lands; but in all the land of Egypt there was bread.

55 So when all the land of Egypt was famished, the people cried out to Pharaoh for bread; and Pharaoh said to all the Egyptians, "Go to Joseph; whatever he says to you, you shall do."

56 When the famine was *spread* over all the face of the earth, then Joseph opened all the storehouses, and sold to the Egyptians; and the famine was severe in the land of Egypt.

57 And *the people of* all the earth came to Egypt to buy grain from Joseph, because the famine was severe in all the earth.

As we review these verses, our minds are freshened to remember that God did warn of what was coming and it actually *did* occur. God also told them what they should do to prepare for the coming disaster. They faithfully got busy immediately making the preparation that God had suggested.

Have you ever wondered what would have happened had these people not heeded God's warnings and made those preparations? What would have happened had they not stored up food? The critical question is: if they had ignored God's warnings, was God still under any obligation to take care of them when the famine came? The Scriptures are silent on this, but in my spirit I feel that, had they ignored God's warnings, God would have not been obligated to take care of them. If God is indeed warning His people today of impending disasters and telling them to prepare, the ignoring of such a warning could have dire consequences.

However, I hasten to add that our confidence must *always* be in God, and not in our preparation. Returning to the account in Joseph's life, if the famine had lasted fourteen or twenty-one years, rather than just seven, I am sure that Joseph would have been confident that God would have miraculously taken care of them. If God leads some of us to store up food, we must be careful that our confidence is not in the food, but in God. Although God may tell you to store up food, you may never eat any of it. You may sell it, give it away, share it, or eat all of it yourself. What God leads you to do with that food, once you have stored it, is up to God. Our responsibility is to make whatever preparations He tells us to make, but to keep our hearts and our confidences in God.

NOAH IS WARNED AND PREPARES

We are all familiar with the story of Noah and the ark. God came to Noah, told him that He was going to destroy the inhabitants on the earth, and told him how to prepare for that coming disaster. This is recorded in Genesis 6:

> 13 Then God said to Noah, "The end of all flesh has come before Me; for the earth is filled with violence because of them; and behold, I am about to destroy them with the earth.
>
> 14 "Make for yourself an ark of gopher wood; you shall make the ark with rooms, and shall cover it inside and out with pitch.
>
> 15 "And this is how you shall make it: the length of the ark three hundred cubits, its breadth fifty cubits, and its height thirty cubits.
>
> 16 "You shall make a window for the ark, and finish it to a cubit from the top; and set the door of the ark in the side of it; you shall make it with lower, second, and third decks.
>
> 17 "And behold, I, even I am bringing the flood of water upon the earth, to destroy all flesh in which is the breath of life, from under heaven; everything that is on the earth shall perish.
>
> 18 "But I will establish My covenant with you; and you shall enter the ark—you and your sons and your wife, and your sons' wives with you.
>
> 19 "And of every living thing of all flesh, you shall bring two of every *kind* into the ark, to keep *them* alive with you; they shall be male and female.
>
> 20 "Of the birds after their kind, and of the animals after their kind, of every creeping thing of the ground after its kind, two of every *kind* shall come to you to keep *them* alive.
>
> 21 "And as for you, take for yourself some of all food which is edible, and gather *it* to yourself; and it shall be for food for you and for them."
>
> 22 Thus Noah did; according to all that God had commanded him, so he did.

God warned Noah, told him what to do to prepare, and Noah did it. We see this pattern repeated over and over again. It is these three steps that we want to be sure to follow:

1.   God warns His servants of disaster.

2.   They (we) are told how to prepare.

3.   They (we) make the preparations.

It is also significant that, both in the case of Noah and of Joseph, God only warned one time. He did not keep repeating his warning.

GOD MIRACULOUSLY PROVIDES FOOD

Most of us are well acquainted with the story of the Israelites wandering in the wilderness and God raining down manna from heaven in order to feed them. He did this during the period in which they were unable to provide for themselves. They had made all the preparations that God had told them to as they left Egypt; they needed food and were helpless. God caused food to rain from the sky each morning. However, this manna ceased once they entered the Promised Land, and were able to provide their own food.

There is another case of God miraculously providing food with which you may not be familiar. It is found in 1 Kings 17 and 18:

1 Now Elijah the Tishbite, who was of the settlers of Gilead, said to Ahab, "As the LORD, the God of Israel lives, before whom I stand, surely there shall be neither dew nor rain these years, except by my word." . . .

8 Then the word of the LORD came to him, saying,

9 "Arise, go to Zarephath, which belongs to Sidon, and stay there; behold, I have commanded a widow there to provide for you."

10 So he arose and went to Zarephath, and when he came to the gate of the city, behold, a widow was there gathering sticks; and he called to her and said, "Please get me a little water in a jar, that I may drink."

11 And as she was going to get *it,* he called to her and said, "Please bring me a piece of bread in your hand."

12 But she said, "As the LORD your God lives, I have no bread, only a handful of flour in the bowl and a little oil in the jar; and behold, I am gathering a few sticks that I may go in and prepare for me and my son, that we may eat it and die."

13 Then Elijah said to her, "Do not fear; go, do as you have said, but make me a little bread cake from it first, and bring *it* out to me, and afterward you may make *one* for yourself and for your son.

14 "For thus says the LORD God of Israel, 'The bowl of flour shall not be exhausted, nor shall the jar of oil be empty, until the day that the LORD sends rain on the face of the earth.'"

15 So she went and did according to the word of Elijah, and she and he and her household ate for *many* days.

16 The bowl of flour was not exhausted nor did the jar of oil become empty, according to the word of the LORD which He spoke through Elijah. . . .

1 Now it came about *after* many days, that the word of the LORD came to Elijah in the third year, saying, "Go, show yourself to Ahab, and I will send rain on the face of the earth."

The key verse is 17:14. It says that the flour and the oil would not be empty *UNTIL* there was rain again. This means that God would only miraculously provide as long as the widow could not provide for herself because of the famine (which was caused by the lack of rain).

There is a very important lesson for us to learn. When God warns us and tells us to prepare, He expects us to obey. If, after our preparations have all been exhausted, there is still a need, God *can* and *will* provide for our needs—even in a miraculous way. I believe, however, that His miraculous provision is somehow related to our heeding His warnings, remembering that He does not make this type of provision as long as we are able to work and provide for ourselves. "He who does not work shall not eat" (II Thessalonians 3:10—*The Living Bible).* His miraculous provisions will stop once we can again provide for ourselves.

IS GOD WARNING US TODAY?

I believe that today God is using the voices of many to warn His people of the coming disasters. He is placing an urgency and expectancy on men's hearts, along with a conviction that we are indeed living in the end times of this present age. We could quote book after book concerning the admonitions that God is giving to His people.

Many of the outstanding leaders of Christianity in America today are all stating publicly that they feel that Christ is coming back soon, which means the Tribulation would soon begin. Demos Shakarian, founder and president of the Full Gospel Businessmen's Fellowship recently said: "We are in the generation that can bring the gospel to every person. And isn't this what Jesus said would happen before He would return? I feel He is coming back very soon."

Along with warnings of impending disasters, God is telling His people *how* to prepare. That, of course, is one of the purposes of this book: to bring together many of the major things that God is saying to His people, both about physical and spiritual preparation for the Tribulation.

What will happen to the Christians who do not heed God's warnings and prepare? I do not know. I feel in my spirit that they will severely regret not having listened to God. Just as in the case of Noah or Joseph, I am not sure that God is under an obligation to take care of an individual who does not heed His warnings.

God Must Speak to You Personally

I do not believe that God is going to lead everyone to prepare in the same manner. As some Christians pray about the eventuality of not being able to buy or sell, and what they should do about it, God may lead them to move to a farm in Canada, for example, and to live in a self-sufficient manner. Another Christian praying about the same disaster might be led of God to store up a seven-year supply of food, and to remain in a rural community. God might tell still another Christian to stay right where he is in the city, to make no physical provision, to proclaim the gospel, and He would miraculously provide his food. Another Christian, God might lead to move to a smaller town, get enough land to have a garden, and have a self-sufficient house. God *does* have a plan for you!

The important and critical thing is that each Christian humbly ask God to show him what he should do. We have not, because we ask not (James 4:2). Possibly you have no guidance in this area because you have not been asking God for it. And you must not ask just once; all the way through the New Testament, when Jesus talked about prayer He said to *keep on* asking, *keep on* knocking, *keep on* seeking. As an example of prayer, Christ talked about a man who kept on knocking on his neighbor's door at midnight for bread. He got the bread *because* of his persistence. The widow who kept on pestering the judge until he finally granted her desires is another that He gave as an example of prayer. As you pray, God will show you personally what preparations He wants *you* to make—both in the physical and the spiritual realms—for the crises that lie ahead. I urge you to take the time to ask God, and then to listen to Him. Once He has spoken to your heart, be sure to be a *doer* of the word and not a *hearer* only.

God appears to be warning us now of multiple disasters that are impending. If this is true, we *dare* not ignore His warnings. The thing to do is to find out, individually, what He would have us do to prepare. Then we must be diligent to make those preparations.

The next two sections of this book will deal with some suggestions and alternatives for preparing for various disasters. Possibly God could use these words to help guide you into the preparations that He would have you to make. He may lead you to do all of these things, some of them, or none of them. They are presented here with the prayer that God would make your heart respond to the things that He would have you to do. Before proceeding, I encourage you to breath a prayer, asking God to give you guidance through what is written in the remainder of this book.

"These things I have spoken unto you,
that in Me ye might have peace,
In the world ye shall have tribulation:
but be of good cheer . . ." (KJV)

—*Jesus Christ*

PART 2

PHYSICAL PREPARATION

6

PREPARING TO SURVIVE

NUCLEAR WAR

First I would like to point out that I am not sure that we should split things up into "physical" and "spiritual." They are both "us" and anything we do in either area should be controlled by God. However, for ease in discussing them, I have made this arbitrary separation.

There are Christians who feel that we should not discuss the physical at all. For those, I would like to suggest that Christ is just as concerned about our physical well-being as He is about our spiritual well-being. As we read in the gospels of His earthly ministry, we find that He spent as much time dealing with physical needs (healing, providing food, providing wine, raising from the dead, and so forth) as He did with the spiritual needs. He has not changed. He still is just as concerned about our physical well-being.

As we approach the subject of preparing for physical survival, we must first acknowledge that the subject is very vast, and many of the topics that will be discussed in the next five chapters could easily have an entire book written about them.

Another difficulty in writing this section is that many of the topics would apply to several chapters. For example, the storing of water would be very critical in both a nuclear war and an earthquake. The storing of food would be important in all of the catastrophes that we will be discussing in this section. The consideration of moving to a self-sufficient farm would be applicable to preparation for nuclear war, for famine, and for the time when Christians can no longer buy or sell. What we will attempt to do is to discuss these various topics in depth when we first encounter them, and then refer back to them in later chapters.

As you read the chapters on these four coming crises, the question may well cross your mind of where you can purchase things such as water purifiers, and dehydrated food. Chapter 11 will give a summary of the things that we have discussed and will include all of the names and addresses that you might need.

My deep desire is that you will read these chapters on physical preparation prayerfully and with an open heart, regardless of what you might believe about the Tribulation. You may believe that Christians are going through the Tribulation, but should make no preparation. This is okay. However, we do have an obligation to take care of our families. There are certain things, independent of the Tribulation, that we do to prepare physically for emergencies. An example of this could be the purchasing of a fire extinguisher for the kitchen. Similarly, the suggestions in these chapters could be very valid and worthwhile simply for preparation with regard to any emergency—Tribulation-related, or not.

THE TRIBULATION STARTS WITH
WORLD WAR III

In both Revelation 6 and Matthew 24, we see that the first major event in the Tribulation is war. Revelation 6 tells us that this war is going to be worldwide:

> **1 And I saw when the Lamb broke one of the seven seals, and I heard one of the four living creatures saying as with a voice of thunder, "Come."** . . .

> **3 And when He broke the second seal, I heard the second living creature saying, "Come."**

**4 And another, a red horse, went out; and to him who sat on it.
it was granted to take peace from the earth, and that *men* should
slay one another; and a great sword was given to him.**

Since this is a worldwide war (there is no peace on the
earth), we can be certain that we are reading prophecies con-
cerning World War III. This war occurs at the beginning of the
Tribulation, about seven years before the Battle of Armageddon.
Dr. Charles R. Taylor, on pages xii and 1 of his book, *World
War III and the Destiny of America* (published by Today in
Bible Prophecy, Inc., P.O. Box 104, Redondo Beach, CA 90277)
summarizes it this way:

"The thermonuclear war, oft referred to as 'The Battle by Fire,' in
accordance with many Bible prophecies which shall be quoted and corre-
lated in the course of this book, is destined to occur approximately and
almost exactly seven years before 'The Battle of Armageddon.' It shall be
very short in duration, but it shall be of tremendous devastation. . . .

"Since 'The Battle of Armageddon' will see the vast armies of the
world gathered together against Jerusalem; but since the ultimate destruction of those armies will be by the power of the Resurrected Christ when
He returns into this earth with His saints to reign as King of Kings and
Lord of Lords (Revelation 19:11-20:4); therefore, 'The Battle by Fire'
which is prophesied throughout the Scriptures must be before that time."

In order to further show that these are two separate and
distinct battles, Dr. Taylor later (pages 135-137) summarizes
the differences between World War III (which occurs at the beginning of the Tribulation) and the Battle of Armageddon
(which closes the Tribulation):

"From each, every and all of the aforementioned contrasts, any
truthful and thinking person can see that it is absolutely impossible for
the two great wars depicted herein to be considered as one and the same
battle. In summary:

"A.   World War III involves but one-third of the world. The Battle
of Armageddon sees the whole world gathered unto battle.

"B.   World War III will have its climaxing battle on 'the mountains
of Israel' (The Lebanese and the Syrian area Anti-Lebanese Mountains).

"The Battle of Armageddon will have its climaxing battle in the
Valley of Meggiddo, called Armageddon, just north of Jerusalem.

"C.   In World War III the full-scale battle takes place when the U.S.S.R., as 'the king of the north' comes 'against him' (Israel's pseudo-protector, the selected king or leader of the Western European Revived Roman Empire area and probable Commander of the W.E.U. and/or NATO forces which would, by treaty, involve and include the United States of America with its 'super-power' Sixth Fleet of the Mediterranean war theater, its Polaris-Poseidon nuclear missile submarines, its ICBMs and other nuclear devices (over 10,000 nuclear warheads or bombs being presently deployed in Europe alone), and its highly potent Strategic Air Command) 'like a whirlwind,' as portrayed in the prophecy recorded in Daniel 11:40.

"In the Battle of Armageddon the real battle takes place when 'the kings of the whole world' are gathered unto 'a place called . . . Armageddon,' near Jerusalem, 'to make war against him that sat upon the horse (Christ) and against his army.' (Rev. 19:19).

"D.   THE RESULTS OF THE BATTLES CONFLICT COMPLETELY.

"In World War III 'the king' becomes identified with 'the beast' referred to in Revelation 13 and with 'the scarlet-colored beast' described in Revelation 17 when he usurps his power for his own glory, claiming full credit for the victory wherein 'many countries shall be overthrown, and the land of Egypt shall not escape, but he shall have power over the treasures of gold and of silver, and over all the precious things of Egypt, and the Libyans and Ethiopians (the other Arab League nations) shall be at his steps,' as depicted in Daniel 11:41-43.

"The end result of the Battle of Armageddon is the absolute destruction of this 'beast' when Christ and His army of saints come forth from heaven. Christ, as 'KING OF KINGS AND LORD OF LORDS' (Rev. 19:16), defeats the armies of the whole world gathered together, and casts the 'beast' and his false prophet into the lake of fire and brimstone. This prophecy is specifically recorded in Rev. 19:11-21.

"E.   World War III establishes the end-time king-despot in his place of power.

"The Battle of Armageddon brings about his defeat and establishes the real rule of PEACE on earth by the real KING OF KINGS AND LORD OF LORDS, the resurrected and glorified Lord Jesus Christ."

World War III Most Likely will be Nuclear

If there is going to be a war involving the whole earth, it is hard to imagine it without some use of nuclear weapons. It is possible that a small country, which has nuclear bombs, would use these to defend itself. With all of the submarines from the U. S. and Russia armed with nuclear missiles, it is difficult to imagine a war without some of these submarines being hit and their nuclear devices exploding. Once the first one is exploded, we could subsequently see—in domino fashion—an extensive use of nuclear devices.

There is also a heavy arms buildup, particularly by Russia. Their naval force now far exceeds that of the United States, and their nuclear missiles are much more numerous. With continuing arms buildup, the likelihood of nuclear war becomes even greater.

In addition to nuclear war, there is Scriptural evidence which could lead one to believe that chemical and biological warfare will also be used. As we saw earlier, biological warfare could be responsible for the pestilences described in the fourth seal.

THE TWO PHASES OF A NUCLEAR EXPLOSION

If there is nuclear war, it is possible that a nuclear bomb (or bombs) could be exploded near where you live or work.

I have found that there are two distinct phases involved in a nuclear explosion, and different actions are required in each of the phases. The first phase is the initial blast wherein you have the thermal waves, the initial radiation and the wall of fire. During the second phase, the materials that were blown to fine bits in the initial explosion (earth, trees, buildings, and such), which have become miniature transmitters of radiation (alpha, beta and gamma particles) and have been lifted 70,000 to 120,000 feet, gradually float back to the earth. This is the "fallout" of the nuclear cloud that was created.

The Initial Blast

It is possible that there would be some warning of a nuclear attack. If this is so, in the U. S. the warning sirens would sound a steady tone for about three to five minutes and when they started warbling, that would mean *take cover*. For detailed information at that time, you should dial the emergency frequencies on your AM radios, which are 640 and 1240.

However, let's assume the worst case, where there is no prior warning. The first thing you would notice would be a very bright flash (*do not* look at the light) and, likely, an earthquake-type tremor. Within a very few seconds, you would get the blast wave and also the thermal and radiation impact. One thing to note is that this wave travels in a straight line. It does not go around corners. If there were a large rock between you and the blast, this wave would go over your head, if you sat in the "shadow" of the rock. At first, the blast wave will move outward from the nuclear explosion and then, almost like the tide, come back into the vacuum that was left from the explosion. This surge out and then back could take as long as two minutes.

All is not total destruction in a nuclear blast. There *is* a central area, of course, that will be totally annihilated. However, it is interesting to note that in the Hiroshima blast, the Hiroshima Electric Building was just 1 mile from ground zero and was basically undamaged. In Table 6.1, we can see the effects of a nuclear explosion at various distances from it.

Table 6.1

EFFECTS OF A NUCLEAR EXPLOSION
(Approximate maximum distance from explosion in miles)

Weapon Yield	Fireball Diameter	Severe Damage to Homes	Window Shattering	Paper Ignites	Second Degree Burns
20 KT*	.3	3	4	4	4
100 KT	.6	4	5	5	5
1 MT	1.4	5	9	9	10
5 MT	2.6	6	14	14	17
10 MT	3.5	8	19	23	25
20 MT	4.6	10	24	35	32
30 MT	5.5	12	27	40	40
50 MT	6.6	14	32	50	50
100 MT	9.0	17	41	65	70

KT = Kilotons (1,000 tons of TNT, equivalent)
MT = Megatons (1,000,000 tons of TNT, equivalent)
 * = Size of Hiroshima bomb.

As you can see from this table, even with the largest of these nuclear devices, if you are beyond 70 miles from the point of explosion, there will be very little damage. Even in the larger explosions, the wall of fire will only go out about 25 to 30 miles. With the average nuclear device, if you are beyond 30 miles from the point of detonation, you should be in pretty good shape. That far out wood will not burn from this type of fire wall. Things such as cloth, paper and trash, however, will catch fire readily.

This brings us to what you should do in the event of such an explosion. If you see a nuclear flash, you should immediately *dive for cover*. When the blast hits, it will shatter windows. There will be thousands of needle-like fragments of glass flying at very high speed. If you are at an office, crouch behind your desk so that the desk is between you and the blast. If you are outside, dive for a ditch or lay down behind a log and shield your eyes and face. If you are at home, dive under a coffee table or bed. One of the main things to do is to get away from windows because of the glass, radiation and heat that will be coming through them. The closer you are to the explosion, the less time there will be between the flash and the blast wave. Even at 30 miles, you probably only have about 20 or 30 seconds. This means that you are going to have to move, and move *fast*.

It is likely in a nuclear attack that two missiles would be sent to each target, which means that possibly a second explosion is coming. Therefore, once you take cover, remain there for at least two minutes. Do not try to run to another room or change position until both the outward surge and the inward surge of the blast have occurred, and you are pretty sure that there is not going to be a second explosion. Then you should have time to do a number of things, such as put out fires and move to a shelter. Depending on your situation and the wind conditions, the fallout will probably not occur for twenty minutes to eight hours. Only a tiny percent of the people will be killed in the initial blast. The vast majority of the deaths will occur because of the subsequent fallout. That is the real danger, and the one from which you must protect yourself. Before looking at *how* to protect yourself from fallout, let us first examine exactly what it is.

Radioactive Fallout

Tiny particles of material are rapidly carried upward in the great boiling mushroom cloud by the intense heat and upward air currents created by the fireball. When the particles are at 70,000 to 120,000 feet, the heat in the air currents will have largely dissipated. This radioactive "cloud" is then caught up in the prevailing winds of the stratosphere, and is carried away from the point of detonation. The particles of debris begin gradually to sink back towards the earth, since they no longer have the heated air to support them. They "fall out" of the nuclear cloud toward the ground below. These particles range in size from coarse grain sand down to very fine, powder. The larger particles resemble grit or dust, while the smaller ones look like fine ashes.

Each of these particles emits three types of rays—alpha, beta and gamma. The alpha rays can only travel through 1 inch of air. The beta particles can travel through 10 feet of air, but the gamma rays are capable of traveling half a mile through air and can penetrate considerable thicknesses of solid material with ease.

These particles are like microscopic bullets. When they pass through your body, they actually do internal damage. If you get enough of them passing through in a short period of time, your body's natural healing processes cannot work fast enough to heal you, and you will die. On the other hand, you can take the same amount of particles over a longer period of time and your body will be able to repair itself and recover from the damage. Because of the extreme short range of the alpha and beta particles, you do not have to worry about them unless you actually get fallout on your person (clothes, skin or hair). Assuming that you take care to prevent this, the major danger then is from the gamma radiation. Remember that the gamma rays travel in straight lines and are stopped by approximately 2½ feet of dirt or 18 inches of concrete. If you had a pile of gamma-producing radioactive material in one place, and a large pile of dirt between you and it, you could sit safely behind the dirt. The rays would pass over your head and around you.

Another important thing to know is the rapid rate of the radioactive decay. Three or four days after an explosion, the radioactivity transmission from the particles is only about 1/100 of the level that it was at the time the bomb was exploded. Figure 6.1 shows this rapid decay rate.

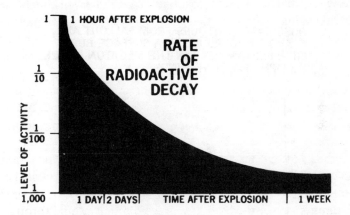

Figure 6.1

It is very important to understand the measurement of this radiation. The basic measurement is the roentgen. This is sometimes referred to as REM (roentgen equivalent man). Frequently, in tables or graphs, it will be shown as "R" for an abbreviation. Table 6.2 (from *Scientific American,* November, 1976) shows the dosage it would take over a one week period compared to a one month period in order to have the effects that are listed.

Table 6.2

DOSE (IN REMS)		EFFECT
IF DELIVERED OVER ONE WEEK	IF DELIVERED OVER ONE MONTH	
150	200	THRESHOLD FOR RADIATION ILLNESS
250	350	5 PERCENT MAY DIE
450	600	50 PERCENT MAY DIE

Figure 6.2 shows the number of roentgens per hour that you would receive standing in an open field at various distances from the point of the explosion. As can be seen, the winds carry the radioactivity only in one direction. This shows that if you were 200 miles from a blast, even downwind, you would have about eighteen hours to prepare before the fallout began.

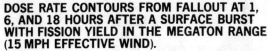

DOSE RATE CONTOURS FROM FALLOUT AT 1, 6, AND 18 HOURS AFTER A SURFACE BURST WITH FISSION YIELD IN THE MEGATON RANGE (15 MPH EFFECTIVE WIND).

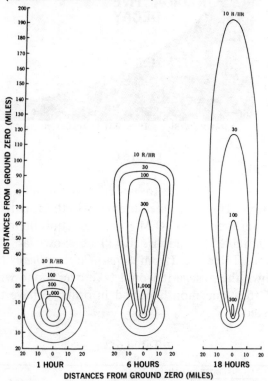

Figure 6.2

A HYPOTHETICAL ATTACK

From pages 96-70 of *Survival Handbook* (publisher given later) we quote:

"The hypothetical attack consisted of a total of 1,446 megatons of nuclear weapons yield delivery to 224 targets in the United States in the form of 263 bombs of 1, 2, 3, 8, and 10-megaton yield. Targets included 70 metropolitan areas of importance in terms of population, communications, industry, military bases, and Atomic Energy Commission installations. All the bombs were ground burst. The pattern of fallout from these hypothetical weapons bursts is shown on the maps. The fallout distribution is shown as it would be at two different times after the initial attack, illustrating the manner in which fallout spreads with the prevailing wind, covering tremendous areas of the country."

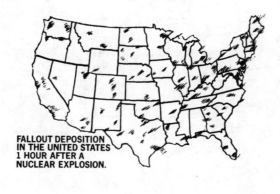

FALLOUT DEPOSITION
IN THE UNITED STATES
1 HOUR AFTER A
NUCLEAR EXPLOSION.

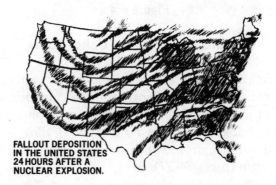

FALLOUT DEPOSITION
IN THE UNITED STATES
24 HOURS AFTER A
NUCLEAR EXPLOSION.

Figure 6.3

Another hypothetical attack was shown in a *Scientific American* article (November, 1976 issue), wherein all I.C.B.M. bases would be attacked with two 1-megaton surface blasts per silo. The Titan missiles are the white squares and the Minuteman missiles are the solid squares. The inner contour delineates a 450 roentgen dose measured standing indoors and the dotted contour represents a 200 roentgen dose indoors.

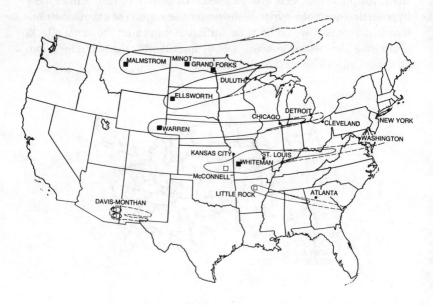

Figure 6.4

Potential Targets in the United States

The following table shows the most likely nuclear targets in the United States. The original listing, as compiled by Martin and Latham in *Strategy for Survival,* was given in a condensed form in the book, *World War III and the Destiny of America* (mentioned earlier), from which Table 6.3 and the following quote are taken (pages 34-37):

"It should be borne in mind that this tabulation was published in 1963: there may have been a few changes since that time; for example, several of the smaller defense establishments have been closed and consolidated with larger bases. Also, the Atlas ICBM launching sites have been 'salvaged'; and the following listing does not include reference to naval bases. Martin and Latham do provide a separate tabulation of naval base target-areas, which may be obtained by referring to Appendix 10 of their book. That which is listed here is but a condensation of the list of cities, according to category. It is a sample of potential targets in the U.S.A."

Table 6.3

KEY

1. SAC bomber base.
2. SAC missile base.
3. ADC base.
4. AF support base.

5. Population, 50 largest cities.
6. Population over 200,000.
7. Population over 50,000.

City	Target Category	Possible Attack Level Megatons	City	Target Category	Possible Attack Level Megatons
ALABAMA			Riverside-		
Birmingham	5	10	San Bernardino	3,6	5-7
Huntsville	7	1	Sacramento	1,3	7-12
Mobile	4,6	10	San Diego	5	10
Montgomery	4,7	1	San Francisco	5	30-40
Tuscaloosa	7	0.5	San Jose	6	6
ALASKA			San Rafael	3	2-5
Anchorage	4	2	Santa Barbara	7	0.5
Fairbanks	4	1-2	Victorville	3	2
ARIZONA			**COLORADO**		
Phoenix	4,5	10	Colorado		
Tucson	1,2,3,6	185	Springs	4,7	20-40
ARKANSAS			Denver	1,2,5	95
Blytheville	1	5	Pueblo	7	0.5
Fort Smith	7	0.5	**CONNECTICUT**		
Little Rock	1,2,7	185	Bridgeport	6	10
CALIFORNIA			Hartford	6	5
Bakersfield	7	1	New Haven	6	5
Fairfield	1	5	Norwalk	7	1
Fresno	6	2	Stamford	7	5
Lompoc	1,2	5-25	Waterbury	7	2
Long Beach	5	1	**DELAWARE**		
Los Angeles	5	50-100	Dover	3,4	2
Marysville	1,2	50	Wilmington	6	5
Merced	1,3	5	**DISTRICT OF**		
Oakland	5	2	**COLUMBIA**		
Ontario-			Washington	3,4,5	8-15
Pomona	7	2	**FLORIDA**		
Oxnard	3	2	Ft. Lauderdale-		
Pomona	7	2	Hollywood	6	5

City	Target Category	Possible Attack Level Megatons	City	Target Category	Possible Attack Level Megatons
Homestead	1	5	Des Moines	6	5
Jacksonville	6	5	Sioux City	7	2
Miami	5	10	**KANSAS**		
Orlando	1,6	5-7	Salina	1,2	65
Panama City	3	2	Topeka	1,2,7	10-14
Pensacola	4,7	1	Wichita	1,2,4,6	185
St. Petersburg	6	4	**KENTUCKY**		
Tampa	1,4,5	5-10	Lexington	7	0.5
Valparaiso	1,4	5	Louisville	5	5
West Palm Bch.	7	5	**LONG ISLAND**		
GEORGIA			Westhampton		
Albany	1,7	5	Beach	3	2
Atlanta	4,5	20	**LOUISIANA**		
Columbus	7	4	Alexandria	4	2
Macon	1,4	5-6	Baton Rouge	7	2
Marietta	3	2	Lake Charles	1,4,7	5
Savannah	1,7	5-7	New Orleans	5	10
HAWAII			Shreveport	1,6	5-7
Honolulu	4,5	5	**MAINE**		
IDAHO			Bangor	1,3	5
Mtn. Home	1,2	50	Limestone	1,3	5
ILLINOIS			Portland	7	2
Aurora	7	0.3 to 0.5	**MARYLAND**		
Belleville	4	1-2	Baltimore	5	20
Chicago	5	30-60	Camp Springs	3,4	2
Davenport-			**MASSACHUSETTS**		
Rock Island-			Boston	5	20-50
Moline	6	5	Brockton	7	1
Decatur	7	0.5	Chicopee	1,3	2
Joliet	7	1	Falmouth	3,4	2
Peoria	7	2	Holyoke	1,3	5-7
Rock Island	6	5	Lowell	7	0.5
Springfield	7	1	Pittsfield	7	1
INDIANA			Springfield	1,3,6	5-7
East Chicago	7	0.1	Worcester	6	2
Evansville	7	1	**MICHIGAN**		
Fort Wayne	7	1	Ann Arbor	7	0.5
Gary	7	2	Bay City	6	0.5
Hammond	7	0.5	Detroit	5	10
Indianapolis	6	5	Flint	6	2
Peru	1,3	5	Grand Rapids	6	5
South Bend	6	2	Kalamazoo	7	1
Terre Haute	7	1	Lansing	7	1
IOWA			Kinross	1,3	5
Cedar Rapids	7	1	Marquette	1,3	5

City	Target Category	Possible Attack Level Megatons	City	Target Category	Possible Attack Level Megatons
Oscoda	1,3	5	Rochester	5	5
Saginaw	7	0.5	Rome-Utica	1,2	5-10
MINNESOTA			Syracuse	3,4,6	2
Duluth-Superior	3,7	5-7	Troy	7	0.5
Minneapolis	5	40	NORTH CAROLINA		
Saint Paul	5	2	Ashville	7	1
MISSISSIPPI			Charlotte	6	2
Columbus	1		Goldsboro	1,2	5
Jackson	7		Greensboro	7	2
MISSOURI			Raleigh	7	1
Kansas City	3,4,5		Winston-Salem	7	1
Saint Louis	5		NORTH DAKOTA		
Sedalia	1,2		Grand Forks	1,3	5
Springfield	7		Minot	1,2,3	505-1505
Warrensburg	1,2	505-1505	OHIO		
MONTANA			Akron	5	5
Billings	7	0.2	Canton	6	2
Glasgow	1,3	5	Cincinnati	5	20
Great Falls	1,2,7	505-1502	Cleveland	5	40
NEBRASKA			Columbus	1,5	5-15
Lincoln	1,2,7	65	Dayton	1,3,5	5-10
Omaha	1,2,4,5	50	Hamilton	7	2
NEVADA			Shelby	4	1
Las Vegas	4,7	2-3	Toledo	5	5
Reno	4,7	0.25	Warren-Youngstown	6	5
NEW HAMPSHIRE			OKLAHOMA		
Manchester	7	1	Altus	1,2	65
Portsmouth	1	5	Burns Flat	1	5
NEW JERSEY			Elk City	1	5
Atlantic City	7	2	Lawton	7	0.25
Jersey City	6	0.25	Oklahoma City	4,5	20
Newark	6	0.50	Tulsa	6	2
Trenton	6	2	OREGON		
Wrightstown	3,4	2	Eugene	7	1
NEW MEXICO			Klamath Falls	3	2
Albuquerque	4,6	2	Portland	3,5	20-22
Clovis	4	2	PENNSYLVANIA		
Roswell	1,2,3	65	Allentown-Bethlehem	6	4
NEW YORK			Erie	7	2
Albany	6	1	Harrisburg	6	1
Buffalo	5	10	Middletown	4	2
Newburgh	3,4	2	Philadelphia	5	30
New York	5	100	Pittsburgh	5	20
Niagara Falls	3,7	2-4			
Plattsburg	1,2	65			

City	Target Category	Possible Attack Level Megatons	City	Target Category	Possible Attack Level Megatons
Reading	7	1	Laredo	4,7	0.2
Scranton	6	4	Lubbock	4,7	2
Youngstown	6	5	Port Arthur	7	2
RHODE ISLAND			San Antonio	4,5	10
Pawtucket-			Waco	4,7	2
Providence	6	6-9	Wichita Falls	1,7	5
SOUTH CAROLINA			UTAH		
Charleston	3,4,7	3.5-4.5	Ogden	4,7	2
Columbia	7	2	Salt Lake City	6	5
Greenville	3,4,7	2	VIRGINIA		
Myrtle Beach	4	2	Hampton	3,6	10-12
Sumter	4	2	Newport News	3,6	10-12
SOUTH DAKOTA			Norfolk	3,5	10-12
Rapid City	1	50	Richmond	6	5
TENNESSEE			WASHINGTON		
Chattanooga	6	5	Everett	3	2
Knoxville	7	2	Moses Lake	1,2,3	50
Memphis	5	10	Seattle	5	10
Nashville	6	4	Spokane	1,2,3,6	12-17
TEXAS			Tacoma	3,4,6	5-7
Abilene	1,2	65	WEST VIRGINIA		
Amarillo	1,7	2	Charleston	7	2
Austin	7	5	Wheeling	7	0.5
Dallas	5	40	WISCONSIN		
Del Rio	4	1-2	Green Bay	7	1
El Paso	1,6	5-10	Madison	3,4,7	2
Fort Worth	1,5	20-25	Milwaukee	5	20
Galveston-			WYOMING		
Texas City	7	10	Cheyenne	1,2	19
Houston	5	20			

Wherever the nuclear bombs fall, the fallout will be downwind of the explosion. Most of it will land on the ground, and some on the roofs of buildings and houses. It is very important to know when the fallout is actually beginning, so that you can take shelter. One easy way to do this is to place clean plates (preferably of a solid pastel color) outside on each side of your house. These can be checked periodically; you will actually be able to see the fallout land on them. Once this begins to occur, it is time to take shelter.

SHELTERS TO SHIELD AGAINST RADIATION

The first question is: what about public shelters of the Civil Defense? In checking these, I found them to be totally inadequate. The metal water containers are empty, so that they will not rust. The cereal-based crackers stored there are quite old, and in many cases would cause you to be sick if you ate them. You are expected to bring your own bedding and flashlights to these public shelters. Even if they were in top-notch shape and completely stocked, living in a shelter like that from four to forty days could be quite a messy situation. You could have all sorts of sociological problems—everything from people panicking to somebody, who has snuck a gun into the situation, setting himself up as a miniature dictator.

Therefore, you should probably consider your own family fallout shelter. My recommendation is that you do not attempt to design one, but that you use professionally designed fallout shelters. If you do decide to do it on your own, there are a number of things of which you should be aware. To shield yourself from the gamma rays, you would need one of the following: approximately 2½ feet of earth, 18 inches of concrete, 3½ feet of water or 6 feet of wood. The ideal, of course, is to have a shelter underground in your backyard or built in your basement. It must have a minimum of 10 square feet per person, although an 8- by 12-foot shelter is usually recommended for a family of four. Figure 6.5 shows a house with a basement before and after protection is installed for fallout. It includes things to do between the time of the blast and the time when fallout begins.

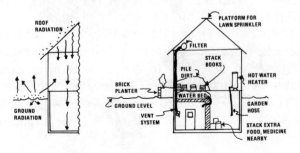

Figure 6.5

You will note that the corner of the basement where there are no vents was chosen for the shelter, and that a water bed was placed on top of the shelter, both for drinking purposes and additional protection. On the floor above the shelter books (and anything with mass) were placed to absorb additional radiation. The shelter has a venting system with a hand crank, which is necessary because there may not be electricity. The air in the shelter will become stale; therefore the occupants will have to take turns cranking the ventilator fan. The air intake of the vent should be filtered. The door has a 6- by 6-inch slideable opening to view outside and to hold out your radiation rate measuring device.

Shown below are some typical family shelters from *Survival Handbook*.

Figure 6.6

If a blast were to occur and no shelter had been provided, there would be time between the blast and the fallout to construct a makeshift shelter. If you were in a home with a basement, you should pile books, cement blocks, bricks, and so forth on the floor above where you were going to be. You could break open a window and shovel dirt inside. In the basement, you could move chests of drawers and work benches to form a rectangle, and on top of this pile bags of cement, bags of fertilizer—anything with mass. If there were a vent into the basement, you could shovel dirt from outside in on top of your makeshift shelter.

For a makeshift shelter in a home without a basement, you could go in the crawl space beneath the floor and dig a hole, piling the dirt up around. This should be done in a corner where there are no vents. If you were outside and there was no way that you could possibly get to a shelter area, you could drive your car over a ditch and get under it. These solutions are crude, but it is better to lie in a hole for four days and be protected from radiation, than to go out in it and experience a sure death.

Water Storage

The first and most important thing that you will need in the shelter is water. You are going to have to be there for at least four days, and up to forty. You can go without food for four days, but you can't go without water. A water bed stored in the basement will provide a good source of drinking water. It doesn't matter if radiation passes through it—the water is still very drinkable. When the blast occurs cut off the main water valve to your house. There is enough water in the hot water heater to last for awhile. A hose should be connected to the drain valve and be run down to the fallout shelter.

While we are on the subject, let's cover water storage in general, since it is most critical in many emergencies. If you are going to go about storing water, the first question that probably comes to your mind is: *how much* water should I store? My stock answer to that is as much as you can. The minimum you should have stored is 15 gallons per person. You should also have some method of purifying more. This 15-gallon minimum will allow you to live thirty days or more if some natural or man-made disaster cuts off the water supply.

The next consideration is *how* to store the water. The good thing about water is that it will store for long periods of time if proper preparation is made. Enough chlorine or other chemical must be added to make sure there is no bacteria or fungus growth. The only thing that happens to prepared water after long periods of storage is that the air separates out and the water tastes flat. This is corrected by aerating the water, which can be accomplished by pouring it from container to container, by shaking it, or by mixing it vigorously.

If money is no object, you can build your supply rapidly and without much fuss by buying enough Sparkletts or Arrowhead 5-gallon containers of drinking water. In checking with the drinking water suppliers, I learned that there can be fungus growth if their water is exposed to sunlight for extended periods. Therefore, each container should be placed in a heavy-duty plastic trash sack and stored in a cool dark place.

One thing to remember when using glass containers is never to stack them tightly together, or on shelves. In case of an earthquake or explosion they might fall or be knocked together.

Another way to store your water is to put it in fairly airtight plastic containers. These could be anything from 5-gallon plastic pails with tight-fitting lids to large 55-gallon drums that were used for shipping bulk products such as apple cider. Be very careful that you do not use a drum which has been utilized to ship dangerous chemicals. Normally these are very difficult to clean thoroughly and therefore may be fatal to use. Whatever size you choose, be sure that the containers are clean and then fill them with ordinary tap water. Add enough *fresh* bleach to make a ratio of 1 tablespoon of bleach for each 5 gallons of water in the container. This is about twice the amount recommended by some books, but I have found that it has stopped all fungus growth for over ten years. I would rather be safe than sorry when it comes to my water supply.

A more economical, but somewhat slower way to build your water storage is by using your empty Purex or Chlorox bottles. I know of ladies who have had all of their friends on the block save their empty bleach bottles so that they could increase their supply faster. After you have used the last of the product, turn the bottle over and let it drain and dry. Do not wash the container out; you want enough of the bleach to remain dried on the inside to protect the water when you refill and seal it. After filling it with water, store it in a cool place. Under the house is an excellent place to store these bottles, and they are out of the way as well.

In case of an extended shutoff of water, or if you had to pick up and move, you would need a way to get good drinking water. This is the time when you would need a good portable water purifier. You should have one that is not dependent on electricity, and that needs no chemical catalyst to make it work. Many purifiers are dependent on chlorine or other chemicals to activate the purifying substance. This would make them useless for purifying river, lake or rainwater. The purifier you need will cost from $30 to almost $200, depending on size, how many gallons it will purify, whether it is gravity or hand pump fed, and whether it has replacement cartridges or you just use it until it stops purifying and then throw it away.

A good portable water purifier will eliminate suspended material, chlorine, some salts and heavy metals, some poisons, and it will kill most bacteria, including deadly coliform bacteria. You can expect a purifier to handle 600 to 3,000 gallons per filter cartridge. I would definitely recommend that you have one.

If you do not have a purifier, you can destroy most bacteria by boiling your water before use. All you need to do is boil it for about three minutes and then let it cool. The flavor of boiled water can be improved by aerating it before drinking it. If the water source is full of debris, the water should be strained before boiling. Boiling will not remove heavy metals, salts or most poisons.

Another method of purifying water for drinking is to use commercial purification tablets. These usually release a measured dose of iodine or chlorine into the water, and directions on the package should be followed. Most commercial purification tablets do have a storage life; you should note the purchase date on the container.

Water can also be purified by distilling. In fact some of the best and cleanest drinking water can be obtained by this method. However, I cannot in good conscience recommend a distiller that takes electric power to run unless your family has its own electricity generating equipment.

There is some good distilling equipment available that uses heat from fires as a power source. This would be fine as long as you make sure you have a dependable source of wood or other fuel. Another alternative is to build a simple distilling unit that uses fire as the power source. Such a unit is illustrated in *How To Be Prepared For Any Crisis,* by Roland Page, Hawkins Publishing. With this as a guide, smaller or larger units could be built by someone handy with tools.

Another type of distilling unit is the *Solar Still.* This is a simple do-it-yourself method that uses the normal water evaporation cycle to trap water from the ground, sand, or plants. It is basically a plastic sheet that is draped over a plant or a hole in the ground and traps the water that rises each day as part of the water cycle. It is explained and well-illustrated in *Outdoor Survival Skills,* by Olsen, BYU Press.

In case of an emergency that abruptly cuts off your water supply, it is good to know that you have between 40 and 60 gallons of good water trapped in the water pipes, hot water heater, and toilet bowl in your home. Before drawing any of this water, you must turn off the main inlet valve to prevent contamination by dirt in broken water mains from entering your system. You should also turn off the gas to your hot water heater to make sure that it does not overheat as the water supply goes down, and to keep the water from becoming cloudy. Then you can safely draw water from the tank's drain valve. You may need to open a faucet somewhere in the house to provide a vent which would allow a good flow of water. If you have a two-story home, this should be an upstairs faucet. Water in toilet tanks will have to be scooped out for use.

Other sources of water include lakes, rivers, ponds, creeks, streams, ditches, swimming pools, ornamental fish ponds or even puddles. Water should be strained and then purified to kill bacteria. Sea water cannot be used as a drinking water source, unless you have a distiller.

Rainwater can be a great source of water if you are prepared to collect and store it. Most new homes do not have rain gutters, but if yours does you can just collect the water at the downspouts. If your home does not have gutters, you can use tarps or plastic sheets to catch the roof runoff and direct rain, and then store it in kettles or drums. Since the rainwater may pick up debris and contamination before it is gathered, it should be strained and purified before using it for drinking or cooking.

To recapitulate, you should take the following steps to insure that you will have water to drink in an emergency:

1.   Locate the water inlet valve to your home, and teach each member how to turn it off in case of disaster.

2.   Using one of the suggested methods, store at least 15 gallons of water per family member.

3.   Buy a water purifier to meet your family's needs.

4.   Learn alternate water sources around your home. Have a plan for using them—that is, how to get the water to your home, how to purify it, and how to store it.

Returning to the specific situation of a nuclear war, we have additional cautions concerning the drinking of water that is from outside. Do not drink water that could have fallout particles suspended in it. You must avoid ingesting these particles. If it is necessary to use water from a source which has been exposed to fallout, the heavier particles will be at the bottom, so skim the water off of the top. Run this water through a purifier, which will remove the radioactive particles. If this is not possible, anything you can do to strain it, like running it through several layers of paper towels, will help to remove fallout particles.

Stocking the Shelter

In considering food for the fallout shelter, remember that there will be *no cooking* because of the small, enclosed space and ventilation problems. This means that you are either going to have to have survival rations like the ones you can buy in hiking stores, or food that is already precooked. Most of the dehydrated food that requires cooking will be useless in this situation.

Concerning waste disposal, you can always use garbage bags for both human and food waste. Tie the bags up tightly and occasionally open the door of the shelter to set them outside. The ideal would be to have a port-a-potty or chemical toilet. Additionally, a large garbage can with a very tight-fitting lid would be helpful.

Your lighting will be primarily from flashlights. After an explosion, you should have the time to gather up all the flashlights and take them to your shelter along with bedding. Don't forget to have special provisions for babies, diabetics, and so on. Also, don't forget your radio because you are going to want to be listening to the emergency frequencies.

The first aid kit should be heavily oriented towards burns. Burns are something that you must prepare for. It is also very desirable to have some tools in the shelter. If the house or building on top were to collapse, you would need saws, axes and hammers to help work your way out. Also bring in books, games and toys for children, as well as productive, quiet things to keep everyone busy.

Measuring Devices

After water, the most important things to have are two types of measuring devices. The first type is called a dosimeter. There should be at least one for each member of the family. In its most common form, it looks like an oversized fountain pen. This instrument gives the total amount of roentgens that an individual has absorbed. The other device is a ratemeter, which gives the number of roentgens that are being absorbed per hour.

Only one ratemeter is needed per shelter. I like to compare these to the speedometer in an automobile. The ratemeter tells us how fast we are going and the dosimeter gives the total miles we have come. Both measuring devices are absolutely necessary. As soon as the nuclear blast occurs, one of the first things that should be done is to give a dosimeter to each individual in the family. Ideally, you would have one at the office and enough in the car for each person, as well as an adequate number at home. It is also necessary to have a dosimeter charger. This works on a C battery. Adequate instructions are included with the charger, so there should be no difficulty in using it to recharge the dosimeter.

The ratemeter is used to determine hot spots within the shelter. Additional protection can be piled up in that area or, if that is not possible, members of the family can rotate so that each spends an equal amount of time in the hot spots. The ratemeter is also necessary to determine when it is safe to go outside. Figure 6.7 shows the scales on these two devices. Addresses at which these measuring devices can be purchased will be given later.

Figure 6.7

Leaving the Shelter

Excursions from the shelter *can* be made. Table 6.4 shows valid reasons for excursions.

Table 6.4

*Reasons for Leaving Shelter at Various
Radiation Levels*

RADIATION RATE OUTSIDE THE SHELTER (r/hr)	ACCEPTABLE REASON FOR LEAVING
MORE THAN 50	Only destruction of the shelter. All other needs must be postponed at least one day.
50 TO 10	Only: a. Destruction of the shelter. b. Removal of dead. c. Severe illness, necessitating immediate treatment with medical help close by.
10 TO 2	a. Obtaining water, if very near. b. Obtaining food, if very near. c. Leaving shelter for nearby shelter with better protection factor.
2 TO 0.5	All rescue, repair, communication and decontamination work. Remain in shelter for sleeping, rest, and meals.
0.5 TO 0	Normal workday can be spent out of doors.

If the rate is 60 roentgens per hour (r/hr), a ten minute excursion will add 10 roentgens to your personal dosimeter.

After making an excursion, it is extremely important not to track any radioactive material into the shelter. Baggies could be placed over your shoes, raincoats could be worn, hats would be essential. Before reentering the shelter, all of these "outside" clothes should be removed. Ideally, the person should strip and wash off thoroughly with water. Any fallout tracked back into the shelter will be damaging to all people inside, as the shelter will not afford protection from radiation within its boundaries.

The canned food in your kitchen is still good and very usable, even though radiation may have passed through it. This does not harm it at all. If there is any radioactive fallout on the cans, it should be washed off prior to opening them. At some point, it would be wise to wash off the roof of the house to eliminate the roof radiation. If thought has been given to this situation beforehand, a small 1-foot square platform could have been erected on top of the house with a lawn sprinkler on it. Between the time of the blast and the fallout, the garden hose could be connected to this, making it easy to wash off the roof.

After the roof is rinsed, the ground at the bottom of the rain gutters will be highly radioactive. As part of the decontamination process, this soil should be scooped out and buried. The soil around your house can be plowed to bury the radioactive dust, and cement surfaces can be washed off. Check for radioactive hot spots with the ratemeter.

Remember that the radioactivity will probably kill most of the animals, both wild and domestic. Protein food will be at a premium after such a nuclear attack. Garden food is still edible, but all radioactive fallout must be washed off. New gardens can be planted; thus a can of survival garden seeds is desirable as part of shelter supplies.

PLAN OF ACTION FOR THE HOME

A plan of action should be developed for your family, if you do not already have one. The following are some suggestions for such a plan. During the time between when the blast occurs and the fallout begins:

1.   Extinguish fires.

2.   Turn off the main water valve to the house.

3.   Put on dosimeters.

4.   Place plates outside to detect fallout.

5.   Repair shelter damage, finish an incomplete shelter, or create a makeshift shelter.

6.   Move water into the shelter. Connect a hose to the hot water drain and put the nozzle inside the shelter.

7.   Move canned food from kitchen to shelter (leave the food in the freezer).

8.   Take the following to the shelter: flashlights, plastic garbage bags and baggies, a radio, bedding, books and recreational materials.

Once you are inside the shelter and the door is closed or, if there is no door, sandbags have been placed across the opening, you should do the following things:

1.   Inventory all food and water supplies.

2.   Establish a rationing procedure.

3.   Delegate important tasks, such as radiation monitoring and food preparation.

4.   Set up schedules of eating, sleeping and daily tasks.

5.   Establish a schedule for cranking the ventilator fan.

6.   Begin constructive activities to occupy the minds of the shelter occupants, to keep them busy.

Plan of Action for the Office

We have already mentioned that if you are at your office when you see the initial flash, you should crouch behind a desk so that it is between you and the windows on the blast side. Once the initial blast is over, you should first extinguish all fires. Water is going to be important. Therefore, you could go into the washrooms and fill all of the sinks, along with anything else that will contain water (waste baskets, pitchers, vases, pencil holders, plastic bags and so forth). If you can get home to take care of your family before the fallout begins, you will probably want to do this. However, for a number of reasons this may be impossible. It may be that the blast occurred between your office and your home, and the roads are out. It is also unlikely that you will be able to phone your home to find out how they are doing. A quick decision must be made as to whether to try to go home or to remain in the office building.

If you decide to remain, you will want to be in one of two places. If it is a tall office building, the center of one of the middle floors is quite safe from fallout radiation. The fallout that will land on the top of the building will be stopped by the mass of the floors above you. The radioactive "ground shine" will be below you and you will only be exposed to some radiation from "sky shine." If the building has a subterranean parking lot which goes several floors below the surface of the ground, the bottom floor of that would be fairly safe from radiation. If you go down to the parking lot, carry with you all the water that you can, and anything else that will make life there more comfortable for four days. Having a package of large plastic garbage bags in your desk could be a tremendous help, both for carrying water down to the basement and for use in disposing of human waste. Don't worry about food at this point. You can fast for several days.

Books and Information

After reading many books on this subject, there is one that I feel is absolutely head and shoulders above everything else that I have read. I think every family should read it. It is *Survival Handbook,* by Robert C. Suggs, and it covers the entire subject very well. It is published by The Macmillan Company, New York and is in the Library of Congress, Catalogue No. 62-19430. If you cannot buy a copy, it is in most public libraries. The book number is 623.38-S94S. Some of the illustrations and tables in this chapter are taken from it.

There are many booklets available from the Civil Defense. I understand that they are free. Their main publication center is:

U.S. Army AG Publications Center
Civil Defense Branch
2800 Eastern Boulevard (Middle River)
Baltimore, MD 21220

In addition, there are eight regions in the United States designated as the civil defense regions. The following is a list of the region headquarters from which booklets and local information are obtainable:

OCD Region 1
Oak Hill Road
Harvard, Massachusetts

OCD Region 2
Olney, Maryland

OCD Region 3
P. O. Box 108
Thomasville, Georgia

OCD Region 4
Battle Creek, Michigan

OCD Region 5
P. O. Box 2935
University Hill Station
Denton, Texas

OCD Region 6
Denver Federal Center
Building 50
Denver 25, Colorado

OCD Region 7
Naval Auxiliary Air Station
Santa Rosa, California

OCD Region 8
Everett, Washington

From these, you can get a book list and the following booklets:

#814   *In Time of Emergency—A Citizen's Handbook on Nuclear Attack and Natural Disasters*

#812-1   *Home Fallout Shelters, Outside Concrete Shelter*

#812-2   *Above Ground Home Shelter*

Summary and Conclusion

Based on the prophecy in the Bible, we know that a world war is coming. In all probability it will be a nuclear war. The doomsday people that say if a nuclear war hits, humanity will be nearly wiped out, and then they won't want to be alive. I be-

PLEASE INSERT THIS BETWEEN PAGES 230-231

SURVIVAL INC. has just changed hands and
I can no longer recommend them. For
survival food, equipment and supplies,
I would suggest that you write instead
to a Christian organization, which was
created for the express purpose of
suppling food and other supplies to
the body of Christ:

> OMEGA FOOD AND SUPPLIES
> P.O. Box 546
> Eagle Point, Oregon 97524

Send $1 for their catalog. This $1
will be credited to your first order.

I believe you will receive excellent
service and top quality goods from them.

God bless you,

Jim McKeever

Jim McKeever

lieve that such people are not speaking words of truth from God. *Many* people will survive. The Christians who survive will have a real ministry, both in helping those in need and in witnessing to them. In a time of chaos like that, people are much more open to turning to God. I believe that it is the duty of every Christian to do everything he can to stay alive so that he can share the good news with the victims of the nuclear war.

A little preparation will go a long way towards helping you stay alive. A package of garbage bags at the office, a very inexpensive shelter in your home, some stored water—simple things such as these do not take much money at all. Storing up a little bit of water and purchasing some fire extinguishers are good steps to begin with. The main thing is to pray about this matter and to do whatever God leads you to do. It is very possible that He wants you to survive World War III and to share the precious story of Christ with non-Christians who also survive.

7

PREPARING TO SURVIVE

FAMINE

Food shortages are coming. The worldwide trends are well-defined and there is nothing on the horizon that appears able to prevent severe shortages of food.

Today the world consumes almost all of the food that it produces. If a very bad year were to occur, wherein little food was produced, there would be sizable shortages worldwide. The world food supply is precariously balanced and cannot tolerate a single year of poor food production.

One of the things that climatologists tell us could affect our food production is that we are coming out of a thirty- or forty-year cycle of very good weather into a cycle of chaotic weather. If the weather acts up drastically, it could cause our food production to drop significantly. This could be from a simple thing like too much or too little snow. If there is too little snow, the winter wheat crop, which relies on a heavy covering of snow to protect it from freezing, could be in danger. Also, the spring runoff, that farmers rely on for water, would be inadequate. Obviously, with drought conditions much less food would be produced. Then there is the other side of the coin, which most people are not aware of. The Irish potato famine that occurred early in this century was not due to too little rain, but rather the potatoes rotted in the ground because they had *too much rain.* So we see that weather conditions could certainly cause food shortages or famine.

If weather does not cause food shortages, the size of the population will. The book *Famines,* by Dr. Larry Ward, President of Food for the Hungry and a dear friend of mine (published by G/L Publications, Glendale, CA 91209), gives the following estimation of what the world's population growth will be (page 11):

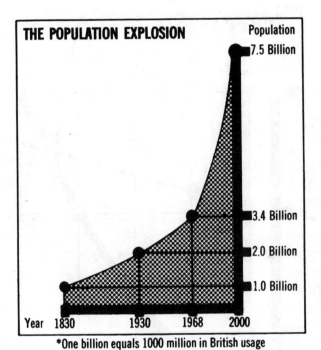

Figure 7.1

As we can see from this graph, between 1968 and the year 2000 the world's population will more than double. We are definitely *not* going to be able to double our food production during that same period of time. The world's food production cannot keep up with the exponential growth in population.

At some point in time, the U. S.—breadbasket of the world —will not be able to produce enough surplus grain to feed the rest of the world. Dr. Ward shows this very graphically on page 39 of his book as follows:

WHEN THE U.S. CANNOT FEED THE WORLD

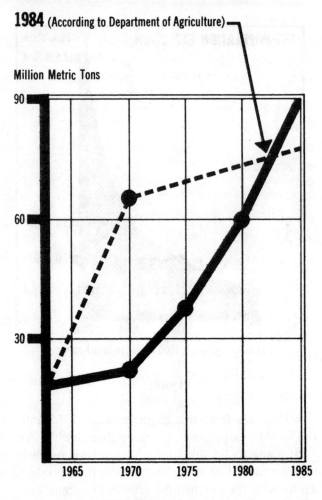

- - - Grain that the U.S. could produce over and above the amounts needed for domestic use and commercial exports.

▬▬ Additional food needed in 66 developing countries

1984 (According to Department of Agriculture)

Million Metric Tons

Figure 7.2

Thus, we see the threat from this rapid population growth, which Dr. Ward terms the disaster of "birthquakes."

FAMINE PREDICTED IN THE BIBLE

We do not know what will cause the famine that is predicted to occur in the early part of the Tribulation. It could be one of the causes mentioned above, or it could be that World War III, with its potential nuclear exchange, could burn up a year's worth of crops. Let us review what Revelation 6 says about the coming famine:

> 5 And when He broke the third seal, I heard the third living creature saying, "Come." And I looked, and behold, a black horse; and he who sat on it had a pair of scales in his hand.
>
> 6 And I heard as it were a voice in the center of the four living creatures saying, "A quart of wheat for a denarius, and three quarts of barley for a denarius; and do not harm the oil and the wine."

If you recall, we pointed out earlier that a denarius was worth approximately 18 cents in silver. In those times this was a day's wage, so what this passage is telling us is that the average working man will have to spend his full day's wage in order to buy enough food for his family and himself.

Being an economist, I would love to delve into the economic and social implications of this. Let it be sufficient to say that the result would be a total upheaval in our economic and social systems as we know them today. Frequently out of such upheaval comes a dictator. Since we know for sure that food shortages are inevitable, we should examine various ways to prepare for these coming disasters. There are five basic strategies that I see employed today. These are:

1. Do nothing; trust the system to take care of you.
2. Have a food storage program.
3. Have a well developed garden.
4. Use hydroponic food production.
5. Move to a farm.

Do Nothing—Trust the System to Take Care of You

In my opinion, the man who adopts this "do nothing" strategy is violating some basic principles of God. The Bible says that if a man does not take care of his own family, he has denied the faith and is worse than an infidel (1 Timothy 5:8). A Christian man who does not make preparation in order to be able to take care of his family in times of emergency in my mind is lower than one who does not profess to be a Christian. If a man makes no preparation for emergencies he is more foolish than the five virgins who did not take extra oil with them when they went out to meet the bridegroom. Here we are not talking about extra oil, but extra *food.*

THE BASIC COMPONENTS OF
A FOOD STORAGE PROGRAM

Food storage is certainly not something new. From the earliest recorded history, people have been storing up food that they produced during times of plenty for use during the winter or during times when food was scarce. Many of our grandparents used to can and preserve foods that they grew on their farms. Often they would have a root cellar for storing vegetables, they would smoke hams and so forth. These were all methods of storing food for the time when it was needed. Only in the last twenty to fifty years has the storing of food been forgotten by most people in the industrialized nations. I would suggest that it is time to return to this activity which proved so beneficial for many thousands of years.

Today, with regard to a food storage program for the average U.S. family, we are looking at four basic types of food for storage:

1.   Wet pack food—everyday foods that you buy in the grocery store.

2.   Air-dried (dehydrated) foods.

3.   Freeze-dried (dehydrated) foods.

4.   Bulk storage of basic foods such as wheat, powdered milk, honey, salt, rice and beans.

Looking at an overall comprehensive program, I would suggest that a family have a three-month supply of wet pack foods, and at least a twelve-month supply of air-dried and freeze-dried dehydrated foods. Some families may want to add the bulk storage of some basic foods to this. Let's examine these categories one at a time.

Wet Pack Foods for Storage

First, let's be sure we agree on what is meant by wet pack. By this I refer to all the items that you find in a supermarket, such as canned fruits, vegetables, meats, cereals, grains, flour, sugar, and prepackaged meals. Wet pack includes items that are packaged for everyday use in the home, without being especially prepared for long-term storage, as well as frozen foods, and home canned foods.

A major advantage of wet pack foods is that you are used to preparing them for your family. In an emergency, your family would hardly notice the change in their diet. A major disadvantage is the fact that the maximum storage life of most of these foods is one to two years. Another problem is storage space; a year's supply of wet pack food for a family of five would take up 60 percent of a two-car garage.

But disadvantages aside, wet pack is an excellent way to build your storage up to a two- or three-month supply. If you do this wisely, you can be sure that none of it will spoil. It can be stored in cupboards in your kitchen and in a small part of your garage. Also, you can build your supply in small increments that fit easily into your budget.

The important thing to remember is to buy the items that you *use* frequently, and in quantities that you can use up in a maximum of three months. Too often I find people buying cases of "specials" for their storage which they then allow to sit unused on shelves until they spoil, because they are not the brand that the family usually uses, or because the amount stored is far more than the family uses in a year. While it is wise to look for the best bargains, it is foolish to buy something just because it is on sale. A good way to build up your supply is to buy an extra can or two each time you go shopping. Soon you will find your supply growing and you will hardly notice the difference in your grocery bill.

Food should be stored in the coolest possible places. Try never to store your supply in the attic, in the top of a garage, in a heater room or over a stove. The cooler the food is kept, the longer it will store. Items that are packaged in paper sacks or boxes should not be stored where there are pungent odors, as the food will pick up the odor. Try not to store your food in deep cabinets where items can be pushed to the back and left to spoil because they are inconvenient to get out and use.

You can increase the storage life of canned foods, such as fruits, vegetables, and meats, by turning them upside down periodically to let the juices run back through the product. In some cases this will double the shelf life of the items that you store. However, if you are storing large quantities of wet pack food, it is best to date the cases and be sure to use them in date sequence. This is not necessary if your storage of wet pack is small.

Flour is one of the hardest items to store. It will almost always wither, turn dark and strange tasting, or hatch weevils. The best way I have found to store flour is to put it into tightly sealed plastic containers with a layer of bay leaves every 3 inches. This seems to help retain the flavor, stops it from packing and stops insect growth. Even with these precautions, flour should be stored no longer than eighteen months.

Fats and oils are also important in your storage. I suggest that you store only vegetable oils since shortening, such as animal fat has a very short storage life. Vegetable oils will store three years or more. Vegetable shortening will store eighteen months to two years without problems, unless it is exposed to high heat.

When you open a package of powdered milk, put the unused portion in the refrigerator and you will find that it will not turn rancid as you get to the bottom of the package.

Air-Dried Dehydrated Foods for Storage

Wet pack foods have a shelf life of about two years. After that time they begin to deteriorate in nutritional value, and frequently the cans will become puffy. Even though the food remains edible longer than that, my experience has been that you can not *depend* on canned food for longer than two years.

There are many companies today producing air-dried dehydrated food for a longer-term storage. This food is usually packed in the large number 10 cans and has a shelf life of at least ten years. It also has significant advantages over wet pack food, in that it weighs much less and is about one-fourth the volume (size) of wet pack food. Enough dehydrated food to feed an individual for a year can be stored in a 1-foot by 4-foot space.

To many who were in the service the phrase "dehydrated food" brings back very unpleasant memories. However, the current dehydrated foods are delicious, and in most cases indistinguishable from wet pack foods.

Most of these food companies have various prearranged groups of foods that would provide you with a balanced diet for say a one-year period. This is very important since most of us are not professional dieticians. However, you will find that these usually do not contain any real meat, but instead, a meat substitute. You may therefore wish to supplement this with the freeze-dried meats that we will discuss later.

The cost will vary, depending on the company that canned the dehydrated food. One of the reasons that there is a variance in cost is that there are different ways of removing the oxygen from the cans. (It is the oxygen that causes food to go bad.) Some of them simply stick a hydrogen wand into a can filled with dried food, stir it around and then seal the can. A more expensive but much more efficient way is to place the can in a vacuum chamber, remove all of the air and oxygen and then introduce hydrogen into the chamber. The can is sealed while it is still in that environment. In Chapter 11 we will give a list of most of the food companies, but the only one that uses this superior method of canning, to my knowledge, is Ready Reserve.

Freeze-Dried Dehydrated Food

Freeze-drying is a very different process than air-drying. In the freeze-drying process, much more of the moisture is removed. The reason for this is that the food (fruit, vegetable or meat) is frozen, and then is quickly exposed to heat so that the water crystals inside go directly to steam without becoming water again. This leaves holes, like in Swiss cheese, and makes the food very light, much like styrofoam. It is so funny to hold pieces of "styrofoam" in your hand that look like quarters of a pear. Even dry these are delicious to eat. Put them into water and they turn back into pears!

Freeze-drying is usually used for meats and many of the premixed meals. If one can afford it, a certain amount of freeze-dried foods should be added to an air-dehydrated food storage program in order to give some real meats and some interesting varieties. There is basically just one brand of the freeze-dried food, and that is Mountain House (Oregon Freeze-Dry).

How to Store the Basic Foods

Wheat has been a basic storage food from almost the beginning of history. It was the staple of the Old Testament, the Roman Empire, and early America. In fact, up until the last ten to twelve years, those who wanted to store food for long periods of time could only turn to basic foods such as wheat, rice, corn, honey and so on. Even today, with all of the high quality dehydrated foods that are available, this basic type of storage is an excellent way to store foods.

Before going into the basics of this type of storage, let us look at the advantages and disadvantages. The major advantage is that you can do it yourself and save some money. Not only can you save money by packing the food yourself, but the ingredients are lower in cost than those of other programs. You will find that the cost per meal for a 2,600 calorie a day diet will run only 25 to 50 percent of that of any other program.

The major disadvantage is the very limited menu, both in variety and color, that can be offered if you store only the basic foods. Also, there is that mental shock of switching from a regular diet to one that contains only four to eight ingredients. This change is especially hard for the very young and the old. That is why it is so important to be sure to use the foods you have stored in your everyday cooking. You learn to use the products correctly, and with confidence, and your family learns to like them.

WHEAT: If you are only using basic foods in your storage, you will need about 300 pounds of wheat or other grains per person per year. Care should be taken to purchase number 1 or 2 hard red winter or spring wheat. Number 1 is preferable, as it has a protein content of over 12 percent and a moisture content under 9 percent. From a nutrient and a storage-life standpoint, it is worth paying a little more to get the best. If you cannot find good wheat by yourself, I would suggest that you contact the Mormon chapel in your area. They have been storing food for a long time and usually know where to get the best wheat for the best price.

Wheat is easy to store. Many people have different ideas, but I am giving the one that I have found to be the best. I have not known this method to fail, if done properly. For every 100 pounds of wheat, you will need three 5-gallon cans. I suggest screw top cans, but the 7½ inch double-lipped cans work almost as well. *Do not use plastic containers* unless they have screw tops. You will also need dry ice, which you can get at an ice house, fire extinguisher shop or sometimes at an ice cream store. Using rubber gloves to protect your hands from the extreme cold, crush the dry ice and place two to three ounces in the bottom of each container. I have found that it is most convenient to do a maximum of three containers at a time. Immediately fill the containers with your wheat and lay the lids on the cans. *Do not tighten the lids even slightly at this point. Wait about thirty minutes* and then tighten the lids as much as you can. Check the cans again in about twenty minutes. If they have started to bulge, loosen the lids and let the excess gas out. This step is necessary if you used too much ice, didn't crush it fairly fine, or tightened the lids too soon after putting in the wheat. The cans should now be painted, marked with contents and date, and stored in a cool, dry place. The paint should be oil-based enamel. I have seen wheat, that has been stored this way for over twenty years, not only make great bread, but sprout well.

RICE: You can store rice by using the same method for wheat. Due to the fat content of the husk, however, you cannot store brown rice for long periods of time. Therefore, use a good quality fortified white rice for your long-term storage.

BARLEY, DRIED CORN, MILLET, CORN MEAL, BEANS, MACARONI, AND SUCH: All of these can be stored in the same manner as wheat, as explained above. Always try to get the best quality available.

SOYBEANS: Raw soybeans cannot be stored for long periods of time. TVP, TSP meat substitutes, or very dry whole soybeans can be used for long-term storage.

POWDERED MILK: This is one of the hardest items to store. First you must decide which type to store—

1. Nonfat, Instant: Easy to mix, good tasting, longest storing due to low fat content. More expensive than nonfat regular. This is the type that I suggest.

2. Nonfat, Noninstant: Least expensive, hardest to mix. Be sure not to get a baker's type if this is to be for drinking. Once mixed it is good tasting. Higher fat content than instant.

3. Noninstant Whole Milk: Most expensive, shortest storage life due to fat content, somewhat difficult to mix, excellent tasting.

At best, expect six months to two years storage from powdered milk that is not stored in cans with most of the oxygen removed. There is no way to do this yourself. Therefore, if you want long-term storage milk, you must go to one of the specially-packed milks from one of the dehydrated food companies such as Rainy Day Foods of Provo, Utah.

For temporary storage of powdered milk, of up to two years, here is the best program that I have found. Place a heavy-duty plastic trash sack inside of a good quality 5-gallon plastic container with a tight fitting lid. Fill the bag with powdered milk, twist the top of the bag to close it, and seal it with the supplied tie. On top of the closed bag place a sack of rock salt about the size of your fist. *Be sure that this is not in contact with the milk.* The salt will absorb moisture and keep it from the milk. Put on the lid and seal the edge with heavy masking tape. Date the lid and store the container in the coolest, driest place around your home, preferably in a dark area. *Never store milk in the top of a garage or attic.* Check the milk every six to nine months, replacing the salt if necessary. If you find any milk caked or rancid smelling, it should be used only in cooking or for feeding animals. It will not be good for drinking. I have seen milk that was stored this way for four years that was still excellent. If you are using a basic foods storage program, you will need 100 pounds of powdered milk per person per year.

Hint: If you are having trouble getting your family to drink powdered nonfat milk, it may be that you are not preparing it correctly. Start rehydrating your milk 18 to 24 hours early. Mix it very well and place it in the refrigerator until it is needed. Mix it again before you serve it.

HONEY: Honey is one of the easiest foods to store. The important criterion here is the amount of water in the honey. If the water content is too high, the honey will not crystallize, but will usually turn black and be useless. You may use any type of honey for storage—clover, alfalfa or whatever. It does not have to be processed. However, I suggest that it be cleaned of most parts of comb and bees before storing. All you need to do is pour the honey into a clean plastic container and seal it tightly. Depending on the moisture content, it will crystallize within one to three months. To use it, just heat the container in a tub of hot water. If you are using a basic foods storage program, you will need 100 pounds of honey per person per year.

SUGAR: 100 pounds of sugar can be stored instead of honey. I have found that the same method used for storing powdered milk works well. You do not have to check the sugar, unless it is stored in a moist area. *Be sure that the salt is not touching the sugar, but is on top of a closed sack.*

SALT: Salt can be stored in almost anything, but be sure that it is kept as dry as possible. Salt can lose savor if allowed to become too moist and hot. Ten pounds is a year's supply for one person.

GARDENING, HUNTING AND FISHING

Another way to supplement your food supply is to have a garden. We won't get into any of the details on gardening, since numerous very good books are available at your local book store. Suffice it to say that a garden, approximately 20 by 20 feet, would supply all of the vegetables that a family of four could eat for a year. All it takes is a little effort, and it could become a fun hobby.

If you enjoy hunting or fishing, either of these could be a very good method of supplementing your meat and protein supply. If you do not practice these sports, but think that you would enjoy one of them, take it up now *before* food shortages occur. The exercise and being out-of-doors would be healthy. You could enjoy yourself while, at the same time, be providing a supply of meat for yourself and those that you care about.

The preservation of the food is one thing that must be considered in conjunction with any one of these three activities. It is easiest for most of us to freeze the food. Hopefully electricity will continue to be available without restriction, and as long as it is, this is a good method. However, looking further ahead to when Christians will not be able to buy or sell, that would include not being able to buy electricity. If you are concerned about the future to that point, you should investigate and learn other methods of preserving food.

There are the traditional canning and preserving methods, such as those that our grandparents used to preserve the surplus from their gardens. Today there are also home food dehydrators that can be purchased very inexpensively (under $50). These allow us the option of dehydrating our own food as a preservative method. Many of the outdoor books, outline ways to preserve meat, such as smoking it, or using salt as a preservative. Before you set out to produce huge amounts of food, you should give careful thought to how you will preserve that food.

Hydroponics to Supplement the Food Supply

Many people may not be familiar with hydroponics. This refers to the growing of plants in a nutrient solution, often with an inert medium, such as fine sterile gravel, providing mechanical support. The nutrient-laden water is poured into the hydroponic gravel "bed" twice a day, left for a short period of time, and then is drained into a container to be used again at the next feeding. Results are optimum in a controlled greenhouse environment where plants are independent of climatic conditions. Since the nutrients are recycled until the plants use them, plants grow faster and produce larger fruit. It is also interesting to note that hydroponic gardening uses 90 to 95 percent less water than traditional gardening, wherein the water—once used—soaks down ultimately to the water table. Only a small portion of the water used in a garden leeches out nutrients from the soil and passes them by the roots of the plants. In hydroponics, all of the water is nutrient laden and it is used multiple times. Chapter 11 will give addresses to write to if you are interested in hydroponics.

Moving to a Farm

Obviously moving to a farm where you can be totally self-sufficient would be of tremendous benefit in a time of severe worldwide famine. Remember that the farmers during the Depression never went hungry, but people in the cities did. This is a vast subject and rather than going into it now, we will cover it in detail in Chapter 10 where we will talk about living in a totally self-sufficient manner.

Protecting Your Food Supply

Christians frequently ask this question: if I have a nice supply of food stored and famine times occur, what do I do if a bunch of people decide to come and take my food? Do I give it to them? Do I kill them? How far do I go in protecting my food supply?

This is one of the most difficult questions that I have to address in this book. I will first give you the answer that obviously must be:

YOU MUST DO WHATEVER GOD TELLS
YOU TO DO AT THE MOMENT.

You might say, "Jim, that's a real cop out." In a way it may be, but in a very real way it is not. I believe that God might lead one Christian family to protect their food with all their might, even to the point of killing those who would attempt to steal it. I also believe that God would lead other Christians to give most or all of it away. (Remember our confidence is not in the food we have stored, but in God!)

Let me share with you a few thoughts on both sides of this question. For those inclined to be more militant in their defense, there is ample Scriptural justification for this stance. For example, it would have been a sin for Aaron, in the Old Testament, to have learned to be a swordsman. God had called him to be a priest. On the other hand, it would have been a sin for Joshua not to have become one of the best swordsmen in the world. It is almost inconceivable to most of us that God would have commanded Joshua to go into a certain town and kill everyone in it, including the old people and the babies. But God actually commanded him to do that very thing. In doing otherwise Joshua would have been disobeying God.

Some Christians, who tend to be pacifists, think that if another Christian is learning karate, or taking shooting lessons he is violent and out of the will of God. We cannot know what God's will is for another brother. Each Christian must do what God leads him to do. I am perfectly convinced in my heart that God leads some Christians to learn these skills.

Another justification for "keeping what you have" is the parable of the ten virgins. As you remember, five virgins brought extra oil, and five did not. When the lamps of the five who did not have the extra oil went out, just about the time the bridegroom was coming, they asked the five virgins who had extra oil for some of theirs and they were denied it. Those who had prepared did not give of their surplus to those who had not prepared. I think that, without violating any of the principles of the Scriptures, we could apply this to the food situation.

On the other side of the question, we see over and over in the Scriptures that if a person is willing to give away his food— as was the boy with the fish and the loaves—frequently God miraculously multiplies the food that is left. God could well lead Christians to give away all of their food so that their reliance would be totally on God.

Those who would say that we should not defend our food supply would point to many of the teachings of Christ, such as going a second mile if a man compels you to go the first mile, and giving a man your coat also if he asks for your cloak. Certainly sharing without resisting would seem to be in keeping with the spirit of Christ's teaching. It is also interesting to note that there is not an instance recorded in the New Testament of God commanding anyone to kill another person. These facts would certainly be Scriptural justification for a Christian who felt that he should store up food but not defend it.

I must state here that I am in favor of free enterprise and individual effort. The one time when the church tried a communal (communistic) way of living was in Jerusalem right after the ascension of Christ. Everyone sold all that they had and pooled their resources. This inevitably leads to laziness, unequal distribution, and so forth. That experiment failed so miserably that eventually the Christians in other parts of the world had to send food and money to these Christians in Jerusalem.

In short I believe that as a man stores up food for his family and himself, that food should be under God's control. God may lead him to give some of it or all of it away, or He may lead him to keep it and defend it. Both are exemplified in the Scriptures. The key is obedience to the voice of God.

Summary and Conclusion

We know that famines are coming. People in the secular world and in the Christian world both are predicting food shortages in the years ahead. We *know* from the Scriptures that famine is definitely part of the Tribulation. This means that at some point food is going to be very scarce and hard to get—likely within our lifetime.

We have examined ways that we can prepare for this inevitable time of food shortage. We can store up food ahead of time, develop skills and begin to practice producing our own food, or we can even take the major step of moving to a farm. There is no *one* answer for all Christians. We must each pray *now* about what God would have us to do. Then we must be very careful to *do* the things that He wants us to do. Remember that this is not a "once-and-for-all prayer." God may not want you to do anything now, but six months from now He may well want you to start storing food. This should be a continual matter of prayer for each Christian.

If God leads us to store some food, we must equally trust Him as to the disposition of it. It is *His* food; we are simply stewards of it. If He leads you to store some, and to keep it for your family and yourself, don't feel guilty about it. If He leads you to give it away, trust that He has something better in mind for you.

8

PREPARING TO SURVIVE

EARTHQUAKES

More precisely the title of this chapter should be "Preparing to Survive Earth Upheavals." To quake means to shake. The earthquakes that we have been experiencing during this century would fall under this category. However, there are earth movements coming that will be far more than a shaking. They will be truly upheavals of the earth. In Revelation 6 we read about one that is coming during the Tribulation:

12 And I looked when He broke the sixth seal, and there was a great earthquake; and the sun became black as sackcloth *made* of hair, and the whole moon became like blood;

13 and the stars of the sky fell to the earth, as a fig tree casts its unripe figs when shaken by a great wind.

14 And the sky was split apart like a scroll when it is rolled up; and every mountain and island were moved out of their places.

15 And the kings of the earth and the great men and the commanders and the rich and the strong and every slave and free man, hid themselves in the caves and among the rocks of the mountains;

16 and they said to the mountains and to the rocks, "Fall on us and hide us from the presence of Him who sits on the throne, and from the wrath of the Lamb;

17 for the great day of their wrath has come; and who is able to stand?"

In verse 14 we see that the earth upheaval was of such magnitude that *every mountain* and *every island* were moved out of their places. The enormity, the violence and the power of such an earth upheaval is almost beyond our imagination.

There have been many such earth upheavals in recorded history. There have been at least seven gigantic geological upheavals that are recorded in the Old Testament. We would like to review some of these.

THE JOSHUA EARTH UPHEAVAL

As Joshua was conquering Israel, we all remember the time when he prayed and the sun stood still. It is recorded in Joshua 10:

> 10 And the LORD confounded them before Israel, and He slew them with a great slaughter at Gibeon, and pursued them by the way of the ascent of Beth-horon, and struck them as far as Azekah and Makkedah.
>
> 11 And it came about as they fled from before Israel, *while* they were at the descent of Beth-horon, that the LORD threw large stones from heaven on them as far as Azekah, and they died; *there were* more who died from the hailstones than those whom the sons of Israel killed with the sword.
>
> 12 Then Joshua spoke to the LORD in the day when the LORD delivered up the Amorites before the sons of Israel, and he said in the sight of Israel,
>> "O sun, stand still at Gibeon,
>> And O moon in the valley of Aijalon."
> 13   So the sun stood still, and the moon stopped,
>> Until the nation avenged themselves of their enemies.
>
> Is it not written in the book of Jashar? And the sun stopped in the middle of the sky, and did not hasten to go *down* for about a whole day.

I have asked many Christians if they believe that the sun actually did stand still and almost invariably the answer is "yes." Then when I ask them what had to physically occur for the sun to stand still, they get a look of astonishment on their faces and say that the earth would have had to stop rotating. This of course is true, and is verified by ancient Mayan and Chinese writings that record a night that was about twice as long as it should have been, which occurred in that same time period.

If the earth stops rotating what happens to the seas? Being a liquid, they would tend to continue to move forward. This would mean that the western shores of the continents would have the seas piled up on top of them. The tidal wave would probably be thousands of feet high. As it surged back and forth many thousands of times it would erode the land and deposit huge layers of sediment.

The core of the earth, being molten, would also tend to continue to rotate; thus, there would be a tremendous tearing effect between the molten core and the hard outer crust of the earth. This would create volcanos and tremendous earth upheavals.

THE AMOS EARTH UPHEAVAL

We see almost the opposite type of earth upheaval related in Amos 8:

> 8 "Because of this will not the land quake
> And everyone who dwells in it mourn?
> Indeed, all of it will rise up like the Nile,
> And it will be tossed about,
> And subside like the Nile of Egypt.
> 9 "And it will come about in that day," declares the Lord GOD,
> "That I shall make the sun go down at noon
> And make the earth dark in broad daylight.

Here we see that the land will rise up as if it were liquid (like the Nile), will be tossed about and then subside. We also see that the sun will go down at noon. I have asked people what would cause the sun to go down at noon and have gotten the reply that there would need to be a tilting of the earth's axis. This tilting of the earth's axis could be caused by many things such as a wandering planet or comet passing very near the earth. This type of earth upheaval would also cause the sea to pour out upon the land, as in Amos 9:

> 5 And the Lord GOD of hosts,
> The One who touches the land so that it melts,
> And all those who dwell in it mourn,
> And all of it rises up like the Nile
> And subsides like the Nile of Egypt;

> 6 The One who builds His upper chambers in the heavens,
>   And has founded His vaulted dome over the earth,
>   He who calls for the waters of the sea
>   And pours them out on the face of the earth,
>   The LORD is His name.

There are other places in the Scriptures that talk about the seas coming out of their secret place and onto the land. Immanuel Velikovsky, on pages 70-72 of his book, *Worlds in Collision* (publisher given later), talks about these huge tidal waves caused by other heavenly bodies passing close to earth:

"The ocean tides are produced by the action of the sun and to a larger extent by that of the moon. A body larger than the moon or one nearer to the earth would act with greater effect. A comet with a head as large as the earth, passing sufficiently close, would raise the waters of the oceans miles high. The slowing down or stasis of the earth in its rotation would cause a tidal recession of water toward the poles, but the celestial body near by would disturb this poleward recession, drawing the water toward itself.

"The traditions of many peoples persist that seas were torn apart and their water heaped high and thrown upon the continents. In order to establish that these traditions refer to one and the same event, or at least to an event of the same order, we must keep to this guiding sequence: the great tide followed a disturbance in the motion of the earth.

"The Chinese annals, which I have mentioned and which I intend to quote more extensively in a subsequent section, say that in the time of Emperor Yahou the sun did not go down for ten days. The world was in flames, and 'in their vast extent' the waters 'overtopped the great heights, threatening the heavens with their floods.' The water of the ocean was heaped up and cast upon the continent of Asia; a great tidal wave swept over the mountains and broke in the middle of the Chinese Empire. The water was caught in the valleys between the mountains, and the land was flooded for decades.

"The traditions of the people of Peru tell that for a period of time equal to five days and five nights the sun was not in the sky, and then the ocean left the shore and with a terrible din broke over the continent; the entire surface of the earth was changed in this catastrophe.

"The Choctaw Indians of Oklahoma relate: 'The earth was plunged in darkness for a long time.' Finally a bright light appeared in the north, 'but it was mountain-high waves, rapidly coming nearer.'

"In these traditions there are two concurrent elements: a complete darkness that endured a number of days . . . and, when the light broke through, a mountain-high wave that brought destruction."

THE JOB AND ISAIAH EARTH UPHEAVALS

The book of Job is probably the oldest book in the Bible. The writer talks about God removing the mountains and incredibly shaking the earth out of its place. This actually means that the earth changed or altered its orbit. We find these events recorded in Job 9:

5 *It is God* who removes the mountains, they know not *how*.
   When He overturns them in His anger;
6 Who shakes the earth out of its place,
   And its pillars tremble;
7 Who commands the sun not to shine,
   And sets a seal upon the stars;
8 Who alone stretches out the heavens,
   And tramples down the waves of the sea;

A similar but separate upheaval is predicted in Isaiah 13:

10 For the stars of heaven and their constellations
   Will not flash forth their light;
   The sun will be dark when it rises,
   And the moon will not shed its light.
11 Thus I will punish the world for its evil,
   And the wicked for their iniquity;
   I will also put an end to the arrogance of the proud,
   And abase the haughtiness of the ruthless.
12 I will make mortal man scarcer than pure gold,
   And mankind than the gold of Ophir.
13 Therefore I shall make the heavens tremble,
   And the earth will be shaken from its place
   At the fury of the LORD of hosts
   In the day of His burning anger.

The fulfillment of this prediction is found in Isaiah 24:

1 Behold, the LORD lays the earth waste, devastates it, distorts its surface, and scatters it inhabitants. . . .

18 Then it will be that he who flees the report of disaster will fall
into the pit,
And he who climbs out of the pit will be caught in the snare;
For the windows above are opened, and the foundations of the
earth shake.
19 The earth is broken asunder,
The earth is split through,
The earth is shaken violently
20 The earth reels to and fro like a drunkard,
And it totters like a shack,
For its transgression is heavy upon it,
And it will fall, never to rise again.

OTHER BIBLICAL EARTH UPHEAVALS

Space does not permit us to go into all of the other earth
upheavals recorded in the Bible. If you wish to pursue them,
some of the others are found in Nahum 1:5-6, Habakkuk 3:10-
11, and Isaiah 2:19-21.

However, the one written of in 2 Kings 20 is very
interesting:

8 Now Hezekiah said to Isaiah, "What will be the sign that the
LORD will heal me, and that I shall go up to the house of the LORD
the third day?"
9 And Isaiah said, "This shall be the sign to you from the LORD,
that the LORD will do the thing that He has spoken: shall the shadow go forward ten steps or go back ten steps?"
10 So Hezekiah answered, "It is easy for the shadow to decline
ten steps; no, but let the shadow turn backward ten steps."
11 And Isaiah the prophet cried to the LORD, and He brought
the shadow on the stairway back ten steps by which it had gone
down on the stairway of Ahaz.

We can see here that the sun descended to where the shadow was long, and then came back up to where the shadow was
short again, before it proceeded to set. As the sun did this zig-
zag in the sky, again we could ask ourselves what happened to
the oceans, the mountains and the rivers? They would have
been in tremendous upheaval, because evidently the earth
stopped rotating, and reversed direction twice before continuing its regular rotation.

CHANGES IN THE EARTH'S ROTATION,
AXIS AND POLARITY

We have looked at changes in the earth's rotations. This subject is spelled out very well on pages 105-106 of Velikovsky's book, *Worlds in Collision:*

"Our planet rotates from west to east. Has it always done so? In this rotation from west to east, the sun is seen to rise in the east and set in the west. Was the east the primeval and only place of the sunrise?

"There is testimony from all parts of the world that the side which is now turned toward the evening once faced the morning.

"In the second book of his history, Herodotus relates his conversations with Egyptian priests on his visit to Egypt some time during the second half of the fifth century before the present era. Concluding the history of their people, the priests told him that the period following their first king covered three hundred and forty-one generations, and Herodotus calculated that, three generations being equal to a century, the whole period was over eleven thousand years. The priests asserted that within historical ages and since Egypt became a kingdom, 'four times in this period (so they told me) the sun rose contrary to his wont; twice he rose where he now sets, and twice he set where he now rises.'

"This passage has been the subject of exhaustive commentaries, the authors of which tried to invent every possible explanation of the phenomenon, but failed to consider the meaning which was plainly stated by the priests of Egypt, and their efforts through the centuries have remained fruitless.

"The famous chronologist of the sixteenth century, Joseph Scaliger, weighed the question whether the Sothis period, or time reckoning by years of 365 days which, when compared with the Julian calendar, accumulated an error of a full year in 1,461 years, was hinted at by this passage in Herodotus, and remarked: *'Sed hoc non fuerit occasum et orientum mutare'* (No reversal of sunrise and sunset takes place in a Sothis period).

"Did the words of the priests to Herodotus refer to the slow change in the direction of the terrestrial axis during a period of approximately 25,800 years, which is brought about by its spinning or by the slow movement of the equinoctial points of the terrestrial orbit (precession of the equinoxes)? So thought Alexander von Humboldt of 'the famous passage of the second book of Herodotus which so strained the sagacity of the commentators.' But this is also a violation of the meaning of the words of the priests, for during the period of spinning, orient and occident do not exchange places.

"One may doubt the trustworthiness of the priests' statements, or of Egyptian tradition in general, or attack Herodotus for ignorance of the natural sciences, but there is no way to reconcile the passage with present-day natural science. It remains 'a very remarkable passage of Herodotus that has become the despair of commentators.'

"Pomponius Mela, a Latin author of the first century, wrote: 'The Egyptians pride themselves on being the most ancient people in the world. In their authentic annals . . . one may read that since they have been in existence, the course of the stars has changed direction four times, and that the sun has set twice in that part of the sky where it rises today.'"

We also know that there have been tilts in the earth's axis. We can see much physical evidence to prove this. The simplest example is the mammoths that were found frozen in Alaska and Siberia. They were standing upright and had tropical vegetation in their teeth and stomachs; they were evidently frozen instantly, because when they were unthawed, dogs ate the meat without any ill effects. All of this implies that they very quickly went from a tropical climate to a freezing arctic climate, which could only be explained by a change in the earth's axis.

In addition, we know that the North and South poles have reversed at least five times. The physical evidence for this has been found in digging down through the fire pits of the Aborigine Indians in Australia and also through the lava flows in North America. In a lava flow, little bits of molten metal tend to line up like tiny compasses in a north-south direction. In digging down through the various layers, you can actually see where the polarity has reversed.

Velikovsky and many Christian scientists believe that some of these earth upheavals were caused as God allowed a comet or a wandering planet to pass near the surface of the earth. These are not events that took place millions of years ago, but within recorded history and they are contained in the Bible. Because of this, I am willing to put faith in their actual occurrence.

If one wishes to pursue an in-depth study on this subject, I would recommend reading the following books in the order that I present them:

Worlds in Collision
by Immanuel Velikovsky
Published by Dell Publishing Co., Inc.

Earth in Upheaval
by Immanuel Velikovsky
Published by Dell Publishing Co., Inc.

The Long Day of Joshua and Six Other Catastrophes
by Patten, Hatch and Steinhauer
Published by Pacific Meridian Publishing Co.

The Jupiter Effect
by Gribbin and Plagemann
Published by Walker Publishing Co., Inc.

The main thing to remember is that God has taken care of His people during the earth upheavals recorded in the Old Testament. He is no less concerned about the physical well-being of His people today. He desires us to be wise about these things and not ignorant. So let's move on and learn more!

The Continental Plates and California

When I studied geology in college, the "continental plate drift theory" was just a theory, and few people believed it. Today you cannot get a job teaching geology unless you subscribe to it. It proposes that all of the land mass was once together in one place and that the continents have drifted apart. Most geologists today feel that this was a gradual process—that the continents drifted apart at approximately 5 centimeters per year. I believe the Bible teaches that they did indeed shift apart, but that it was a sudden movement, not a gradual one. Genesis 10:25 discloses that this earth mass was "divided" during the time of Peleg. Peleg was one of the people involved in the building of the Tower of Babel. After prayerfully reading Genesis 10 and 11, it appears that first the languages were confused, and then the continents came apart.

Most of the continents are floating on single "plates," each of which is bigger than the continent itself. However, the North

American continent is on two plates. The majority of the United States, Canada and Alaska are all on the North American plate, which is moving almost due west (today at 5 centimeters per year). Baja California and the part of California west of the San Andreas fault are on the Pacific plate which is moving northwest, also at 5 centimeters per year. This means that, given enough time, Los Angeles will eventually wind up where San Francisco is today. Along much of the San Andreas fault the plates are "creeping" past each other at 5 centimeters per year. However, because it makes a gigantic S-curve, the part around Los Angeles has been "stuck" for several hundred years. In the book, *The Jupiter Effect,* it is estimated that if this mass of land were to dislodge all at once, it would move northward about 40 yards. The Southern California earthquake is inevitable, although no one knows when it might happen or what might trigger it.

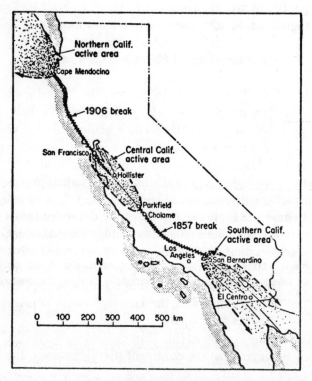

Figure 8.1

The Jupiter Effect puts forth the theory that the lining up of the planets will possibly trigger this earthquake. The planets are normally distributed randomly about around the sun. Once every 179 years they line up in a straight line on one side of the sun. This will occur in 1982. (Actually, they line up twice during 1982, once in April and once in September.) This may or may not be the thing that will actuate the Southern California earthquake.

It is very likely that we will have many major earthquakes before the occurrence of the gigantic earth upheaval that will be part of the Tribulation. It would therefore be wise to prepare for earthquakes. I believe that this is valid advice in whatever part of the country or world you might live.

On pages 32 and 33 of *The Vision,* David Wilkerson tells of earthquakes that he foresees occurring in the United States and the rest of the world:

"The United States is going to experience, in the not-too-distant future, the most tragic earthquake in its history. One day soon this nation will be reeling under the impact of the biggest news story of modern times. It will be coverage of the biggest, most disastrous earthquake in history.

"It will cause widespread panic and fear. Without a doubt, it will become one of the most completely reported earthquakes ever. Television networks will suspend all programming and carry all-day coverage.

"Another earthquake, possibly in Japan, may precede the one that I see coming here. There is not the slightest doubt in my mind about this forthcoming massive earthquake on our continent. I believe it will be many times more severe than the San Francisco quake.

"I am not at all convinced that this earthquake will take place in California. In fact, I believe it is going to take place where it is least expected. This terrible earthquake may happen in an area that's not known as an earthquake belt. It will be so high on the Richter scale that it will trigger two other major earthquakes. I also believe we are going to see, later, a major earthquake in the Aleutian Islands, which will result in a number of smaller earthquakes and aftershocks all along the west coast of the United States.

"Without a doubt, earthquakes are going to strike the United States and other parts of the world with growing intensity. Concern about earthquakes will be uppermost in forthcoming years. News about government scandals, news about war and even economic problems will be completely overshadowed by earthquakes. Within minutes after this quake hits, the whole country will know it, and millions will be stunned and shocked. Thousands will be affected with much loss of life and millions of dollars' worth of damage. Minor earthquakes, aftershocks, and tremors will be recorded almost daily throughout the world. Earthquakes will become the number one cause of fear and consternation.

"The earth is actually going to shake, and there will be numerous other earthquakes in various places throughout the world. This is one kind of judgment that cannot be explained by the scientists. It is supernatural intervention into the affairs of men. It is an act of God causing havoc and judgment, calling men to repentance and reverence. It can strike at any time, and there is no way to deter it. Men will just have to stand back in awe and terror as the power of God is demonstrated in the earthquake."

SAFETY DURING THE ACTUAL EARTHQUAKE

Since God is concerned about your physical safety during earthquakes, let's examine where the basic dangers lie. The big danger is from falling objects. Most deaths and injuries result from objects that fall and crush or maim individuals, or from flying glass that can severely cut. The ideal place to be when an earthquake hits is in a flat, treeless meadow. Ground ruptures are seldom, if ever, the cause of casualties. Most of the hazards are man-made. It is best not to be under signs or poles that can snap or fall, buildings and bridges that can collapse, or wires that can break. Neither is it safe to be near reservoirs and storage tanks, as they can rupture and spill their contents.

If you are inside a house or building when an earthquake hits, stay inside. It is best to move quickly to a position under a doorway, in a bathroom or in a corner. The reason for choosing these areas is that they have extra structural reinforcement and will tend to hold up ceilings and roofs, preventing them from collapsing on you. It is also wise to grab a coat or blanket to put over your head to avoid facial cuts from flying glass.

If you are outside, stay outside. Many accidents and injuries during earthquakes occur when people are leaving or entering buildings. You should try to get out from under things that could fall on you—telephone and electrical poles, signs, trees and the like. Also, the walls of buildings can fall outward during an earthquake; therefore, it is best to move to as open an area as possible. It is likely that during the earthquake electrical wires will be snapped and fall. It is unnecessary to mention that you should at all cost avoid these falling electrical wires.

Once the shaking has stopped, there will be time to evaluate your position and plan what actions to take. It is very likely that there will be fires (created from broken gas lines) to be extinguished. When a big quake hits, any or all of the following could occur:

1. The power may go off.

2. Water supplies may dribble dry.

3. Phones may be dead or tied up.

4. Sewer and gas lines may be broken.

5. Roads and freeways may be blocked by collapsed bridges, landslides, downed power lines, debris and stalled vehicles.

6. Fires may break out and there will be no water with which to put them out.

7. Police and fire services may be unable to help you.

8. The bottled goods in drug stores and grocery stores could all be smashed and unusable.

Take the Three-Day Test

Having been through earthquakes, I find that they hit suddenly and without warning. One could hit your area tonight. Would you like to find out how prepared you are for it? I would encourage you to take the three-day test (suggested by Bill Pier). Here is what you do. First thing tomorrow morning, go out to the water meter and turn off the water, go to the electrical box and throw the main switch, and go to the gas meter and turn off the gas. Place a restriction on your family that they cannot buy anything at the drug store, grocery store or gas station. Then plan to live this way for three days, without making preparation. This will show you how prepared you really are, and will point out dramatically things that you need to do in order to be more prepared.

If you take this test, you will find that if you do not have some water stored you will be in trouble. It might take days to truck water to some areas after an earthquake. After the California 1971 earthquake, water in the San Fernando valley was selling for $2 a gallon. For drinking and cooking, allow a minimum of a half gallon per person per day. Since there will not be enough water to wash dishes, you will also find that having a supply of paper cups and plates is highly desirable.

Another discovery that you will make is that there is a problem with waste disposal, since after one flush, the toilet will no longer be usable. You will find that a port-a-potty would be an invaluable asset.

If you are reading this book in the winter, heating will also be a major consideration. If an earthquake were to occur in the winter, and gas lines were broken, which would likely happen, how would you heat? Good wood stoves would provide a valuable alternative source of heating.

Cooking is less important in that we can go up to forty days without food, and we can sustain ourselves on uncooked food, if necessary. However, being able to cook on one of the Coleman propane camp stoves, or on a wood stove, would make survival during these times much easier and more pleasant. What would you do for lighting if the power were off? Battery-powered lights are best in an earthquake and I believe kerosene lamps to be an excellent addition for longer-term use. Kerosene will store indefinitely, and you can buy several 1-gallon cans of it or even a 55-gallon drum.

What would you do in the evenings during the time of crisis following a large earthquake (or even during your three-day trial period)? Battery-operated cassette players and radios would provide entertainment, as would games to play by kerosene light and books to read. Therefore, a supply of good books and games would be a highly desirable provision for such times.

In addition to the things that you will discover during the three-day test, there are other things that you will want to consider having in order to be prepared for an earthquake. A fire extinguisher is one, since during an earthquake there would probably not be any water pressure, which is needed to fight fires. Fire was the big killer during the 1906 San Francisco earthquake. Also, do not forget to include in your first aid kit items geared for cuts, broken bones and burns.

HOME SAFETY PREPARATION
FOR EARTHQUAKES

I was in Guatemala in 1976 between the two big earthquakes. My wife and I were there a little later and talked with people who had experienced these quakes. The universal comment was that the noise was so deafening that it sounded like they were in the middle of a battlefield. Can you imagine for blocks around everyone's bookcases tumbling over dumping out books, tall China cabinets falling over, breaking all of the dishes in them, grandfather clocks crashing over, wall units falling and spilling their contents as well as cans and dishes flying out of the cupboards? The first big quake happened at night in Guatemala. After it was over, people went into their living rooms to find books, broken mirrors and broken dishes strewn everywhere.

This brings us to one of the first things that we can do in preparing our homes for an earthquake. We can put eye screws in the back of tall pieces of furniture, and eye screws in the studs in the walls behind them, and wire them to the walls so that they will not topple over. Probably the worst potential accident is the hot water heater. During the 1971 California earthquake, a friend's hot water heater "walked" from one side of the garage to the other, obviously breaking the gas pipe and water pipes that connected it. A hot water heater is already top heavy and unstable, and is usually a prime victim of earthquake damage. The diagram on the next page shows how the water heater might be cabled to the wall.

In addition, in an earthquake drawers will fly open and tend to spill their contents. Thus, positive action drawers, such as are found in most boats, would be very nice to have in a home. Since dishes will tend to fall out of cupboards, at a mini-

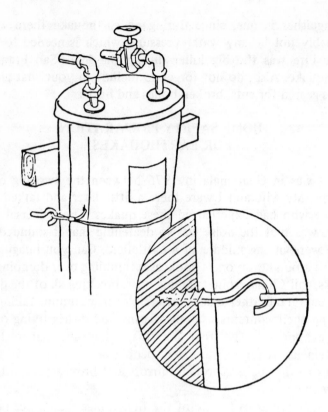

Figure 8.2

mum, a screen-door-type hook could be placed on the outside of each cupboard in the kitchen, and latched when not in use. Another possibility would be to nail a small piece of wood about 1 inch high inside the cupboards on the front of each shelf to form a lip, so that the dishes would not fall out even if the doors swung open.

Heavy, hanging mirrors and things of this nature will tend to come off of their hooks and crash to the floor during an earthquake. Anything that is tall and heavy, especially if it is near your bed, should be properly secured to the wall.

Most people, if they would make a complete check of their home, trying to imagine what it would be like if the Jolly Green Giant were to grab it on each side and shake it vigorously, will be able to discover things that they need to take care of in a preventive way. The way to prevent damage to your property and harm to your family is to take a little time to provide precautionary measures.

After the Quake is Over

Once the quake is over, if you are unhurt, your priorities should be:

1. To keep from getting hurt.
2. To help as best you can those who are injured.
3. To prevent further injuries and property damage.

If medical help is unavailable, do all that you can to aid, comfort and reassure those who are hurt or frightened. Do not move injured people unless they are in immediate danger of further injury. As you go out on your patrol to help people in need, move cautiously and wear protective shoes. Be constantly alert for hazards that could be magnified by aftershock.

Even a tiny spark from an electric switch, cigarette or flame can ignite accumulated gas. Should you suspect that there are damaged lines or possible leaks, immediately ventilate the area and turn off the gas main. Indoor candles and open flames, such as matches and cigarette lighters, are earthquake "no-no's." Aftershocks may cause gas leaks, or even tip over your unattended candles. If the fire department cannot reach you, the smallest flame, unchecked, can touch off a neighborhood holocaust. As far as extinguishing flames, wet towels can be used and reused to beat out small fires, extending precious water supplies. Shoveled dirt, potted plants, and even potato salad can be used to snuff out flames that could destroy a house.

Fallen electrical wires can be a real hazard. To rescue someone from wires is to seriously risk your life. A wrong move can kill you. If you attempt such a rescue, you must stand on dry, nonmetallic surfaces (ground, paper or rubber matting, and such), remaining totally and continually insulated from both the victim and the wires. The victim and the wires must be separated, by pushing or pulling them apart, using only bone-dry, nonmetallic, nonconducting objects (broomsticks, long boards, plastic pipe, and so forth).

Do not waste food. Use first defrosted food out of your refrigerator. After this is used up, begin to utilize the frozen food out of your freezer. Even if the electricity has been turned off, the freezer still may preserve the food for several days.

Makeshift toilets must be kept thoroughly disinfected and tightly covered. Their contents should be buried deep, or kept in sealed plastic bags or trash containers along with other garbage and refuse. Keep refuse away from hungry and homeless animals that might gather around it.

Keep your transistor radio tuned in for broadcasts of conditions and emergency recommendations.

There is a real danger of an aftershock or second earthquake that can be as damaging as the first. Frequently, the first big aftershock will create more damage than the initial quake, since many of the structures that have been weakened by the first shaking, will topple with the second. It has been my experience that less severe aftershocks will continue for many days after the first one or two big quake movements.

EARTHQUAKE-CREATED TIDAL WAVES

The severe Alaskan earthquake of 1964 created tremendous tidal waves that were experienced as far away as South America. We have already seen in the Old Testament where massive earth upheavals created gigantic tidal waves. We looked at the tremendous earth upheavals in Revelation 6, where every mountain and every island were moved out of their places. It is reasonable, then, to expect tidal waves of several thousand feet. When these things occur, let anyone living along a coastline flee to the mountains. As we saw in Revelation 6, even the kings of the earth and the great men hid themselves in the caves and among the rocks of the mountains (Revelation 6:15). These potential tidal waves should be a point of prayer if you are considering moving your residence (especially if you are considering moving next door to the sea).

TAKE THE TIME TO PREPARE

We have seen that earthquakes are coming. During the latter days there will be earthquakes in many places. There are major upheavals that will definitely occur after these, during the Tribulation. For about $50 you can make a home fairly safe from earthquakes. A few eye screws and pieces of wire and cable will attach tall furniture and the water heater to the walls behind them. Installing hooks on cupboards, and purchasing some water storage barrels (less than $20) and a port-a-potty could make the survival of you and your family much easier during an earthquake. All it takes to make these preparations is a very little bit of money and a little time.

There are three books that I have found helpful with regard to details about how to prepare for an earthquake. The first two are smaller—almost booklets—and the third one is an extensive volume which even gets into construction considerations for making new buildings more earthquake proof. If you are interested in pursuing the subject, I trust that you will find these books useful:

The Earthquake Handbook
by Chuck Coyne
Published by Cucamonga Press
P. O. Box 632, Cucamonga, CA

Earthquake Home Preparedness
by Ruth Brent
Published by DeVorss & Co., Inc.
Box 3848, Downey, CA 90242

Peace of Mind in Earthquake Country
by Peter Yaney
Published by Chronicle Books
870 Market Street, San Francisco, CA 94102

You may be lulled into thinking that you do not need to prepare, since you do not live in earthquake country. However, I agree with Dave Wilkerson who feels that we are due for some major earthquakes where we least expect them. This might even be in your own home town.

9

PREPARING TO NOT

BUY OR SELL

I would first like to review the verses which say that Christians who do not accept the mark of the beast will not be able to buy or sell. This is recorded in Revelation 13:

16 And he causes all, the small and the great, and the rich and the poor, and the free men and the slaves, to be given a mark on their right hand, or on their forehead,

17 and he *provides* that no one should be able to buy or to sell, except the one who has the mark, *either* the name of the beast or the number of his name.

18 Here is wisdom. Let him who has understanding calculate the number of the beast, for the number is that of a man; and his number is six hundred and sixty-six.

In Chapter 4, we looked at what will happen to anyone who receives the mark of the beast and worships his image. We learned that anyone who receives this mark will reap the full wrath of God and will be tormented day and night forever. This is found in Revelation 14:

9 And another angel, a third one, followed them, saying with a loud voice, "If any one worships the beast and his image, and receives a mark on his forehead or upon his hand,

10 he also will drink of the wine of the wrath of God, which is mixed in full strength in the cup of His anger; and he will be tormented with fire and brimstone in the presence of the holy angels and in the presence of the Lamb.

11 "And the smoke of their torment goes up forever and ever; and they have no rest day and night, those who worship the beast and his image, and whoever receives the mark of his name."

12 Here is the perseverance of the saints who keep the commandments of God and their faith in Jesus.

13 And I heard a voice from heaven, saying, "Write, 'Blessed are the dead who die in the Lord from now on!'" "Yes," says the Spirit, "that they may rest from their labors, for their deeds follow with them."

To cover the vast subject of Christians not being able to buy or sell would require an entire book (at least). One would need to discuss the present and future monetary systems, paper money becoming worthless, electronic money, the mark of the beast, living on a farm, having a self-supporting house, raising and preserving food, and bartering, to name just a few. Perhaps someday God will tell me to write that book, but for now we will have to but touch on many of these topics very briefly. We will be dealing with *how* the future world economic system *might* work. This may or may not be the way it will actually occur. Nonetheless, the Scriptures tell us loudly and clearly that for a Christian to remain true to God, he cannot accept the mark of the beast, and in declining the mark of the beast, the Christian will not be able to buy or sell in the world economic system. The computer power exists today to implement such a controlled economy, and God tells us that it is coming. Therefore, it is prudent for a Christian to consider this coming system and how he might provide for his loved ones and himself, without denying Christ and accepting the mark of the beast.

ELECTRONIC MONEY

I was with IBM for ten years, in the computer business for twenty, and have written books on the subject of computers, management and management information systems. During my time in the computer field, I was exposed to much information not available to the general public. One of the things that I was well aware of was the trend towards electronic money to solve some basic problems. A summary of some of this information may be helpful at this point.

Many years ago, before dial telephones, the telephone company did a study in order to project their requirements for telephone operators. At the rate they were growing, they could see that in a number of years they would need more telephone operators than there were employable people to fill these jobs. They concluded that, of necessity, they had to develop dial telephones. More recently the telephone company did another study and projected that they would need more long distance operators than there were people available to fill those positions. They then concluded that it was necessary to develop direct dialing, so that the individual telephone subscriber could dial his own direct long distance calls.

Similar studies were done in the banking field. Checks at one time were all handled and distributed manually. It was projected that the volume of checks would increase to the point where they could not be managed by hand. Therefore, the MICR (Magnetic Ink Character Recognition) was developed. The funny-looking numbers printed along the bottom of your checks are called MICR numbers. These are readable by automatic check-handling machines. Another study was later developed, showing that we would still be buried under a pile of paper checks unless something more were done. Investigators found that there was no way to speed up the flow of these pieces of paper. Therefore, research began into methods of eliminating checks.

The following example illustrates the problem of being buried under a pile of paper. For an individual to get paid, deposit his check, purchase a belt on credit at a department store, and subsequently pay that bill upon receiving the monthly statement from the store, it requires approximately 17 pieces of paper, which are handled over 30 times. The papers would include the paycheck, a deposit slip, an envelope to mail the deposit slip, a stamp, the sales slip at the department store, the customer's ledger card, his monthly statement, the envelope for the monthly statement, the customer's check, the return stub of the department store invoice, the envelope which the customer uses to mail this check, the stamp, the department store's deposit slip and so on.

As the number of transactions of this type increases, the amount of paper that must be handled increases geometrically. Thus, as the number of transactions increases tenfold, the amount of paper will increase about one hundred times.

Federal Government Moves Toward Electronic Money

Evidently the federal government agrees with this problem, for we read in *The Houston Chronicle,* January 10, 1975:

"Cashless Society Said Possible in Decade: All Transactions Would Be Electronic . . . New York (UPI)—A cashless society, in which all transactions from buying groceries to paying the telephone bill are handled electronically, is possible within 10 years, according to a Federal Reserve Bank officer. Thomas G. Waage, senior vice president of the Fed's New York Branch, said that unless a new system of exchange is developed the nation's banking system will 'choke' under an avalanche of checks.

". . . To reduce check volume, Waage proposed a system whereby personal bills would be paid directly by a bank to the creditor. All bills and computer programming would have to be standardized for 'a uniform transfer.' A national standard for all bills would have to be adopted so they contained 'all the necessary information' and could be translated by either magnetic tape or optical scanning devices.

"Under this system, an individual would take or send his bills to the bank, which would make direct payments from the individual's account to the creditor's bank account through electronic transfers of money between the banks. The Federal Reserve would act as an automated clearing house. Again, no paper would change hands.

"'This system,' Waage said, 'has been used successfully in Europe. In the Netherlands, 90 percent of all house payments and rentals are made this way,' he said.

"'Such a system could be implemented in a year's time,' Waage said, 'if everybody would do it. IT WOULD BE A FIRST STEP,' Waage said, 'TO A CASHLESS SOCIETY THAT COULD BE REACHED IN 10 YEARS.'"

How Would an Electronic Money System Work?

I would like to take the same example as before—that of a person getting paid and purchasing a belt. Under an electronic money system, instead of the individual getting a paycheck, the company where he works would type its payroll into a computer terminal. This terminal would be hooked to the central financial computer for his town. The computer would automatically take the money out of the company's bank account and deposit it in the individual's bank account. Then as this individual went to the department store to purchase the belt, he would present his "super" credit card to the clerk. The clerk would enter the item number for the belt and the credit card into a computer terminal. Money would immediately be transferred from this individual's account into the department store's bank account. The department store's inventory record would also be updated. All of this would occur electronically, without any paper changing hands. At the end of the month, the individual would receive from his bank a detailed printout of all of his transactions during the month. Thus, only one piece of paper would be utilized. The savings in paper and handling, as well as in pure cost, are obvious.

In this electronic money system, all other transactions that a person would make would be done in basically the same manner. Actually, this is not as far-fetched as it may seem. A person can live today only writing one or two checks per month. With his Mastercharge card he can purchase food, gasoline, hardware, clothes, and all the other basic necessities of life. At the end of the month he can write *one* check to Mastercharge to pay for all of these expenses. There may have to be another check or two written to pay the rent and utilities. However, in some places this too can be done with a credit card. All that would have to be done to make the electronic system a reality would be to have the funds automatically go to Mastercharge, rather than writing that one check.

Some people may panic when they hear about such a system, because they tend to start writing "hot" checks a day or two before payday. This has been thought out and taken care of in the electronic credit system. You could apply for credit in advance. This is being done today in the checking accounts, otherwise known by various names such as "balance plus accounts." In this type of account, you are authorized to overdraw by $100, $500, or whatever is your approved credit limit. The bank will then automatically loan you the money and charge you the interest. Sometimes this loan is actually taken from your credit card. However, in an electronic system, once you have reached the point of your credit limit there would be absolutely no additional purchases.

Problems with Electronic Money Systems

For such a system to work there would have to be a single identifying number for each individual. This implies that there would probably also be a single "world credit card." Many people look at the social security number as the number that will likely be used for this. I seriously doubt that. There are a vast number of individuals in the United States who have the same social security number as someone else. There are also many individuals who have multiple social security numbers. A number of years ago, insurance companies tried to use the social security number as a means of identification; they found it impossible to use and subsequently terminated their efforts in that direction. The other difficulty with the social security number is that it does not have a self-checking digit.

A self-checking digit is usually a single digit at the end of a number which insures that the number has been entered correctly. Usually this self-checking digit is generated by taking something like every other digit and doubling these. The alternate digits and these products might then be added, and the right-hand digit of the sum would become the check digit. Thus, if we had the number 1234-5678-X, we would double the 1, 3, 5, and 7, which would give us 2, 6, 10, and 14. We would add these numbers to the 2, 4, 6, and 8. The total of these numbers is 52. The "2" would be the check digit, and therefore our complete number would be 1234-5678-2.

The self-checking digit would prevent most errors when "account" numbers would be entered into computer terminals. For example, if someone typed a 9 instead of a 3, 18 would be added into the total rather than 6 (this was one of the doubled digits). This would change the sum and, therefore, the check digit. It also would prevent two numbers being transposed.

Given the problems with the social security number, when such a system begins to be used widely, I look for a renumbering of the population. Possibly it could be based on the social security number, with the addition of a three-digit country number on the front, to represent the U.S., and a trailing self-checking digit. You would then have 12 or 13 digits for your identification number, rather than the present 9 digits of our social security number.

The System will be Implemented Gradually

Let me first state that I do not think this coming system is good. Today I regret some of the efforts that I expended in conceiving and designing portions of this system. Back in my more naive days, while speaking to a group of bankers, I labeled this system SAVE (System for Automatic Value Exchange). Today it is known as EFTS (Electronic Funds Transfer System).

Even though I now do not like the idea of such a system, nor want it imposed upon us, I still believe it is inevitable. There are too many forces pushing us in that direction. The "big brother" implications are horrifying. The government could keep track of all of our expenditures. They could put us on a budget, allowing us use of only a portion of our funds each week. The IRS could tag your account, preventing you from making any purchases. If a dictator were ever to arise, he would have the technology that would enable him to totally control the population.

This electronic money and credit system will not be instituted all at once. There will be bits and pieces of it implemented here and there. At times these pieces will seem unrelated. However, ultimately they will all become part of this net that will encase us. First we will see our regular credit cards come more and more into prominence. Eventually these will probably be merged into a single credit card. This might be privately owned, or might ultimately be taken over by the government. If we have a depression and people in mass cannot pay for their credit card charges, it is likely that the government will have to nationalize this card(s). We will see more terminals appearing in stores.

We might begin to see heavy charges for using checks. Bit by bit the system will take shape.

Banking and Purchasing

There are two basic elements of the system. The first is the automatic, electronic deposit of funds. The second is the computer terminal controlling the purchases. Let us first look at the electronic banking. Automatic depositing by electronic means is well under way. In the *Columbia Record* of January 31, 1975, we read:

"There'll be no more paychecks for some 60,000 airmen in the Western states—they're paid electronically. This means they are paid right on time, there is no more danger that a paper check may be lost in the mail and the federal government is saving thousands of dollars in paper and handling. From now on the Federal Reserve Bank, with blips and bleeps on magnetic tape, will move millions of dollars to Air Force personnel. 'The program is entirely voluntary,' a Federal Reserve official said, 'But already two out of every five airmen have chosen the new medium and it's expected that nearly 300,000 will take advantage of electronic payments.' A single reel of magnetic tape can store 14 million characters which can be retrieved and read in a few minutes. One reel replaces almost 190,000 checks or a stack of paper 70 feet high. By 1980, officials said, as many as 16 million recurring federal payments will be transferred directly to the accounts of recipients along the Fed's electronic funds network."

It is estimated that almost 4 million social security recipients are now receiving direct deposits of federal payments. The electronic banking is going further. Under a ruling issued by James E. Smith, the controller of the currency, electronic banking for consumers will soon be available on street corners and in supermarkets. The controller's ruling will allow customers to make deposits, withdrawals, transfers between checking and savings accounts, and payments to other persons, without even going near the bank.

This trend was pointed out in more detail by the *New York Times* News Service of April 13, 1975:

"Banking In Style In The Supermarket—Electronically: Instant Transfer by Computer May Do To Checks What Checks Did To Currency; Experts Ponder Other Effects:

"Burbank, California—Richard DeCarlo did his banking the other day at his supermarket. DeCarlo, a professional musician here, drove to the Hughes market here, picked out some groceries and then told the clerk he wanted to withdraw money from a savings and loan association several miles away. A few moments and a few flashing lights later, he had the money to pay his grocery bill, and some spare cash for himself.

"The medium DeCarlo used for his banking was a small counter-top computer terminal about the size of an electric typewriter. It is a symbol of an emerging technological upheaval that is sending tremors through the banking world and promising to alter fundamentally the way Americans handle their money. Within recent months, 14 commercial banks in nine states, and 117 savings and loan associations in 17 states, have installed such devices, or notified Federal authorities that they intend to do so. . . ."

These conveniently located banking terminals are going interstate. In the March, 1976, issue of *Supermarket News* we read:

"Chicago—The two largest banks in the Midwest—First National Bank of Chicago and Continental Bank—are moving ahead with plans to expand electronic funds transfer systems in supermarkets, despite a Federal judge's ruling that limits the systems to performing check cashing and authorization and bank credit-card authorization. . . .

"A total of 56 Chicago area savings and loan associations have filed applications with the Federal Home Loan Board, Washington, to share the Continental Bank's electronic network at 199 National Food Stores and Dominick's Finer Foods supermarkets.

" . . . Continental Bank also disclosed it would establish, during the third quarter of 1976, a computer link with Milwaukee Midland National Bank, enabling Midland's customers—and customers of 48 S & L's (Savings & Loans) in Illinois and Wisconsin to share Continental's electronic network at National and Dominick's supermarkets in the Chicago area."

Stores Going Electronic

Many of the major merchandising organizations, such as Sears Roebuck and Co., are operated almost exclusively with computer terminals. The information is entered into the terminal as you are purchasing the merchandise. The clerk enters the product numbers and quantities. The computer automatically updates your account, extends the amount based on quantity, and calculates the tax. The only thing that is lacking is the connecting of this into banking terminals. This would complete the circuit and move the money from your account into the stores.

Similarly, supermarkets are going to laser checkout stands, based on the UPC (Universal Product Code). This code is the strange-looking series of lines, about the size of a large postage stamp, found on most grocery items in stores today. These lines depict numbers. The code is usually 12 numbers—the first 6 identify the manufacturer of the product and the last 6 identify the product. Any price changes will be registered within the store's computer. The computer will simply look up the item number and find the exact price for the day. (In a runaway inflation this will be very handy when prices are going up daily or even hourly.)

On the back of most of the major credit cards is a black line about 3/8 of an inch wide. This is a strip of magnetic tape on which your name and account number are encoded. Once terminals are more widely spread, they will begin to use this magnetic coded information, rather than the visual raised numbers.

The same type of magnetic strip could ultimately be used for money and small change. This is currently being used in the San Francisco BART (Bay Area Rapid Transit) system. You can deposit some amount of money—say $5—and get a card. Every time you ride the BART train in San Francisco you put your card in the turnstile, which deducts the amount that you are using, prints the new amount on the card, and returns it to you. When the amount remaining gets low enough, you can add to the amount on the card by inserting it with additional money into a special machine. An example of a Bart card is shown on the next page.

Look closely at it, for it could eventually be the kind of money that you will use for taxi cabs, baseball games, buying cokes, and so forth. In this instance, these vending devices will take the card, deduct the amount, and then return it to you, with the new amount both printed and encoded magnetically. In the future electronic system, you would insert your "super" credit card in a machine and get one of these temporary "money cards" for small purchases.

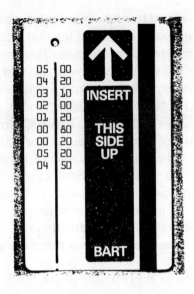

05 00
04 20
03 10
02 00
01 20
00 80
00 20
05 20
04 50

INSERT

THIS
SIDE
UP

BART

Figure 9.1

There is a book that deals with this cashless economic system in detail. It is:

Cashless Society: A World Without Money
by Wally Wood
Published by The Southwest Radio Church
P. O. Box 1144, Oklahoma City, OK 73101

A Credit Card You Cannot Lose

Looking at such an electronic money system, wherein you would have a universal credit card that would represent your entire assets, the question then arises: what if you lose your credit card? If you were to lose your credit card, or if it were stolen, someone could wipe you out and spend all of the money that you had saved all your life. I say this as a computer expert, realizing the use of security codes, key words and the other security measures that can be built into an electronic system. There is still a danger that this could occur, especially to the rich. Therefore, the solution would be to make the credit card unlosable.

At first fingerprints were investigated as a possible alternative. However, the problems in pattern recognition became too difficult to handle. The simplest solution would be to tattoo a number in ultraviolet ink on each individual. The number would be invisible except when held under an ultraviolet light (such as the stamp they put on your hand so you can go in and out of an amusement park). A logical place to put it would be some place where it would normally be visible, even if a person were bundled up. A likely place would be the back of the right hand. For those without a right hand, the forehead might be used as an alternative.

This idea of an invisibly tattooed number I first mentioned in a radio interview in 1964. Since then it has been picked up by many authors and speakers. In the September 20, 1973 edition of *Senior Scholastics* they say:

"There is a huge conviction in financial circles that EFT in one way or another will become a major means for transferring money in the near future. All buying and selling in the program will be done by the computer. No currency, no change, no checks. In the program people would receive a numbered TATOOED IN THEIR WRIST OR FOREHEAD. THE NUMBER IS PUT IN BY LASER BEAM AND CANNOT BE FELT. THE NUMBER IN THE BODY IS NOT SEEN WITH THE NAKED EYE AND IS AS PERMANENT AS YOUR FINGERPRINTS. All items of consumer goods will be marked with a computer mark. The checkstand will pick up the NUMBER IN THE PERSON'S BODY and automatically total the price and deduct the amount from the person's 'Special Drawing Rights' account. . . ."

This idea of branding with laser beams is actually being done today. *Oklahoma City Times,* in their November 6, 1975 issue, pointed out that this is presently being done with fish:

". . . a university professor believes a 'laser iron' may be in (the) future. The laser beam branding iron marks steers and horses—and swimming salmon. It is quick and painless, says its inventor, R. Keith Farrell, a Washington State University veterinary medicine professor . . . Only two of the devices, which resemble thin telescopes, exist. One is used by the state Fisheries Department to brand thousands of salmon.

"The laser destroys skin pigment. In thirty-billionths of a second a technician can stitch a brand . . . or just initials—on fish or livestock."

The *Chicago Daily News,* in March, 1974, reported: "Permanent I.D. on Newborns Urged For Counting Population." Whenever this type of system is actually implemented a number of justifiable reasons will be given, such as keeping track of the census. The government will probably also cite certain "womb to tomb" benefits people can have with such a number. The Christian, however, wants to avoid this type of system like the plague.

New World Economic System

A logical question might arise as to how this electronic money system fits in with a potential new world monetary system. The current world system has been in shambles since President Nixon closed the gold window in 1971, leaving all paper money backed by nothing. There is a need for a new system which would stabilize the floating exchange rates and establish some semblance of stability in the monetary chaos that presently exists.

At present I believe that the new monetary system and the electronic money system are independent, but parallel in their development. However, when the new world monetary system is implemented, it could well be that the electronic money system will be one of the key building blocks of it. They are both being sponsored by the same group of banks.

As an economist I would love to dig deeply into the present economic system and this future one, and delve into all the reasons why a new system is inevitable, and why the present system has within it the seeds of its own destruction. However, space will not allow me to even begin that. What is important now is that the Christian will not be able to be part of the new economic and new monetary systems. Whether it occur as I have envisioned it here, with electronic money and invisible tattoos, or whether it takes some other form really doesn't matter. The key thing is that Christians at some point will not be able to buy or sell, and therefore must make preparations to live independent of the economy.

BECOMING SELF-SUPPORTING

You will notice that I did not say "self-sufficient." No man is ever self-sufficient. We all need God and His power. However, God does expect us to support ourselves, regardless of the political or economic system under which we live. To become truly self-supporting there are four basic approaches that you could take:

1. Move to a farm (a single-family farm).

2. Move to a farm (a group or community of families).

3. Have a retreat (a place to go during time of crisis).

4. Have a self-supporting house in the city.

We will discuss each of these approaches in detail in just a minute. Prior to that, there are certain things that are going to be needed, whichever approach you might be led to take. The first thing that is obvious is that we are going to need to learn how to barter instead of purchase. Most Christians are so accustomed to "purchasing" things in stores that a face to face negotiation for an item would be a frightening experience. If this is your case, I would encourage you to begin to attend swap meets, garage sales, flea markets, and other places where this type of negotiation goes on. After you are comfortable negotiating with money, take the next step; try doing it without money. For example, you could take a couple of cans of a good brand of peaches to a garage sale to see what you could trade them for. You should also remember that bartering with people you know and trust is much easier than bartering with strangers. In the Christian group with which you fellowship you could begin to barter with one another. You can also learn to exchange services. Get used to lending people a helping hand and doing nice things for them. This bread that you cast on the waters can come back to you manifold.

If you are going to barter (with goods), this necessitates the storing up of barterable items. Various writers have suggested numerous things that might be used for barter, such as nails, ammunition, toilet paper, food, and medicine. My suggestion is that you don't blindly follow anyone's advice, but that you figure out for yourself what the people you know would really want, if things began to be in short supply. It is ideal if the items are storable for long periods of time and are contained in small units. Once you have decided on certain barter items, lay in a supply of these. (Don't put all of your eggs in one basket.)

Just as most Christians today do not have items with which to barter, they also do not have skills that are barterable. For example, there may not be much demand in your neighborhood for the repairing of giant electronic computers, but there may be for the repairing of television sets or lawn mowers. It would therefore be wise for a computer repairman to take some courses and training in these other types of repairs, so that his skills will be in demand when he cannot buy or sell. There are many other types of repair skills that would be very valuable during a time when one cannot buy or sell.

In addition to repair-type skills, skills for producing essential items would be much in demand. For example, if you had a wheat mill you could grind wheat into wholesome, fresh flour for people, in exchange for whatever items or services they might want to give you for it. Knowing how to can and preserve would also be valuable during such a time. You could do the canning and preserving for somebody else's garden for a certain percentage of the final preserved output. Or you could become an expert in vegetable gardening, and help people with their gardens in exchange for some of the produce.

Storing up barter items, learning new skills, moving to a farm, or making your city home self-supporting all imply major changes in life-style. They also all require time to achieve. Therefore, you should prayerfully consider what, if anything, you should do, and then go ahead and get started, since it may take several months or even years to accomplish.

A Self-Supporting Home in the City

Many Christians feel that they are not able to move to a farm and must survive in the city. Usually the reason for this is that the city is where their job is. When the time of the mark of the beast comes, I do not believe that Christians will be able to work for pay in jobs as we know them today. If this is true, a home in the city may not be that desirable during the Tribulation.

However, if you are going to try to have a completely self-supporting house in the city (or even on a farm), there is one book that I feel is an absolute must:

The Autonomous House
by Brenda and Robert Vale

Unfortunately, I have not found a place to purchase this in the United States, since it is a book I picked up in my travels. You can order it from:

Thames & Hudson
30 Bloomsbury Street
London WC1B 3QP
England

The price of the book is 2.50 pounds in the United Kingdom. My guess is that if you sent them $10 they would airmail you a copy of it. Their definition of an autonomous house is as follows (pages 7-8):

"The autonomous house on its site is defined as a house operating independently of any inputs except those of its immediate environment. The house is not linked to the mains services of gas, water, electricity or drainage, but instead uses the income-energy sources of sun, wind and rain to service itself and process its own wastes. In some ways it resembles a land-based space station which is designed to provide an environment suitable for life but unconnected with the existing life-support structure of Earth. The autonomous house uses the life-giving properties of the Earth but in so doing provides an environment for the occupants without interfering with or altering these properties. . . .

"The autonomous house is not seen as a regressive step. It is not simply a romantic vision of 'back to the land,' with life again assuming a rural pace and every man dependent upon himself and his immediate environment for survival. Rather, it is a different direction for society to take. Instead of growth, stability is the aim; instead of working to earn money to pay other people to keep him alive, the individual is presented with the choice of self-autonomy or working to pay for survival. No such choice exists at present. 'Dropping out' now is a game for those with private means. . . .

"However, the attractive idea of a house generating its own power and recycling its own wastes is almost as difficult to realize as the idea of a stable economy. Apart from the physical limitations of income-energy sources, the system can be made only marginally competitive with existing methods of servicing houses. This difficulty could be removed if autonomy did not have to fit within the present system."

We may never reach the ideal of having a totally autonomous house, with no requirement of inputs from outside sources. This is very difficult to achieve even on a farm. I found this when I lived in a cove on Catalina Island for a year. There was no electricity, telephones or roads into the place. The only way in was by boat. The cabin that I built was powered by propane. I would have to take my boat into town to buy two tanks full of propane. I would then throw them into the ocean (they float even full), tie them onto the back of the boat and tow them out to the cove, anchor the boat and swim them ashore. The propane provided us with light, refrigeration and heat. Similarly, on most "self-sufficient" farms today, people rely heavily on outside supplies of electricity, gasoline, diesel fuel and feed grains.

If necessary, one can live in a lean-to covered with leaves and branches, cook freshly killed wild game on a stick over a campfire, and sleep on the ground. This may be fun on a camping trip but would be difficult, at best, as a way of life for several years. A friend of mine spent summers at his father's ranch, living in a tin shed with a wood stove and outhouse. This is better than a lean-to, but it is far from an ideal situation for your family.

We will be discussing something closer to the ideal. No one family will likely do everything that we are going to suggest. However, there may be many valuable ideas that you will gain as you read about making a house self-supporting. If you find yourself getting bogged down in the details of say "wind-powered electricity generation," I would suggest that you just skim through that section and go on to the next. However, I must hasten to add that information on such a subject may prove to be very valuable when we can no longer buy electricity, because we have refused to accept the mark of the beast.

Since it is almost unheard of in our society to be totally self-supporting, those Christians who move in this direction will really be pioneering new ground. This is a difficult task on a farm, and it will be even more difficult in a city.

Three Basic Approaches

In order to have a more self-supporting house, there are three basic approaches that can be taken:

1.   Modify the existing house.

2.   Build an auxiliary house behind the present one.

3.   Buy land (a lot) and build a new house.

Deciding which approach to use requires much careful thought and consideration. What you decide depends on how autonomous you want to be, how much land there is available at your present site, how much sentiment is attached to your present house and so on. One thing that should be investigated while you are considering your approach is the zoning law, as well as other laws that could influence your decision. For example, in some communities it is illegal to raise small animals, such as rabbits and chickens. In other communities, having a septic tank may be against the law. There are many places in the nation where drilling a well without permission is violating the water laws. Also consider how your neighbors might react to your putting up a wind electrical generator. These are all very important considerations when deciding which approach to take.

1.   Modify the existing house.

This is by far the hardest approach. Just to modify an existing house for solar heating is quite a task. If you include things such as modifying the plumbing so that the toilet can be flushed with used bath water, you will have to do major ripping out of walls to make the changes. There are certain things, however, that can easily be done to an existing house, such as adding wood stoves and having an alternative electrical supply. The nice thing about this approach is that you do not have to move.

2. *Build an auxiliary house behind the present one.*

This approach was used by a family who saw the movie, "Wilderness Family." They were so inspired by this film that they decided to make a "move." Their property is about an acre in size and has an old stable in the back, with an adjoining room. They bought a wood stove, made bunks and actually moved into this room next to the old stable. They live there without electricity or television, and feel that it has brought their family closer together. They say that they are much happier. They go "up front" to their plush, luxurious house occasionally to pick up items that they need. In considering this approach, we are not looking at anything quite this drastic, but rather at the building of a "guest house" (perhaps even on top of the garage) that would be totally self-contained. Your family could spend several evenings a week there to become accustomed to the changes. This could be a worthwhile experience, as well as being a lot of fun. It could possibly improve the value of the property too. With this approach, you remain in your home while building the guest cabin, which would provide a self-supporting refuge in time of an emergency.

3. *Buy land (a lot) and build a new house.*

This is by far the easiest and, I believe, the best approach, if one can make the move. You can find a piece of land that is just right and build from scratch a house that has all of the survival features that you want. If you purchased a lot on which a productive well could be drilled, a septic tank installed, and a wind electrical generator put up without any objections from the neighbors, you would be well on your way to having an autonomous house. You could then have your home customized for your family's specific needs. You could have a basement built that would provide protection from nuclear radiation.

Rainwater collectors and large water tanks could be installed, as well as large fuel tanks (diesel or propane).

THE BASIC CHECKLIST

The basic items worth consideration that we will be discussing, with regard to making a home more self-supporting, apply to any one of the three approaches. These items are as follows:

1.   Water supply
2.   Waste disposal
3.   Heating and air conditioning
4.   Heat for cooking
5.   Lighting
6.   Refrigeration
7.   Entertainment
8.   Food production
9.   Food preservation

I would like to begin our discussion with the most important one . . .

Water Supply

After any emergency, such as an earthquake, the three most important things that you will need are water, water and water. The same thing is true when considering a self-supporting home, whether in the city or in the country. If you can't buy water, you must be able to supply your own. There are a number of ways to acquire an independent water supply. The ideal is to have a spring on the property, which will gravity feed enough water for all of your needs (house, garden, and so on). Probably the next most desirable water supply would be by rainwater collection, if you live in a part of the country where there is sufficient rainfall. The water for homes in the Cayman Islands is supplied by rainwater. Collecting rainwater is not as

simple as having an old rain barrel. One necessary step is to separate out the first flow rainwater from the roof (which will be
dirty) and discard it, while collecting the remainder. This can
be achieved by the device shown in Figure 9.2.

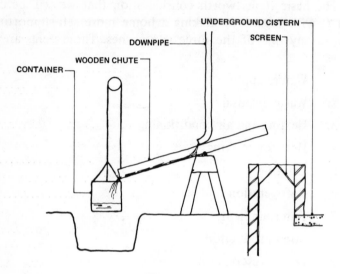

Figure 9.2

Water that is to be collected must be filtered before it enters the tank. Such a filtering and storage system is shown in
Figure 9.3

Another approach is to drill a well. This is feasible in more
parts of the country than one might realize. A friend of mine
in Dallas, Texas, had a well drilled in his backyard, which he
now uses to water his lawns. The supply of the water there,
however, is ample to furnish all of his household needs, if necessary. Chances are that the well you drill will not be flowing,
and that the water will have to be pumped. The simplest thing
is to have an electric pump, with which you can pump water
into a very large storage tank. It is possible that this tank could
combine the well water with rainwater. By pumping a large
amount to storage while public electricity is available, you
would have to do little manual pumping, if any, during an
emergency.

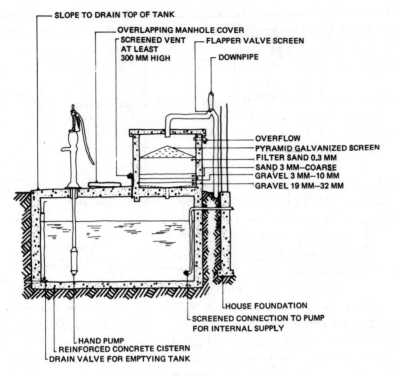

Figure 9.3

If water is in a short supply, reusing some of it would be highly desirable. Your system might include a solar still for distilling dirty shower water.

Such water could also be utilized to flush the toilet (W.C.). A complete system of the reuse of water is shown in Figure 9.4, shown on the next page.

Waste Disposal

Very few Christians ever give much consideration to the disposal of waste. They assume that the sewers are going to work forever and that garbage will always be picked up. However, in a situation wherein we can neither buy nor sell, we will not likely be able to utilize the sewer and garbage services of our cities. On Catalina, garbage disposal was a major problem for us.

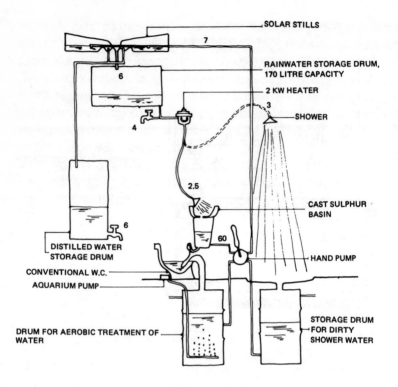

Figure 9.4

We had to separate our waste into three piles. The edible portion I took up the canyon and put out for the wild boars. The burnable part I burned once a week. The rest—bottles and cans—I took out to sea once a week and dumped overboard. If one has animals that he can feed the edible wastes to, and a burn barrel for the burnables, he is partway there. The rest can be stored and hauled away periodically, assuming that it has been washed and is free of food particles.

By far the type of waste most difficult to dispose of is human waste. On Catalina we had the traditional outhouses, as well as the covered pail under the bed for nighttime emergencies. This is quite primitive and there are better ways. In most places a septic tank can be installed for the collection of waste. If a septic tank is not legal on the property that you have in mind, you should consider a composting toilet. (For those not familiar with compost piles, this is where manure, straw and such are stacked up and left to decay. This material is subsequently used for fertilizer.) These composting toilets operate without water and collect the residue in a large container. About once a year, dry fertilizer can be shoveled out of the toilet. One of these composting toilets would be good either for a guest house or for one of the bathrooms in a new home. In a guest house, one could also use one of the chemical recirculating port-a-potties. Whatever method is used, careful consideration must be given to the disposal of garbage, human waste, and used water. Addresses will be given in Chapter 11, for those interested in receiving information on these.

Heating and Air Conditioning

There are three basic methods to consider with regard to space heating independent of public utility systems:

1.   Solar

2.   Wood burning

3.   Wind-generated electricity

In considering the use of solar energy to heat your home, it is obvious that it will be much easier to utilize if you are building a new home than if you are trying to "retrofit" solar heating into an existing structure. The main motivation for installing solar heating, as far as I am concerned, is not economics but independence. Solar heating will tend to make you less dependent on the utility systems.

There are two basic types of systems in solar heating: passive and active. In a passive system, one does not have the pipes and pumps that are involved in an active system. The simplest form of a passive system is to have all of the south side of a house glassed in, and perhaps no windows on the north side. While the drapes are open all day, the sun shines through the glass. This heats the air in the room, the furniture and, if there is a thick concrete floor, it heats the floor. In the evening the drapes are shut (or a movable insulation is placed across the inside of the windows), and the heat is slowly released from the furniture and floor to keep the house warm all night.

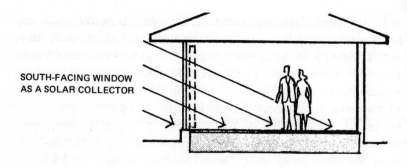

Figure 9.5

Another passive system also utilizes a glass wall on the south side, but drums of water are stacked inside, and the end of each of these that is next to the window (sun) is painted black. All day these drums collect heat, which they release during the evening and night. These are but two of the many variations on passive systems. The nice thing about them is that if the electricity went off, they would still work.

Figure 9.6

Another advantage of the passive systems is that they are more easily installed in existing structures. For example, one could fairly inexpensively add another window to the south side of one's house—or more ideally, several giant floor-to-ceiling windows. However, this will only heat rooms on the south side of the house. This leaves something to be desired, unless the house is built as a long narrow structure running east and west, so that every room has a southern exposure. This means that most houses will probably require an active system.

There is a huge variety of active solar heating systems. All of them consist of four basic components:

1. Collection
2. Transportation
3. Storage
4. Distribution

There is some type of a collector, usually placed on the roof, to convert the incident solar radiation into usable thermal energy. The collectors are usually metal boxes with glass or plastic covers. The interior of these gets very hot and pipes are run through them. In the simplest case, water is circulated through these collectors and becomes hot. This water is then stored in a hot water tank. Air is heated as it is passed around the hot water tank. The hot air can then be moved through ducts to heat the house. Thus, we can see the other components of the system—that of transporting the hot water to the storage tank and the distributing of the hot air through the house. Such a system normally requires an electric pump, and also an auxiliary heat source in the event of a large number of contiguous overcast days.

In an integrated system, the heating of the house and of the hot water would be combined into a single system. This can be seen in Figure 9.7, on the next page. In this house hot water is circulated, whereas in some solar systems, hot air is circulated. We will not attempt to get into a comparative evaluation of these systems, but will leave that for your individual investigation. The government has established a center to help you in this study. You can contact them at:

National Solar Heating & Cooling Information Center
P. O. Box 1607
Rockville, Maryland 20850

If you write to them, they will be glad to send you their book, *Solar Dwelling Design Concepts,* and their booklet, *Solar Energy In Your Home,* and place you on their mailing list for solar information. One of the better books that you can buy on this subject is:

Designing and Building a Solar House
by Donald Watson
Published by Garden Way Publishing
Charlotte, Vermont 05445

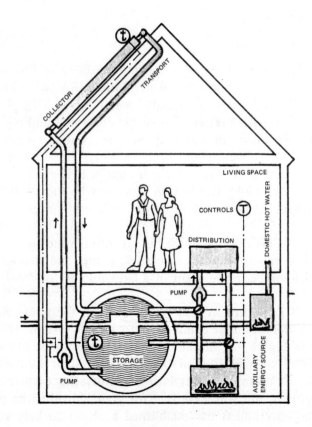

Figure 9.7

As a supplement to solar heat, one could have wood-burning stoves in many of the rooms. Another alternative would be to have supplemental heat by hot water radiators, the water being heated by wind-generated electricity. Wood and wind will be discussed later in more detail as primary energy sources.

One significant consideration when thinking of space heating is the temperature of the space that you need to heat. For example, in an underground home the air is roughly 55 degrees summer or winter. This means that air conditioning in the summer is unnecessary and heating in the winter is minimal—the temperature has to be brought up only a small amount.

By no means are all underground houses ugly. Jack Strickler, a retired assistant vice-president of the engineering division of Bell Aircraft, has built his own underground house. His heating bill is less than $30 per year. He has designed a wind system to generate electricity which is used to heat water. The hot water is pumped in pipes through the floor to provide supplemental heat. His unique windmill design has automatic feathering of the blade, so that it will not spin too fast during hard wind blows. According to Jack, one big problem for homemade power systems is storing the energy. He stores it in hot water rather than batteries, and estimates that he can store as much energy in one 80-gallon tank with 100 degrees temperature rise as he could in twenty-seven 60-amp-hour, 12-volt batteries. He also included several failsafe mechanisms so that certain appliances can operate on both commercial and windmill power. For safety, when the power is turned off, it is turned off from both sources.

Jack collects his own water for household use. He has a plastic-lined, V-shaped pit, of about the same dimensions as the house, to collect rainwater. This pit has a cover. He now has about 20,000 gallons stored. His total construction cost was between $17 and $18 a square foot, for a total cost of between $25,000 and $30,000. A view of this home is shown in Figure 9.8. Because of the large demand for plans of his lovely three bedroom home, Jack is selling them for $150. If you are interested you can contact him at:

John F. Strickler
338 Wind Sun Way
Camano Island, WA 98292

Styrofoam backed doors are closed for the evening on Jack and Billie Strickler's "modern day sod house" on Camano Island. The flat roofed home is banked with dirt on three sides for insulation, but the patio doors across the front let the sunshine in. When the sun gets thin, the inner sliding doors are closed to trap the warmth.

Figure 9.8

Styrofoam backed doors are closed for the evening on Jack and Billie Strickler's "modern day sod house" on Camano Island. The flat roofed home is banked with dirt on three sides for insulation, but the patio doors across the front let the sunshine in. When the sun gets thin, the inner sliding doors are closed to trap the warmth.

There are two books that I would highly recommend in connection with heating (both available from Survival, Inc.):

New Low-Cost Sources of Energy for the Home
by Peter Clegg
Published by Garden Way Publishing

Complete Book of Heating with Wood
by Larry Gay
Published by Garden Way Publishing

The first book is educational, as well as being a catalog of available equipment for solar, wind, water and wood power.

Air conditioning is not needed with an underground house, unless you are in the desert. In Palm Springs, California, they are building underground houses with solar-powered air conditioners. These air conditioners use a heat pump for the cooling.

Heat for Cooking

Another question to contend with is whether or not you will eat your food raw, if the gas and electricity are turned off.

For a temporary form of cooking, the little propane-fueled heaters and cookers are fine. For a more long-term solution other sources are needed. Survival, Inc. (address in Chapter 11) has a fire box stove with an oven for $199, which will burn wood, coal, charcoal or any other solid fuel. It heats, cooks and bakes. They also have a more sophisticated stove available—one with warming ovens and a water reservoir for heating water.

One interesting stove that I have run across recently has electric cooking on the right-hand side and wood cooking on the left-hand side. This combination stove can be used in the regular way during normal times, and the wood-burning aspects can be utilized in times of emergency. It is manufactured by Monarch.

A suggestion is in order. Cooking on a wood stove is very different than cooking on a gas or electric stove. The heat cannot really be controlled. Thus, much more care must be taken to keep things from burning. "Lifters," to raise the cooking pan up off of the stove, are a desirable addition. If you plan to cook with a wood stove during times of emergency, I would strongly recommend that you try it out now. This would be invaluable experience, particularly with the baking oven, since it is all but impossible to maintain a constant temperature.

Lest we become bogged down by specifics, let us pause for a moment to refresh our minds as to why we are discussing these things. God has told us that there is a time ahead when Christians will not be able to buy or sell *anything*. God wants us to provide for our families, even during those times (I Timothy 5:8). Hence, it is pertinent to discuss alternate means of providing the essentials, and some comforts, for our families when we are no longer able to buy water, gas, sewage service, and electricity.

Lighting

Most people would agree that candles or kerosene lamps are fine for emergencies, but they would not be happy using them on a day to day basis, year after year. I have concluded that Americans have been spoiled by too much light. The lighting standard for schoolrooms has increased steadily across the years to where almost ten times as much light is required now as in the 1930's. When we lived in Los Angeles, my wife and I found, while spending some time in the room behind our old garage, which we called our "cabin," that it takes a real adjustment to get used to less light. We used the Aladdin kerosene lamps there—the kind with the mantle. Even two of them in a small cabin do not completely light the room. There are areas in the corners that are quite dark. If you want to see something in one of these corners, you have to carry a lamp over with you. Also, these lamps have to be watched carefully because the mantles can soot up (turn totally black and give off no light at all). It is enjoyable to use them on occasion, and I think that every family should have a couple for emergencies, but for most of us kerosene lamps are not adequate for daily use. This means that we are going to have to have electricity. Speaking of kerosene and electricity, there is a very good combination kerosene/ electric lamp, with a solid brass base, available from Survival, Inc. (Of course we *can* exist without electricity, but if we wish to continue to use it after we can no longer buy it from the utility system, we need to consider alternate ways of providing it.)

There are two basic types of electrical systems: 110 volt and 12 volt. The choice of which of these to have, or whether to have both, is very critical. If you are going to install both, at least some dual wiring will be necessary in the house, guest cottage or cabin. The 12-volt systems are utilized in campers and motor homes, since they run off of the vehicle battery system, which is 12 volt. There are lighting fixtures, refrigerators and a few appliances that will work off of a 12-volt system. If you are generating your own power by wind, the power generated is stored in 12-volt batteries. Thus, if you have 12-volt lights, there need be no conversion to 110, and no energy loss that goes with such a conversion.

I believe that it is essential to have some capability for producing 110 volts, in whatever situation you might find yourself. There are so many critical pieces of equipment that only work off of 110—such as skill saws and electric drills—that having some capacity for 110-volt electricity can significantly affect your life-style. When I lived on Catalina island, we had a

small gasoline-powered electrical generator. While I was building the cabin, in the morning I would measure two-by-fours
that needed cutting and also mark places where I needed to
drill holes for pipes. About lunchtime I would fire up the generator for about thirty minutes and do all of my cutting and
drilling at once. I would then spend the afternoon nailing up
all of the board that I had cut. Having 110 to operate the power
tools and power equipment made our life much easier.

The ideal is to have both systems. Even our mini-motor
home has both 110 and 12 volt. As far as I'm concerned, a self-
sufficient home should be dual-wired.

Wind-Powered Generation of Electricity

All generators utilize some type of motor to turn the generator, which generates the electricity. In the case of nuclear
power, this motor is a steam engine, the steam being generated
by the heat of the nuclear reaction. But any kind of engine will
do—including gasoline, diesel and *wind-powered* engines. The
wind-powered system has something that is unique in that it
runs sporadically. Sometimes it runs very fast; sometimes it
does not run at all. Therefore, there must be a way to store the
electricity generated so that it can be used whenever desired,
even when there is no wind. Normally a wind electrical generator will charge 12-volt batteries. There is a large bank of these,
the number depending on how much electricity you want to
store. These batteries are usually mounted on shelves up a wall.
If you are using a 12-volt lighting system, it can be hooked directly to this bank of batteries. If you want a 110-volt system,
the 12-volt batteries can be hooked to a transformer which con-
verts the 12-volt direct current to 110 alternating current. By
proper wiring, you can have the same bank of batteries run
either system.

The two basic classifications of wind machines are recorded
on page 178 of *The Homebuilt Wind-Generated Electricity Handbook,* by Michael Hackleman (published by Earthmind, 5246
Boyer Rd., Mariposa, CA 95338):

"A wind machine is an aeroturbine; as the word suggests, it's an air-
driven turbine. Mechanical energy from the wind. . . .

". . . there are two classes of aeroturbine: the vertical and the horizontal axis machines. And they're pretty well defined by the name. The vertical axis machine rotates about a vertical shaft (or axis) and the horizontal axis machine—yep, you guessed it—rotates about a horizontal shaft. The sail-wing, wind-sail, prop-types, Chalk turbine, farm waterpumpers, Dutch windmills, are all horizontal axis machines. The Savonius rotor, Darrieus rotor (alias 'eggbeater'), and the hybrid-types are all vertical axis machines."

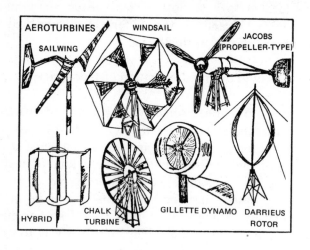

Figure 9.9

As can be seen in Figure 9.9, there are many types of horizontal axis wind machines. These all have to turn into the wind in order to take advantage of it. The ones with a vertical axis are able to receive wind from any direction. Thus, a vertical axis machine might be more appropriate if the wind is quite variable in your area. If there is always a prevailing wind from the same direction, a horizontal axis machine would be preferable. Figure 9.10 shows a large vertical axis wind-powered generator, built in Scotland at the beginning of the century, and a smaller vertical axis (S-type) windmill that is in common use today (from pages 64 and 71 of *The Autonomous House*).

For most situations the horizontal axis wind machine is very adequate and a bit more efficient than the vertical axis one. As for the cost, for $495 you can order a horizontal axis 200-

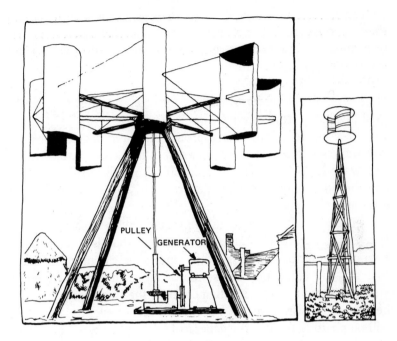

Figure 9.10

watt, 12-volt wind generator from Survival, Inc., which includes the wind turbine tower and completely wired instrument panel. This is a small system and will give a minimal amount of lighting. It would be suitable for a cabin or guest cottage.

Other Forms of Electrical Generation

First I would like to discuss gasoline- and diesel-powered generators. I do not think that anyone would want to have a gasoline or diesel engine running twenty-four or even twelve hours a day. A great amount of fuel would be used; there would be pollution, and a noise that would drive you crazy. On the other hand, one of these generators for periodic use—to provide 110 for specialized tasks such as sewing, drilling, and grinding wheat—could be quite useful. It could be used in conjunction with a 12-volt system that provides the lighting and refrigeration in the home. If you are going to rely on a gas or diesel 110-

voltage generator, you will need to have a 500-gallon tank of the appropriate fuel stored. A 500-gallon tank of diesel fuel will run a diesel electrical generator for half an hour a day for many months. Diesel fuel has the advantage that it will store for long periods of time, and will not turn to vanish like gasoline will. For long-term gasoline storage, an additive must be used (available from Survival, Inc.).

If you are taking this approach, I would suggest having a two-way switch where the power comes into the house. Thrown one way, it would use the electricity from the utility system, and the other way, electricity generated by the diesel or gasoline generator.

There are two possible approaches with regard to these types of generators. You could buy one that is a single unit. I would tend to discourage this, since repair is more difficult. Instead, you could buy a gasoline or diesel motor and the generator that you want, and then connect the two together with a belt or chain. Used in this way, if the motor ever quit it would still be possible to turn the generator with other types of power.

In some unique situations it would be possible to have a waterwheel turn a generator. Two things would be necessary in order to turn a hydroelectric generator; a drop in the water level of at least 7 to 10 feet, and a good flow.

If a property has flowing water with that much grade, this would be my number one choice for a way to generate electricity. It is constant, has no pollution and is quiet. If you are considering purchasing land, this would be one thing to keep in mind. It is possible that there is a stream on the property that could be dammed up to give you the appropriate drop. If there is a stream coming through the property that slopes down enough, water could be directed off at a higher level into a trench or channel that slopes down less than the stream. The channeled water could then be dropped back into the stream at a lower elevation.

There are three books that I would recommend for further pursuit of the subjects of wind and water electrical generation. They are:

Handbook of Homemade Power
by The Mother Earth News Staff
Published by Bantam Books, Inc.

Wind and Windspinners
by Michael Hackleman

Homegrown Energy
by Wade and Hartmann
Published by Oliver Press

This last book is really a catalog giving addresses and descriptions of the various companies that make different types of energy equipment.

Refrigeration

When I speak of refrigeration, most of us think of the refrigerator-freezer that we have in our kitchen. I would like to expand your vision just a little, if I may. There are at least two other forms of cooling that can be utilized. The first is the old familiar root cellar. A ditch is dug about 6 to 8 feet wide and about 6 feet deep. A wooden "room" is built inside of this ditch and the dirt is piled back on top. With an entrance consisting of two doors separated by 3 feet of airspace, the interior will remain quite cool year-round. The root vegetables, such as potatoes, carrots, and beets, can be stored in it from one harvest to the next (twelve months). As an interesting side note, a root cellar is also an excellent nuclear fallout shelter. Keep some water and a few emergency supplies down there (you would already have plenty of food), and you would be in business.

Another way of cooling is what is called the "springhouse." The springhouse in its simplest form is a shed about 6 feet square that has, effectively, no walls. Instead, the sides are covered with burlap. Around the inside top edge is a metal trough with holes in it, about an inch apart. Water is fed into this trough. It drips down through the holes, soaks the burlap and runs out a drain through the bottom. A springhouse is very adequate for keeping butter, milk, eggs, fresh vegetables and most of the things that we would normally put in our refrigerator. It can be 100 degrees outside and yet be very cool inside the springhouse.

With a root cellar and a springhouse for large storage, and a 12-volt refrigerator powered by a wind electrical generator, most of the refrigeration needs of a home could be met on a continuous basis. As long as electricity is plentiful and available, I would certainly recommend having a large freezer well stocked. There may come a day when you can no longer use that freezer, but enjoy it while you can (that will probably be several years). During an emergency, if the electricity goes off, a portable diesel or gasoline electrical generator could maintain the freezer until electricity is restored.

Entertainment

It is important, as we have discussed before, to be able to have some 110-volt electricity to run a mixer, wheat mill, skill saw, electrical drill and other pieces of truly labor-saving equipment. The other major use of electricity is for entertainment purposes. With electricity we power our stereo, television, radios, tape recorders and other such "toys." If we are going to become truly self-supporting, much of this is going to have to be eliminated or altered. Many of these items can be replaced by ones that are battery-powered, and the batteries can be charged with a solar-powered battery charger. Other items can be converted to 12 volt and run off of a 12-volt wind electrical generating system. For example, there are very nice CB's and stereos that work in automobiles and utilize 12 volt. This takes care of everything but television. As far as I'm concerned, you can use the TV as long as there is plenty of power available from your electrical utility. When that ceases you are probably not going to watch TV anyhow; you will be too busy providing necessities for yourself.

For entertainment I believe that we will see a revival of reading, guitar playing, singing, and the playing of table games. These things can all be done with a limited amount of light. My wife and I have even done them by kerosene light. Therefore,

I would consider a good supply of books and games that you enjoy to be essential in a self-supporting house.

THE "IDEAL" HOUSE

We are considering the time when Christians will not be able to buy and sell, and will want to be independent of the utility systems. Let's now look at the ideal self-supporting house, as I envisage it. It would be at least partially "underground," with the south side in glass for passive solar heating. It would have its own water supply, which may be a combination of springs, a well, a stream, and collected rainwater. It would have its own septic tank and a way to dispose of wastes. There would be solar collectors on the roof for active heating, supplemented by wood stoves in several of the rooms. In the kitchen there would be a combination electric-and-wood cook stove.

A 12-volt wind electrical generating system would run the lights and the refrigeration, and a 110-volt dual system would run the freezer. The 110 voltage would normally be drawn from the utilities, but there would be an emergency 110-volt diesel generator which could run the freezer and other power equipment. The stereo, CB and other entertainment equipment would run off of the 12-volt system, and the TV only off of the 110 commercial power.

There would be a garden, and chickens, rabbits and other small animals would be raised. The surplus from the garden and the edible wastes would be fed to these smaller animals. For food preservation there would be a root cellar at least, and possibly a springhouse, in addition to the 12-volt refrigerator.

It may be that an existing home could be modified to incorporate the features that you want. If not, and you really wish to remain on the property where you are, possibly a "guest house" could be built with these features. If neither of these are possible, the only way to move towards a self-sufficient home would be to purchase new property and build from scratch. This isn't all theory; some of the subscribers to my economic newsletter (McKeever's *MISL)* are actually doing this. The following is a letter from one of them:

Dear Jim:

Was most interested in your MISL #146 on the self-suffi-
cient house. We are in the process of expanding on this idea
even more than we have in the past and thought you might be
interested in how we are going about it.

We have moved to Carmel Valley, CA from Salinas and
the Chicago metro area. CV is quite rural and protected by
mountains and is fairly far from the major metro centers. It has
one major road in and out and a quite cohesive population
(8,000 ±). There is even some talk about incorporating the val-
ley (leaving Monterey County rules and regs.—perhaps even
forming a new county!). As this movement grows, I and some
others are implanting the libertarian idea in people's thinking.
Might be nice to have a living libertarian workshop . . .

In this valley, we bought a house that we are converting
to a combination home and office. This will be a 100% solar
heated and hot-water house. We have just finished the roof and
are putting the collectors on shortly. It is a forced-air system
with a heat exchanger for the hot water. (Even the collectors
are forced-air). Storage will be in eutectic salts in a specially in-
sulated "basement" under the living room. Also there will be a
fireplace where we can cook.

The walls are 2x6 and fully insulated and the roof has 1½"
urethane foam (foil coated) where it is open beam and 10" of
fiberglass in other areas. Windows and doors are thermopane
and weather tight. And this is in a very mild marine climate (as
you know).

There are passive collectors also in the form of two large
greenhouses. This will warm the house directly as well as fur-
nishing preheated air to the solar collectors. In addition, the
greenhouses will enable us to garden all year around.

On our acre of land, we have a large orchard (plums, apples,
oranges, lemons, peaches, etc.) and a vegetable garden (mulched
with a special 10 mil black plastic or organic mulch). We also
have 17 New Hampshire Red chickens for eggs and eating. The
whole operation is organic (and the rooster gives us low-choles-
terol eggs as long as he does his thing!).

Much of the lighting and electrical circuits are low-voltage (12vdc). We also have our own well and a well-drilling outfit that is hand-held. And our truck has a gas regulator so it can run on gasoline, natural gas, methane, etc.

Still haven't gotten free of the gas and electric company, but we are working on it. Also have to get back to our plumbing work now. Trying to separate the gray from the septic waste. Putting in two separate lines. Haven't gotten it all worked out yet, but we are getting there.

Keep up the good work.

R. Lundquist

Begin As Soon As It Is Practical

We have already had one oil shortage in the U.S. I firmly believe that there is an electricity shortage coming. It may be as far as five to ten years away, but it is coming. Our country is not moving ahead on nuclear power, and the conversion to coal will take too long to provide the electricity demanded by the U. S. people. It will take a minimum of from ten to twenty years before other forms of electrical generation, such as solar or geothermal, will have any impact on the energy needs. With the present gas shortage, an electricity shortage on the horizon and a potential future shortage in oil, one would be prudent to begin to arrange one's living quarters and life-style so as to be less dependent on the utility systems.

Many large computer installations run off of the regular electricity. However, they have standby diesel generators that automatically switch on in the event of a power failure. We are looking at a similar type of philosophy for our homes. We will continue to utilize utility systems as long as they are functioning. But if there is a disruption, whether from an emergency or a shortage, we would like to be able to switch to alternate systems. The need for alternate systems could arise in a hurry, and the time of an emergency is a little late to begin installing dual systems. The work must be done before the alternatives are needed.

Even if emergencies or shortages do not force us to use alternatives to the utilities, we know that a time is coming when we will not be able to buy the utility services without taking on the mark of the beast.

Food Production and Preservation

Because of the importance of producing food and preserving it for consumption at a later time, I have decided to discuss this, along with the growing trend of Christians moving to farms, separately. These all-important subjects, which are vital to our being able to live without buying or selling, will be discussed in detail in the next chapter.

10

FOOD AND THE FARM

The next most important thing to providing water for your family is providing food for them. Since during the Tribulation you will be unable to buy food, you must either have seven years of food stored or be able to produce your own. If you live on a farm or ranch, producing food will be easier than if you live in a city. However, even in a city you can produce your own food.

PRODUCING FOOD IN THE CITY

There are two basic approaches to raising food in the city:

1. Gardening
2. Hydroponics

Let's look at gardening first. A 50- by 50-foot garden can provide enough vegetables to last the average family for the entire year. Because of various conditions, it may be that some have to start smaller. You might think that you do not have enough land to have a garden, but if you own your own home, you probably have the land. You may have to dig up your front lawn and suffer the embarrassment of teasing by neighbors, but there is likely room for a garden. If your whole backyard is cemented in, take a sledge hammer and knock out part of it to make room for a small garden. If you live in an apartment, own a condominium, or live in a retirement village, frequently there are unused areas of land in the complex that you will be allowed to use for a garden. If you simply do not have any land available to you, then look around for empty land. There is usually land around an airport, where houses have been torn down because of the high noise level, land underneath electrical and power lines, vacant lots and so on. Go down to the city hall and find out who owns the property and ask them if you can use it for a garden. If you can not find any land in the city, find some farmer with a large farm on the edge of your city and ask him if you can use, or rent, a small corner of one of his fields.

Once you find some land, the next thing is to prepare the soil for planting. We won't get into this subject, since books on soil preparation and planting are readily available in any book store. However, there is one form of gardening with which you may not be familiar. It is known as "mulch gardening" and it is one of the best methods known. A layer of old hay is spread across the ground. It is then separated and seeds are planted near the top of the soil underneath. Mulch gardening produces a significantly higher yield than regular gardening. Moreover, if root vegetables such as potatoes are planted, they do not have to be dug out, since they lie between the hay and the soil. A good book on the subject is:

> *The Ruth Stout No-Work Garden Book*
> by Ruth Stout and Richard Clemence
> Published by Bantam Books, Inc.

It is interesting to note that there is a revolution going on in gardening. An organization in Northern California called Common Ground estimated, in 1975, that on one-fifth of an acre (93 feet by 93 feet) a person could make $12,000 a year. Their approach is "companion planting," in which compatible plants are interspersed with each other. They also describe proper soil preparation, which not only allows more plants per acre, but also creates a higher yield per plant. You may want to write for their fascinating book:

> *How To Grow More Vegetables*
> by John Jeavons
> Published by Ecology Action of the Midpeninsula
> 2225 El Camino Real, Palo Alto, CA 94306

PUTTING MEAT ON YOUR TABLE

When Christians can no longer buy and sell, it may be that many of them will have to become vegetarians. For those who still want meat, there remain basically three ways to acquire it:

1. Hunting and fishing
2. Raising your own animals
3. Bartering

If you presently enjoy hunting and fishing, these could be ways to provide meat for your family. They may have to become requisites rather than recreation, but the skills would certainly serve you well during that period.

If you are considering raising your own meat, whether it be in the city or on a farm, I would recommend the small livestock such as: goats, chicken, sheep, geese, rabbits, hogs, turkeys, guinea fowl, ducks and pigeons. There are many reasons why I believe these are preferable. Being smaller units, you would not lose that much if one of them were to die. Another reason is that if you kill a large cow there is the problem of preserving the meat, whereas your family could consume one of these smaller animals before it spoiled. Another factor is that they tend to reproduce faster. You can get milk and eggs from them, as well as meat, which provides a balance to the diet.

Especially if you live in the city, and want to raise meat, small animals are the only choice that you have. In such a case, raising rabbits in an indoor building can help minimize complaints from the neighbors. You should have plenty of windows in the enclosure to let in sunlight and fresh air. A garage can easily be converted into a rabbitry. The concrete floor of most garages makes them easy to clean.

You can even have labor-saving devices such as feed hoppers which can be filled without opening the cages.

There is an excellent book on the subject of small livestock. If you are going to raise any of these animals for meat, you should get a copy of:

The Homesteader's Handbook to Raising Small Livestock
by Gerome D. Belanger

There are many good books on hunting, but the only way to learn it is to do it. This is a way of putting meat on your table that has been used continuously since Adam and Eve. There is a very good book, written by a Christian evangelist, that has an excellent section on foraging in the wilderness. It can be ordered from Alpha Omega Publishing Company (Box 4130, Medford, OR 97501):

Timely and Profitable Help for Troubled Americans
by Hans J. Schneider

Food Preservation

If you are going to provide your own vegetables, you will have the problem of preserving them through the winter, so that you can use them until the next crop is harvested. There are a number of methods that can be used to keep food: canning and dehydrating are two. There are good food dehydrators available that can be used in the home. We will give addresses for some of these in Chapter 11. As for root vegetables (carrots, beets, potatoes, turnips and such), they will tend to keep for the year if stored in a cool place, such as the root cellar that we mentioned in Chapter 9.

The freezer is a handy place to preserve food as long as it is operational. If at some point you can no longer buy electricity, and you are not able to provide your own, a freezer would not be a good thing to depend on.

Meat, like fruit and vegetables, can be preserved in numerous ways. It can be dehydrated, canned in glass jars, or frozen. In addition, a smoke house can be built in which to smoke the meat. Meat can also be preserved by soaking it in a salt brine.

Speaking of food preservation, in our era of fast foods and convenience foods much of the food value is lost in the processing and a lot of undesirable chemicals are added. There is an excellent book that deals with all aspects of food, from a Christian perspective. The authors warn of coming troubled times, advise a food storage program (giving details), and discuss health, weight and proper eating habits. This book can be ordered from

Alpha Omega Publishing Company (Box 4130, Medford, OR 97501):

> *Eat, Drink and Be Ready*
> by Monte L. Kline and W. P. Strube, Jr.

YOUR OWN FOOD FACTORY

An alternative to a garden for raising vegetables is a greenhouse. In a greenhouse fruits and vegetables can be grown year round. The problem of preservation basically vanishes since a supply of fresh produce is continuously available. There are many advantages to raising food in a greenhouse, some of which are:

1. Protection from wind
2. Controlled temperature (no scorching)
3. Controlled moisture (no drought or flooding)
4. Protection from airborne disease
5. Protection from freezing
6. No weeds
7. No bending (you work at table height)
8. Less space used than for a garden
9. The greenhouse is a fantastic place to spend time with the Lord!

In this greenhouse "food factory" you can utilize soil as the growing medium. However, many plants will require soil of a significant depth. There is, in my opinion, a superior method for food production in a greenhouse facility; that method is "hydroponics." In hydroponics, any inert medium, such as plastic foam chips, straw, marbles or sawdust, can be used to provide the mechanical support for the plants. I believe that 3/8-inch, sterile pea gravel is the preference. Twice a day a nutrient solution is pumped onto this gravel, or other such medium, in which the plants are growing. This solution consists of water and a mixture of powdered nutrients. After about twenty minutes, the nutrient-laden water is drained so that air can get to the roots. The typical hydroponic bed is about 3 feet wide, 10 or 12 feet long, and 9 inches deep. Since the roots do not have to search for nutrients because the nutrients are brought to them, hydroponically grown plants tend to produce bigger and nicer vegetables than those grown in the ground.

If you want to experiment with hydroponics, you can do so simply by using large flower pots filled with gravel and a bucket of nutrient-laden water as your basic equipment. Twice a day you would pour the solution into the pots of gravel where you have planted seeds or small plants. To carry this a step further, you could have a little electric pump that would pump the nutrients from a bucket or tank up into the beds. You could simply throw the electrical switch on for fifteen minutes twice a day and have the pump do the work. The next step would be to have the pump switch run by an electrical timer, which would automatically feed the plants. This is one big advantage of hydroponics: the care of the plants can be automated.

With hydroponics you can control the nutrition and watering of the plants. If you place your hydroponic beds inside a greenhouse, you can also control the climate, plant diseases and insects. The food production from a hydroponic greenhouse garden is phenomenal. It is estimated that, in a 10- by 12-foot greenhouse, enough food could be produced for a family of four on a year-round basis. All that it would take is about ten minutes of your time per day. If you would like to have your own fresh vegetables and fruits year round, with about ten minutes of effort a day, a hydroponic greenhouse "food factory" would be the way to do it.

If you wish to pursue this, there are three books that I believe are head and shoulders above all of the other hydroponic books that I have read:

Hydroponic Gardening
by Raymond Bridwell
Published by Woodbridge Press Publishing Company

Hydroponic Greenhouse Gardening
by Joel Hudson

Home Hydroponics
by Lem Jones
Published by Beardsley Publishing Co.

Just as with raising small animals, a hydroponic greenhouse has the advantage that you do not have to worry about preserving the food produced. If you wanted to have tomatoes continuously, you would plant one plant, two weeks later plant another, two weeks later another, and so on. By keeping up this rotation you could have fresh tomatoes year round. The same thing goes for lettuce, beets, strawberries and even corn. Even for those who live on a farm, this type of a "food factory" is well worth considering. I know some people in Oregon who grow all of their vegetables in such a greenhouse.

Plan Your Planting

If you decide to invest in a hydroponic greenhouse, once you have your greenhouse and your beds ready, careful planning is necessary in order to obtain the full potential of this "food factory." Take the time to draw a diagram of your plant arrangement. For example, you will want to plant the tomatoes, cucumbers, and any other vine-type or tall plants, next to the greenhouse wall, and shorter plants progressively in towards the center of the greenhouse. Be sure to plant things that you *enjoy eating,* not simply things that do well in hydroponic environment. After awhile you will learn which varieties you like best, and you will be able to get your rotation going so that you can have a continuous supply of food. Figure 10.1 shows one potential layout for two 12- by 3-foot hydroponic beds.

A Protein Factory

A while back I ran across a very interesting article in *Science Digest* (May 1975, P. O. Box 1568, New York, NY 10019). It deals with having your own "fish factory" in your backyard. This particular one, belonging to Robert Huke, is enclosed under a geodesic dome 17 feet in diameter. There is a fish tank basical-

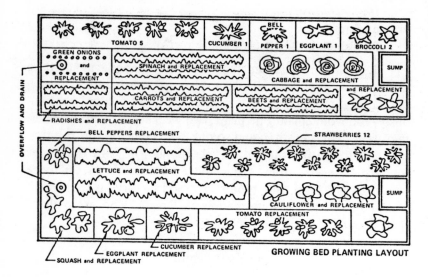

Figure 10.1

ly stocked with Catfish (the larger fish in Figure 10.2) and Tilapia (the smaller fish). The water from the tank is pumped to twin metal drums. The bacteria inside the drums convert the fish excrement to fertilizing nitrate which, through a tube, is sprayed onto vegetation. Some vegetation, like soybeans, can be shredded and put back into the water, which then circulates down a waterfall back to the fish tank and feeds the fish. Periodically the metal tanks are cleaned out, and the fertilizer is used to feed the tomatoes and soybeans. In this way, a full cycle is completed.

Huke estimates that he gets about 100 pounds of fish per year out of this fish factory. He chose Catfish because you can pack them tightly into a small tank without them eating each other. They are also good tasting. Huke estimates that building his dome cost him about $700.

Next to fish, the average city backyard would probably support rabbits better than anything else. As mentioned before, you do not have the noise and commotion with them that you would have with chickens, goats or any other of the smaller animals. If you combine rabbits and gardening, you could have

Figure 10.2

a cycle with surplus vegetables from the garden being eaten by the rabbits, and rabbit pellets being used for fertilizer.

Some people may consider hydroponics and fish farming too artificial and they would prefer to go "back to the land." So let's now discuss the option of moving to a farm.

MOVING TO (OR BACK TO) A FARM

As I travel around the world, I see what appears to be an increasing movement of Christians "back to the land." Many families are moving from the cities to farms. Sometimes one family moves to a single farm; in other cases a group of families purchase a large farm; and in still other situations families from a body of believers will try to purchase farms that are adjacent to each other, so that they can have a "community." I am not saying that this movement is for all Christians. However, it is certainly a matter worth holding before the Lord to see if He would have you become part of it.

If the Lord leads you to move to a farm, in whatever arrangement, the first thing that you are going to have to do is to find the right piece of land and buy it. Before you even begin looking, there is an excellent book that you should read:

> *First-Time Farmer's Guide*
> by Bill Kaysing
> Published by Straight Arrow Books

After reading this book, you will realize that two of the most important things to look for are water and the condition of the soil. It is absolutely essential that there be an ample supply of water. Nothing grows without it. It is not only important to have water flowing by or through your property, but to be sure that you have the "water rights" to use that water for irrigation as well as for your home.

Concerning the soil, you can not tell by feeling or smelling it whether or not it is soil that will be productive. You must have it tested to be certain. You can usually get such a soil test done for free, or at a small fee, by the local county agent. If a good water supply and fertile soil are present, the farm can be a productive one.

In looking for the right piece of land, there are two catalogs that you should send for. Each of these catalogs have farms and acreage listed from all over the United States. They have pictures of the houses and properties along with the descriptions. They also give the realtor's name, address and phone number, in case you wish to contact him. These two catalogs are:

> *The United Farm Agency Catalog*
> United Farm Agency, Inc.
> 612 West 47th Street
> Kansas City, MO 64112

> *Strouts*
> Strout Realty, Inc.
> 150 N. Santa Anita Avenue
> Arcadia, CA

After having read the *First-Time Farmer's Guide* and getting these catalogs, you will be in a position to begin to isolate, of course under the Lord's guidance, the area of the country in which you should concentrate your looking.

In moving to a single family farm, one of the problems is always finding Christian fellowship. It is important to be aware of the spiritual aspects of the community that you are contemplating moving into, as well as the physical. It is good to spend a couple of Sundays in the area, visiting various churches and groups with whom you might be like-minded. If there are not any, it may be that the Lord is moving you to a certain place in order to help establish a Christ-centered fellowship.

There are three other books in this area that I highly recommend reading.

Five Acres and Security
by M. G. Kains
Published by Dover

Farming for Self-Sufficiency
by John and Sally Semour
Published by Schocken Books

The Manual of Practical Homesteading
by John Vivian
Published by Rodale Press

I hope that these books will be of help to those of you whom the Lord leads to move to a farm. It is an exciting adventure to move to the country and begin farming for the first time. There are many rich lessons that God will teach you as you observe His creation. What a magnificent Creator we have!

The Community Farm

There are many obvious advantages to a group of Christian families moving to a farm(s) together. The people already know and love one another, and are used to working together and helping each other. There is already a unity in their fellowship and worship when they come together.

There are many tasks in a farming situation, such as raising a roof, building a barn, pulling tree stumps, and so forth, wherein many hands are required. Harvest is also a time when a number of people working together makes the job easier and more enjoyable.

If a group of Christians are going to move to a single large farm, there are basically two ways that the farm can be set up economically:

1.   Communally

2.   With a free enterprise system

The communal approach has many advantages. There is an economy of scale. One large, 1-acre garden is more efficient than several small ones. One big field of wheat is easier to cultivate than several small ones. Only one bull is needed for a number of cows. Sharing a bull is obviously more efficient than every family owning one bull and one cow. If an electrical generator is put in, it is easier to put in a single large one for an entire community than several small ones.

However, if resources are pooled and then redistributed according to the needs of the families, you have all the inherent disadvantages of communism. There is no incentive to work; there is no incentive not to have an excessive number of children. I have seen this occur on Christian communal farms, where some of the old men did almost no work and the young, strong men resented the fact that all of the work load was falling on them. This can generate a great deal of strife within a community of this type.

With the communal method of running a Christian farm, there is also the key question of how decisions are made. In the Bible we always see the offices of priest and king separated, except in Christ and in Melchizedek. If the spiritual leaders (elders) of the community are also the "management" of the farm, one has—I believe in an unhealthy way—the offices of priest and king combined. If the communal approach is taken, I would suggest that a different group head the physical running of the farm, than the group which has the spiritual responsibility for the believers. The Holy Spirit can use this setup to provide a healthy check and balance, just as He has always done with the priesthood and the kingship.

To help you to evaluate the decision making process of a communal farm, find out how the following two decisions would be made. First, let's suppose that the existing generator on the farm breaks down. The people can spend $500 on repairs, but there is no guarantee that the generator would then work, although there is a pretty fair chance that it would. The other alternative is to spend $5,000 for a new generator. There are people in the group who are strongly in favor of each of these alternatives. How is the decision made?

In a second situation let's say that there is $4,000 in the "kitty." Three projects need doing, each requiring about $4,000. The community needs to build a milking barn, they have to improve the water system, and they need to buy a flatbed truck. Again there are people in the group who consider each one of these projects to be the most important. Only one can be afforded at this time and the other two must be left undone. How is it decided which one is the most important?

The other possibility for a rural Christian community is to have a free enterprise economic setup. This does not mean that there are not things being done communally, such as the installing of an electrical generator, but it does mean that every man has his own piece of land and is responsible for its productivity. There is likely barter between the families and trading of working time for produce or services, and so on. It may be that one man owns the bull and, for some type of payment, the other families can use it to freshen their cows once a year. In this kind of situation, there should be a community meeting monthly in which everything is discussed and each family has one vote. I do not believe that anyone should be forced to do anything against his will. If three-fourths of the families want to cooperate on electrical generation and some families do not, let those who are in favor of it pool their funds for an electrical generation system. Those who were not in favor of it would not be required to participate. Neither would they be given electricity from it. Totally separate from this type of decision would be a group of elders who would have the responsibility of the spiritual shepherding for the church that would likely meet on the property. Here again attendance and participation in the church should be voluntary, not compulsory.

In either case, a nonprofit corporation or church would probably own the land. In the free enterprise case, this organization could either sell or lease parcels to the individual families. In one such free enterprise system that I have seen recently, any improvements to the property, such as building a house, are handled in such a way as to be a loan to the corporation. Under this system, if someone moved to this community farm and built a $30,000 house, it would be considered a $30,000 loan to the church or non-profit organization. If the individual ever left, that loan, without interest, would be paid to him.

Even though I am inclined towards the free enterprise system, let me make an observation on the spiritual side. I believe the Holy Spirit is increasingly making the body of Christ truly "one." We are progressively dying to self in order that we may become *one body* and have a true unity in the Spirit. This is not an easy process, but I believe that the Lord is taking each of us through it. Even if we were to start a farming community with a free enterprise system, the Lord may lead us to give away most of what we produce to our elderly and needy neighbors. It is the Lord who gives. We are simply caretakers of what He gives to us; it is up to Him whether or not He wants us to use ourselves that which He has given, or give it away.

Summary and Conclusion

In the last chapter we looked at the fact that a day is coming when Christians will not be able to buy or sell, and remain true to Christ. This means that we need to be independent of the monetary system under which we live. A key factor to this is being able to provide our own food. We have examined a number of ways in which we could provide food for our family and those for whom the Lord has made us responsible. Preparation for this time may involve making our home in the city much more self-sufficient and being able to produce our own food. It might entail moving to a farm.

If the Lord does lead you in a move to a farm, careful consideration and prayer should be given to whether just your family moves, or you go with a group of families. If you do go as a group of families, a great deal of care should be taken as to how the community is structured. I have seen so many communal farms get into trouble economically and otherwise because, they attract the elderly, who tend to be less productive, and the younger couples tend to have a baby a year. Economic constraints are needed so that every man is motivated to work. I would be inclined more to have individual garden plots, individual homes and kitchens, and each family responsible for providing its own food. Yet I feel this should and can be accomplished with an atmosphere of love and willingness to share with those who have needs, as the Lord directs and commands. For most of us, moving to a farm would be a major step which should only be taken if the Lord clearly gives us "marching orders" to do so.

11

PHYSICAL SURVIVAL SUMMARY

In the last few chapters we have seen that there are certain physical catastrophes coming to the earth, as prophesied in the book of Revelation. Christians can count on these occurring. It therefore behooves each Christian to pray asking God what, if any, preparations he should make. In preparing for the natural disasters that could occur prior to the Tribulation, and specifically for the catastrophes that there will be during the Tribulation, there are certain precautions that would be appropriate for multiple calamities.

Many disasters would cause the water lines to be broken or polluted. Thus, it is wise to have some water stored in case of a short-term interruption of the water service. If one expects a longer-term interruption of the water supply, it is desirable to have a water purifier.

Many of the coming calamities will be accompanied by fires. Having an adequate supply of fire extinguishers is advisable for the control of these fires.

In almost all of the disasters, food will be in short supply. Having a food storage program and/or the ability to produce food yourself may ultimately become a matter of survival.

We have talked about numerous other possible preparations, from having a self-supporting house to building a nuclear fallout shelter. Many of these things require a certain amount of money to achieve. However, there are some things that you can do which cost no money at all:

1. Have an emergency plan for your family in case of a nuclear attack, and actually have a drill every six months.

2. Have an emergency plan and drills for your family in case of an earthquake.

3. Store water in empty Purex bottles, or in empty milk containers with a little Purex added.

4. Dig a hole under your house or in your backyard that could be used as a makeshift fallout shelter.

There are also a number of things that could be done at a very small cost. Some examples are:

1. Keep a flashlight by your bedside in case of an emergency or disaster occurring at night.

2. Have emergency candles that could be used during a power failure.

3. Have a transistor radio handy.

4. Have a box of large plastic garbage sacks in your desk at the office in case of an earthquake or nuclear attack while you are at work.

5. Plant a garden.

6. Buy a little extra food (three weeks' supply).

7. Buy some water purification tablets.

8. Have a good first aid kit.

9. Buy a fire extinguisher.

10. Have a port-a-potty or pail with a lid.

If you want to spend a little bit more, you could add such things as:

1. A Coleman propane (camp type) cooking stove

2. A Coleman propane double-mantle lantern

3. A water purifier

4. A footlocker with survival equipment

5.   Kerosene lamps

6.   A Walle Hawk survival tool (see Survival, Inc. catalog)

None of this should be done without prayer. Once God directs you as to what to do, much can be done with little expenditure of anything but time.

I publish a newsletter (20 issues per year) which deals with these subjects. If you think you might be interested in subscribing, you can write for information to:

McKeever's Investment and Survival Letter (MISL)
P. O. Box 4130-T
Medford, Oregon 97501

In this newsletter I have evaluated many types of equipment and supplies through the years. The following ones I have tried myself and I am able to recommend.

Survival, Inc.

When the Lord first led me into making some physical preparations, I chased all over the countryside to find wheat mills, food dehydrators, dehydrated foods, freeze-dried food, water purifiers, wood stoves and so forth. I thought at that time that it would be great if there was one place that I could go to get all of these types of supplies. Since there was no such store, I felt the Lord wanted me to start a company that would supply this type of service. In 1974 I started Survival, Inc. After getting a number of products lined up and organized and having a productive business, I felt the Lord wanted me to sell it. I sold Survival, Inc. to Bill Pier, whom I personally know to be very honest and service-oriented. You can now get all of the survival supplies that you need in one place. I would encourage you to send $1 for his catalog, book list and food list. The $1 is credited toward your first purchase. Send it to:

Survival, Inc.
Box 4727
Carson, CA 90749

Survival, Inc. mails items all over the world and in their catalog you will find articles such as:

1.   Water purifiers and water purification tablets

2.   Water storage containers and barrels

3.   Complete survival footlockers

4.   Windmills

5.   Wind-electrical generators

6.   Kerosene lamps

7.   Combination electric and kerosene lamps

8.   Wood stoves

9.   Wheat mills

10. Sprouting kits

11. Food dehydrators

12. Almost every survival book printed

13. Dehydrated and freeze-dried foods

I think you will find, as I have, that Survival, Inc. is a place that can meet your needs, at competitive prices, and give you the personal service that you are looking for. If you do desire to chase around the countryside for these types of products, some of the following addresses and information should be helpful.

Dehydrated Food Companies

The following is a list of companies that provide dehydrated and freeze-dried foods. Some of them have a sample trial dinner packed in a number ten can, others do not. Survival, Inc. does have both a freeze-dried and a dehydrated food trial pack. Other food companies that you can contact directly are:

1.   Arrowhead Mills, Inc. (806) 364-0730
     P.O. Box 866, Herford, TX 79045

2.   Bee Hive Food Company (714) 793-0084
     Box 1162, Redlands, CA 92373

3.   Dri Harvest Foods
     2110 E. 37th, Vernon, CA

4.   FSP Foods (415) 483-2855
     Box 725, San Leandro, CA 94577

5.   Neo-Life
     Box 367, San Lorenzo, CA 94580

6.   Oregon Freeze Dry (503) 426-6001
     770 N. 29th, Albany, OR

7.   Rainy Day Foods (801) 377-3093
     Box 71, Provo, UT 84601

8.   Ready Reserve Foods (213) 960-1914
     530 Baldwin Park Blvd., City of Industry, CA 91746

9.   Sam Andy Foods (714) 824-0200
     525 S. Rancho, Colton, CA 92324

10. Vacu-Dry, Utah (Perma-Pak) (801) 972-2809
     Box 26696, Salt Lake City, UT 84125

Food—Doing It Yourself

If you wish to preserve your own food, you can either grow your own or purchase extra fresh foods in the summer and fall when certain items are in abundance. Some of this you could can and some you could dehydrate. For dehydrating you will need a home food dehydrator (several are sold by Survival, Inc.).

If you store wheat, you will need a wheat mill. (It's a little hard to grind the wheat between two bricks.) The one I would recommend is the Magic Mill. If you are going to make your own bread, a mixer that will handle the heavy stiff bread dough is the Bosch mixer. (These too are available from Survival, Inc.).

Composting Toilets

For those who are interested in a more self-sufficient house, and need to—for whatever reason—forego a septic tank, composting toilets are almost ideal. If you are interested in these you can contact:

Mullbank Composting Toilet
9800 West Bluemound Road
Milwaukee, WI 53266

Clivus Multrum USA Inc.
14A Eliot Street
Cambridge, MASS 02138

Solar Energy Equipment

There are two companies that have catalogs with some solar-powered equipment ranging from hot water heaters and house heaters to solar-powered watches and solar-powered battery chargers. You can get these catalogs by writing to:

Solar Usage Now (SUN) Inc.
450 E. Tiffin Street
Box 306
Bascom, OH 44809

Edmund Scientific Company
300 Edscorp Bldg.
Barrington, NJ 08007

In addition, there is a government office set up to assist people interested in solar energy. You can get information from them by writing to:

National Solar Heating & Cooling Information Center
P. O. Box 1607
Rockville, MD 20850

Water Purifiers

There are basically two water purifiers that I recommend, both of which are in the Survival, Inc. catalog. The first one is a PCP portable water purifier. It is about the size of a thermos jug and will treat 1500 gallons of water. I gave one of these to a friend of mine who had a cabin by a lake where the water was heavily chlorinated. All smell and taste of chlorine was removed when he cleaned the water through this, and the family was delighted. There is a bigger water purifier, known as the AQCP, which you can even install in your house.

Nuclear Radiation Survival Equipment

To purchase dosimeters or ratemeters you should contact:

Victoreen Instrument Company
10101 Woodland Avenue
Cleveland, OH 44104

The ratemeter that I recommend for the average family is
Model #493. If you want to get fancy, I would suggest Model
#740-F. The dosimeter that I recommend is Model #541-R and
the dosimeter charger is Model #2000-A.

For hand-cranked ventilators for a fallout shelter you
should contact:

Champion Fallout Blowers
Mrs. Jane T. Mumma
937 Mifflin Street
Columbia, PA 17512

For a metal-foil suit and a respirator that will allow somewhat protected excursions:

Nucle Clean
P. O. Box 299
Livermore, CA 94550

Hydroponics

There are two companies that I would recommend that sell
complete systems. They include the greenhouse, beds, temperature controls, automatic feeding system and everything else
you need to have your own backyard food factory.

Mr. Marlin Meier, President (213) 248-0884
Foothill Hydroponics
2506 Foothill Blvd.
La Crescenta, CA 91214

Mr. Dick Kirk, General Manager (314) 878-4222
Plantworks, Tiffany Industries
145 Weldon Parkway
Maryland Heights, MO 63043

TYRANNY OF THE URGENT

We have just discussed a lot of things that you can do, if the Lord so leads. Every one of them takes time. Almost all of us are extremely busy. There are pressures and demands on our time from every side. We have much more to do than we can possibly achieve in twenty-four hours per day. Many of us have wished for a thirty or forty hour day to help us get everything done. In fact, this is one of the reasons that people subscribe to newsletters such as MISL; it saves them the time that it would take to read numerous books and magazines, and research financial and survival topics.

All of us have long lists of things that we are neglecting to do. There are unanswered letters, books that we have bought but never read, visits with friends, neighbors, and relatives, daily exercising, unfinished projects, courses we would like to take and so on. We feel guilty because we have not done many of these important things.

Creating versus Reacting

At one time in my career I taught management courses to the executives of such companies as Blue Cross, Computer Science Corporation, and IBM. Once in a course I asked the executives what they actually spent more time doing—creating or reacting. Every one of them said that he spent more time "reacting." I then asked them which *should* they spend more time doing. All of them said "creating." They were actually doing the opposite of what they felt they should be doing. The reason for this is:

The urgent things in life absorb all of our time and keep us from doing the important things.

The urgent things in life always have a deadline, while the important things never do. The urgent things might include a report to get out, a sale to make, a dinner party to plan, or a problem to solve. All of these have strict deadlines as to when they have to be done. Important things in life—such as spending time with our children, reading the Bible, taking a self-improvement course, or developing a new skill—do not have deadlines, and therefore get crowded out.

When I was teaching one of these courses to a group of Blue Cross executives, one executive came up to me at the coffee break after we discussed this and said: "Jim, I have just learned an extremely valuable lesson. I could go home now and the course would have been well worth it to me. I'm going to go back and set aside time each day to create." I believe this man was very wise. We have to actually *schedule in the important things* and let some of the less urgent things wait their turn. It is interesting that many things we thought urgent will tend to disappear of their own accord.

BE DOERS, NOT JUST READERS (HEARERS)

There was a young preacher once, fresh out of seminary, who went to pastor his first church. The first Sunday he preached a very good sermon. The next Sunday he preached the identical sermon. Some of the church fathers felt that he had just forgotten that he had preached it the previous Sunday. However, on the third Sunday he preached the same sermon again. After the service, one of the church fathers came up to him and said, "Young man, I don't want to be critical, but do you realize that you have preached the same sermon three Sundays in a row?" The young preacher said, "Well, the people in the church haven't done that yet; why should I go on and preach about something else?"

I am sure that many of you agree with me in your hearts and minds about what is coming, and that you should prepare for it. Unfortunately, the preparation is only an important thing to you, and not an urgent one. Therefore, the urgent things in life prevent you from doing some of the important things. But I believe, with all of my heart, that the day is coming when these important things will become very urgent, but the *time* needed to make preparations will have run out.

Take Time to Plan, and Then Act

We have to be careful not to get excited and just start randomly doing "important" things. The reason for this is that these important things must take us towards our goals, and they also have priorities. Some of the important things are much more important than others. The first thing to do is to sit down and plan intelligently. The steps I suggest that you go through are as follows:

1. *Evaluate your present status*—in all areas of your life: financial, skills, ability to survive various emergencies, and so on.

2. *Formulate your objectives and goals*—This would include such things as investment objectives, retirement goals, and contingent plans of action (that is, whether or not you would flee the U.S. in times of certain crises, whether you would stay or move out of the city in the event of city rioting, and so forth).

3. *Develop your view of the future*—This should be written down and must be updated every few months. Your view of the future is not the same today as it was three years ago or ten years ago.

4. *Write your desired status*—This refers to the changes that you would like to make in your current status— either in the financial, skills or survival environment.

5. *Write a detailed plan of action*—I will have more to say about this shortly.

6. *TAKE THE ACTIONS*—It does no good to do the planning unless the actions are actually taken.

In no way am I suggesting that you do this in the flesh. Your planning must be bathed in prayer and you should be convinced in your own heart that God wants you to take any actions that you plan to take.

YOUR PLAN OF ACTION

To develop your plan of action, write down all of the actions that you need to take in order to prepare for the future as you see it. This should be done in great detail. For example, if you feel that nuclear war is a possibility, among other things you might:

1. Purchase one ratemeter, and also a dosimeter for each member of the family (cost approx. $600).

2. Buy two barrels for water storage ($17 each).

3. Build a makeshift shelter in the basement (approx. $100).

4. Put a sprinkler platform on the roof (approx. $5).

When outlining the actions needed to prepare for the various crises that you see occurring in the future, do not pay any attention to priority. However, you should include the cost of each action.

The next step is to prioritize these (considering cost) in the order of the most important to the least important. Do this on a sheet where you can lay out the following columns:

#	Action	Approx Cost	Individual Responsible	Date Due	Date Completed
1.	Buy Water Barrels	$ 34	John	5/1	
2.	Buy 3 mos Food	$600	Mary	4/20	
3.	Buy Smoke Detector	$ 20	John	5/15	
4.	Buy Fire Extinguisher	$ 30	Billy	5/1	

As you can see, in addition to the action and the cost, a specific person should be named as being responsible that an action be taken. This may be the husband, the wife, a child, relative, or friend. It is very important that each event have a reasonable and achievable date for completion attached to it. Once this date is assigned, mentally take the action out of the category of "just important" and place it in the category of "urgent." Make that a deadline that matters, and try not to miss it. There is a last column provided, in case the action is completed early or a few days late, to record the actual date of completion.

Once you have prayed about what you should do, have developed your plan of action and have taken the actions, relax. Do not live in constant fear and turmoil. We should remember, though, that this is not a once-and-for-all activity. Like everything else in our lives, we should continually hold before God our state of preparedness for physical emergencies, to see if there are any additional things that He wants us to do, or if possibly He would have us undo some of the things that we have done.

If you are far from being rich and feel that there is very little that you can do, don't worry. If elaborate preparations were the thing that was going to see us through the Tribulation, only the rich Christians would make it. That is not God's way. He loves you and He will care for you. However, He does want you to make whatever preparations He lays on your heart. There are some things that everyone can do. The main thing is to do all, but nothing more, that God clearly directs you to do. This applies to both physical and spiritual preparation. Much like Noah, we are preparing when there is not that much calamity in sight. We are preaching righteousness when everyone else is "living it up." As we, in obedience, make our physical and spiritual preparations for the flood of catastrophes that lie ahead, God will bless and prosper us. All of the physical preparations *alone* would be like a bunch of match sticks being washed away by a flood. Let us then take a look at the spiritual preparation which must accompany any physical preparation.

"I love Thee, O Lord, my strength.
The Lord is my rock and my fortress and my deliverer,
My God, my rock, in whom I take refuge;
My shield and the horn of my salvation, my stronghold.
I call upon the Lord, who is worthy to praised,
And I am saved from my enemies."

—David

PART 3

SPIRITUAL PREPARATION

12

SPIRITUAL PREPARATION

IS MORE IMPORTANT —

Called to righteousness

Praise God! I am glad that we have finished with the section on physical preparation and can now move on to the exciting subject of spiritual preparation. Some people who read this book may disagree with the part on the physical preparation. However, with all my heart I hope that you have read it carefully, because the knowledge that you will gain from reading it could someday save your life and the lives of your family. If you have skipped over the previous section, I hope that you will prayerfully consider going back, at some point, and reading it. When the time comes that you need that information, this book may not be handy or available. I believe that God wants Christians alive during the Tribulation. He has work for us to do!

You may wonder why I want to talk about spiritual preparation. Haven't the churches through the years been getting us prepared spiritually? Yes—or at least that is what they *should* have been doing. Unfortunately, many of them have been so involved in organization, programs, standards, church buildings and so on, that they have not adequately prepared their members for the spiritual conflicts of the great Tribulation that is to come. Even if your own church has been doing a good job in this area, I believe that God is today giving a deeper call. Let me hasten to say that the pastors have been doing basically what they were taught to do in seminary, so let's not blame them for what has or has not been done in the past. In Acts 2, Peter said that in the last days the Holy Spirit would be poured out in a powerful way. That is occurring today and we must now be especially careful to flow with this new movement of the Spirit of God.

THE PURPOSE OF THE TRIBULATION

We discussed the purpose of the Tribulation earlier, but I think it essential to review this now. If Jesus Christ were to begin His thousand-year reign on earth tomorrow, the first thing that He would need to do would be to get rid of anything that is wicked, evil, corrupting, false, or based on hatred or malice. This would mean that He would need to destroy the houses of prostitution, massage parlors, magazine factories and everything that would incite an unholy lust in people. He would need to get rid of all of the state and national capitol office buildings, since His would be the only government. He would have to destroy all military equipment, munitions, aircraft, and tank and gun factories. He would very likely terminate the tobacco industry and put the land that is used for growing tobacco to a better use—such as growing fruits and vegetables. He certainly would want to annihilate the headquarters, meeting places, temples and churches of any false religions. Much of the land that we have polluted and corrupted He would want to plow up and make fresh again, so that the earth could become a beautiful garden once more.

Jesus Christ hates all that is evil and corrupt. Those things cannot exist during His reign of one thousand years. A major purpose of the Tribulation, therefore, is to get rid of all unrighteousness *before* the thousand-year reign of Christ begins, so that His reign can commence in love and peace rather than destruction. He wants Christians here on the earth, during the Tribulation, who hate evil as much as He does, who have turned from their wicked ways and are walking in holiness and righteousness before God.

THE CALL TO RIGHTEOUSNESS

There is a call to righteousness going out to Christians all across our nation and around the world. God is using men of God who are truly sensitive to the Holy Spirit to tell Christians to forsake all wickedness and anything that is doubtful, and to walk in holiness.

One of the best analogies for what God is doing can be drawn from the Tabernacle of the Old Testament. Within the walls of the Tabernacle was the outer court. Within that was the Holy Place, where the priests alone could go. Then there was the Holy of Holies, where only the high priest could go once a year. A diagram of this is shown in Figure 12.1:

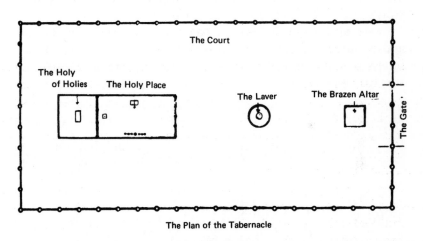

The Plan of the Tabernacle

Figure 12.1

The parallel is that those who are outside of the spiritual tabernacle are those who are not Christians—who have never been "born again" and do not know Jesus Christ as their personal Savior and Master. Those in the outer court are born-again Christians, but they have never been filled with the Holy Spirit and have never allowed God to totally control their lives. In the Holy Place are the Christians who have been filled with the Holy Spirit, and who are seeking to have God totally rule and control their lives. These are the Christians who are trusting in the power of God through the Holy Spirit, rather than in their own strength to accomplish the task that lies before them. These are the Christians who look to God for healing and miracles, when the Holy Spirit directs them to. Unfortunately, the Christians in the Holy Place still have much wickedness and evil in them— in their hearts and also in their conduct. Many actions are still self-centered, independent of God, and unthoughtful of others. There are irritations, words said in anger, and a pushing to get one's own way. And among many of the people, even in the Holy Place, there's even more overt sin. They know what it is and God knows what it is, but it's enjoyable and therefore they "secretly" do it. They think they are very clever because even their fellow Christians don't know about it. However, the One who really counts, knows all about it. He is bidding us to wash our hands, to cleanse our lives, to purify our actions and our words. Yes—He is asking us to be perfect and sinless.

We all believe that we are to obey the commands of God and of Jesus. Jesus gave us a command that is rarely dealt with, but it is in the imperative form and He expects us to obey it. It is found in Matthew 5:

> **48 Therefore you are to be perfect, as your heavenly Father is perfect.**

You might reply, "But that is impossible! It cannot be done." I would have to ask you if Jesus Christ would command you to do something that was impossible. I do not believe that He would. Perfection (maturity), in God's eyes, *must* be possible, by the power of the Holy Spirit. God expects us to exercise our will and to start making decisions that will clean up our lives and move us towards perfection, and the Holy of Holies.

Returning to the example of the Tabernacle, we would have the groups of people distributed as is shown in Figure 12.2. Into which group would you place yourself?

I do not know any Christian who is perfect. I certainly am far from it. Yet this does not negate the call that is going out today. God is beckoning us to move towards perfection and to enter into the Holy of Holies. It is the Christians who heed this call and press forward now who will be the overcomers.

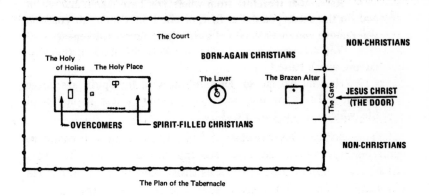

The Plan of the Tabernacle

Figure 12.2

THE OVERCOMERS

In Revelation 2 and 3 there are seven letters from Jesus to the churches. Many Christians place much emphasis on the letters of Paul to the churches, and very little emphasis on the letters of Jesus to the churches. Chapter 2 begins with a letter from Jesus to the church at Ephesus. To examine your own emphasis, just ask yourself how many times you have read Paul's letter to the church at Ephesus (Epheisans), and how many times you have read the first seven verses of Revelation 2, which is Christ's letter to that church. If I had to choose between the two, I would give more weight and importance to what Christ had to say to the Christians there. This is His letter in its entirety, found in Revelation 2:

1 "To the angel of the church in Ephesus write:
The One who holds the seven stars in His right hand, the One who walks among the seven golden lampstands, says this:

2 'I know your deeds and your toil and perseverance, and that you cannot endure evil men, and you put to the test those who call themselves apostles, and they are not, and you found them *to be* false:

3 and you have perseverance and have endured for My name's sake, and have not grown weary.

4 'But I have *this* against you, that you have left your first love.

5 'Remember therefore from where you have fallen, and repent and do the deeds you did at first; or else I am coming to you, and will remove your lampstand out of its place—unless you repent.

6 'Yet this you do have, that you hate the deeds of the Nicolaitans, which I also hate.

7 'He who has an ear, let him hear what the Spirit says to the churches. To him who overcomes, I will grant to eat of the tree of life, which is in the Paradise of God.'

The church (in this case at Ephesus) is made up of born-again believers. In verse 7 we see that some of these believers will be overcomers. Jesus promises those who overcome that He will grant them to eat of the tree of life which is in the paradise of God. This promise is not to all of the believers at Ephesus, but only to the overcomers. An overcomer is a born-again believer in Christ, who is walking moment by moment filled with the Holy Spirit, so that like Christ, he does only those things the Father tells him to do. By doing this, what he says must come to pass and Christ's nature, not his, shines out of his body.

Each of the other six letters follow the same format and include a specific promise to the overcomers. Without comment I would like to present Christ's words and promises to the overcomers in the other six churches.

11 'He who has an ear, let him hear what the Spirit says to the churches. He who overcomes shall not be hurt by the second death.' . . .

17 'He who has an ear, let him hear what the Spirit says to the churches. To him who overcomes, to him I will give *some* of the hidden manna, and I will give him a white stone, and a new name written on the stone which no one knows but he who receives it.' . . .

26 'And he who overcomes, and he who keeps My deeds until the end, TO HIM I WILL GIVE AUTHORITY OVER THE NATIONS;

27 AND HE SHALL RULE THEM WITH A ROD OF IRON, AS THE VESSELS OF THE POTTER ARE BROKEN TO PIECES, as I also have received *authority* from My Father;

28 and I will give him the morning star (Revelation 2).

5 'He who overcomes shall thus be clothed in white garments; and I will not erase his name from the book of life, and I will confess his name before My Father, and before His angels. . . .

12 'He who overcomes, I will make him a pillar in the temple of my God, and he will not go out from it any more; and I will write upon him the name of My God, and the name of the city of My God, the new Jerusalem, which comes down out of heaven from My God, and My new name. . . .

21 'He who overcomes, I will grant to him to sit down with me on My throne, as I also overcame and sat down with My Father on His throne (Revelation 3).

An entire book could be written about the overcomers, the promises to them and the Biblical suggestions for overcoming. Perhaps someday God will lead me to write such a book, but for now we need to realize that the overcomers are a subset of all Christians. To those who overcome, Christ promises many things. Specifically in Revelation 2:26-27, and 3:21, He promises that they will rule over the nations (during the Millennium) and will sit with Jesus on His throne. Jesus would like you, if you know Him as your Savior, to be part of the ruling authority during the Millennium. This is a position, close to Jesus, reserved for the overcomers. I urge you to heed the call of Jesus to the churches to be an overcomer.

If Christ has overcome the world, and He expects us to be like Him, then we should be in the process of overcoming the world. In John 16 we read:

33 "These things I have spoken to you, that in Me you may have peace. In the world you have tribulation, but take courage; I have overcome the world."

Overcoming the world means overcoming self, sin, lusts of the flesh, the world system, the world's worries, nature and Satanic forces. You may be surprised that I include nature in this list. Back in Genesis 1 we read:

26 Then God said, "Let Us make man in Our image, according to Our likeness; and let them rule over the fish of the sea and over the birds of the sky and over the cattle and over all the earth, and over every creeping thing that creeps on the earth."

27 And God created man in His own image, in the image of God He created him; male and female He created them.

28 And God blessed them; and God said to them, "Be fruitful and multiply, and fill the earth, and subdue it; and rule over the fish of the sea and over the birds of the sky, and over every living thing that moves on the earth."

In verse 28 God gave us humans a command to subdue the earth and to rule over it. That command has never been repealed. We know that power over nature has been given to God's people. In the Old Testament we see prophets who could cause the rain to cease and later cause it to rain, for example. I believe that obeying this command in Genesis 1 is part of overcoming the world.

As to how we specifically overcome, one key passage is found in Revelation 12:

10 And I heard a loud voice in heaven, saying,

"Now the salvation, and the power, and the kingdom of our God and the authority of His Christ have come, for the accuser of our brethren has been thrown down, who accuses them before our God day and night.

11 "And they overcame him because of the blood of the Lamb and because of the word of their testimony, and they did not love their life even to death.

Verse 11 says that these Christians overcame Satan because of three things:

1.   The blood of the Lamb.

2.   The word of their testimony.

3.   They did not love their life even to death.

I was going to comment on these verses, but the Holy Spirit said, "No." Therefore, I commit them to you to weigh carefully before the Lord, allowing the Holy Spirit to speak to you.

In Romans 12, Paul gives us further insight as to how to overcome:

9 Let love be without hypocrisy. Abhor what is evil; cling to what is good.

10 Be devoted to one another in brotherly love; give preference to one another in honor;

11 not lagging behind in diligence, fervent in spirit, serving the Lord;

12 rejoicing in hope, persevering in tribulation, devoted to prayer,

13 contributing to the needs of the saints, practicing hospitality.

14 Bless those who persecute you; bless and curse not.

15 Rejoice with those who rejoice, and weep with those who weep.

16 Be of the same mind toward one another; do not be haughty in mind, but associate with the lowly. Do not be wise in your own estimation.

17 Never pay back evil for evil to anyone. Respect what is right in the sight of all men.

18 If possible, so far as it depends on you, be at peace with all men.

19 Never take your own revenge, beloved, but leave room for the wrath of *God,* for it is written, "VENGEANCE IS MINE, I WILL REPAY, SAYS THE LORD."

20 "BUT IF YOUR ENEMY IS HUNGRY, FEED HIM, AND IF HE IS THIRSTY, GIVE HIM A DRINK; FOR IN SO DOING YOU WILL HEAP BURNING COALS UPON HIS HEAD."

21 Do not be overcome by evil, but overcome evil with good.

The last verse said not be overcome by evil. That is the protective, defensive side of it. The aggressive or offensive part is to overcome evil with good. The rest of Chapter 12 (verses 1-20) defines what "good" is. I trust that you will reread even the few verses that we have presented and let God speak to you. If you are not being "good" in this way, fall on your face before God and ask Him to work these things in you and to make you an overcomer. You have not because you ask not (James 4:2b).

UNITED WE STAND, DIVIDED WE FALL

Someday I would enjoy writing a book entitled "The Lone Ranger Christian is An Outlaw." I know that this is true because I have tended to be a lone ranger Christian myself. I think that the days when Christians can survive as loners are gone. Every Christian should be part of a local body of believers. No one of us is complete enough or strong enough to stand alone. In the

first place we should meet together because it is commanded.
In Hebrews 10 we read:

> 23 **Let us hold fast the confession of our hope without wavering,
> for He who promised is faithful;**
> 24 **and let us consider how to stimulate one another to love and
> good deeds,**
> 25 **not forsaking our own assembling together, as is the habit of
> some, but** *encouraging one another;* **and all the more, as you see the
> day drawing near.**

Here we are told not to forsake assembling ourselves together with other Christians. In a body of Christian believers,
when one is discouraged, another is walking close to the Lord
who can lift him up. A week or two later the situation may be
reversed, and the brother who was formerly disheartened can
encourage the other. We also see this harmony in the gifts that
the Holy Spirit gives to the various members in a body of believers. The Holy Spirit will give to each member the gift or gifts
necessary to make the body function well as a whole and glorify
Christ, the head. There is no evidence that God will give *all* of
these gifts to an individual, who would then be able to stand
alone. We all need the edification that comes from the gifts that
the Holy Spirit has given to the other members of the body of
believers with which we meet (or should meet).

It is the Holy Spirit, working *through* the body of Christ,
Who will see us through the Tribulation and give us the power
to become overcomers. Since there is so much misinformation
and misunderstanding about the Holy Spirit, and confusion concerning the gifts of the Spirit, I feel that we need to devote the
entire next chapter to the workings of the Holy Spirit.

13

THE HOLY SPIRIT

AND HIS GIFTS

As an evangelist, pastor and speaker at conferences, it has always been very difficult for me to give a message on the Holy Spirit. The reason is that the Holy Spirit's task is to glorify Jesus Christ. It is difficult to preach about the Holy Spirit without glorifying the Holy Spirit. Yet if someone gives a message on the Holy Spirit that glorifies the Spirit, it is not of the Spirit; if it were, it would glorify Jesus Christ instead. This is clearly spelled out in John 16:

13 "But when He, the Spirit of truth, comes, He will guide you into all the truth; for He will not speak on His own initiative, but whatever He hears, He will speak; and He will disclose to you what is to come.

14 "He shall glorify Me; for He shall take of Mine and shall disclose *it* to you.

I have been to charismatic meetings where the people were so concerned about the gifts of the Spirit, that the Holy Spirit was all that they talked about and, I believe, the only One they glorified. The name of Jesus was rarely mentioned. I do not believe a meeting of this type is *of* the Spirit of God.

Thus, it is my prayer and desire that this chapter, even though speaking about the Holy Spirit and His gifts, be uplifting to our Lord and Savior, Jesus Christ.

THE HOLY SPIRIT IS A PERSON

I hate to begin on such an elementary basis, but some people think that the Holy Spirit is an influence, a feeling or a rosy glow. He is an individual—a person, just like God the Father and Jesus Christ. In fact, Jesus equated the Holy Spirit to Himself in John 14:

> 16 "And I will ask the Father, and He will give you another Helper, that He may abide with you forever;
> 17 *that is* the Spirit of truth, whom the world cannot receive, because it does not behold Him or know Him, *but* you know Him, because He abides with you, and will be in you.

The word used in verse 16 for "another" means "identical to" or "just like." Literally Christ was saying that when He went away, He would give us someone just like Himself who would be with us forever. We see later in that chapter (verse 26) that the Holy Spirit will teach us all things and bring to our remembrance the things that Christ said. John 16:13 says that the Spirit will guide us.

According to psychologists, to be a "person" you have to have three things:

1.   Knowledge

2.   Will

3.   Feelings

The Scriptures attribute all of these things to the Holy Spirit. 1 Corinthians 2:11 tells us that the Holy Spirit gives gifts to Christians as He wills. Thus, we know that He has a will. We know from Ephesians 4:30 that we can grieve the Holy Spirit, and Romans 15:30 tells us that the Holy Spirit has love. It is apparent that He has feelings, as well as knowledge and a will.

So in every aspect the Holy Spirit is a person. He is a person without a body. This is why in the earlier days He was called the Holy Ghost: "ghost" was the term people used for a personality, or a being, without a body. The Holy Spirit is not limited, as Jesus Christ was while He was on earth, to being in one place at one time. In this respect He is like God the Father; He can be everywhere at once (omnipresence). This beautiful person, who loves us and cares for us, yearns to teach us about Jesus and to help us become like Him.

OUR RELATIONSHIP TO THE
PERSON OF THE HOLY SPIRIT

Let's again begin at the beginning. There are several relationships with the Holy Spirit. The first relationship is the receiving of the Holy Spirit, as He comes to dwell within us. This indwelling happens at the time we receive Christ as our personal Savior. If you do not have the Holy Spirit, you do not have a relationship with Jesus Christ, you are not "born again" and according to the Bible, you are not a son of God. Romans 8 has this to say:

9 However you are not in the flesh but in the Spirit, if indeed the Spirit of God dwells in you. But if anyone does not have the Spirit of Christ, he does not belong to Him.

10 And if Christ is in you, though the body is dead because of sin, yet the spirit is alive because of righteousness.

11 But if the Spirit of Him who raised Jesus from the dead dwells in you, He who raised Christ Jesus from the dead will also give life to your mortal bodies through His Spirit who indwells you.

12 So then, brethren, we are under obligation, not to the flesh, to live according to the flesh—

13 for if you are living according to the flesh, you must die; but if by the Spirit you are putting to death the deeds of the body, you will live.

14 For all who are being led by the Spirit of God, these are the sons of God.

Verse 14, in my opinion, is the best definition in the New Testament of a Christian (son of God)—one who is "being led by the Spirit of God." In verse 9 we see that if you do not have the Spirit of God, you do not belong to Jesus. Our relationship with the Holy Spirit is one that grows and progresses throughout our Christian lives. One might think that once the Holy Spirit comes to live inside of us, that is all there is. This isn't true, as we will see as we look at the first apostles.

There is some question as to when the apostles were actually born again. It certainly had to occur after Christ's death and resurrection. After discussing this with two of my dear brothers in Christ, I believe that the apostles' conversion is recorded in John 20:

> 21 Jesus therefore said to them again, "Peace *be* with you; as the Father has sent Me, I also send you."
>
> 22 And when He had said this, He breathed on them, and said to them, "Receive the Holy Spirit.
>
> 23 "If you forgive the sins of any, *their sins* have been forgiven them; if you retain the *sins* of any, they have been retained."

At this point in time, the apostles have believed on Jesus Christ as the Son of God and have accepted His resurrection. In these verses they receive the Holy Spirit and, in verse 23, some measure of spiritual authority. You might think that this was all that they needed. (Many Christians today are living in this realm. They know Christ as their Savior and have the Holy Spirit dwelling inside them, but they have limited effectiveness in their ministry and lack evidence of supernatural power.) In the Bible we see Christ telling these apostles that they need something more. After they had received the Holy Spirit (in John 20), He tells them in Acts 1 what they need:

> 4 And gathering them together, He commanded them not to leave Jerusalem, but to wait for what the Father had promised, "Which," *He said,* "you have heard of from Me;
>
> 5 for John baptized with water, but you shall be baptized with the Holy Spirit not many days from now." . . .
>
> 8 but you shall receive power when the Holy Spirit has come upon you; and you shall be My witnesses both in Jerusalem, and in all Judea and Samaria, and even to the remotest part of the earth."

Here He tells them that they will receive the needed power when the Holy Spirit comes upon them. The fulfillment of this is recorded in Acts 2:

> 2 And suddenly there came from heaven a noise like a violent, rushing wind, and it filled the whole house where they were sitting.
>
> 3 And there appeared to them tongues as of fire distributing themselves, and they rested on each one of them.
>
> 4 And they were all filled with the Holy Spirit and began to speak with other tongues, as the Spirit was giving them utterance.

We see that they are filled with the Holy Spirit, receive power and demonstrate supernatural gifts (speaking in other known, but unlearned languages). In Acts 1:5, Christ told the apostles that they would soon be baptized with the Holy Spirit. After Pentecost, there is no mention in the Scriptures of anyone being baptized with the Spirit. The disciples were also "filled with the Holy Spirit" at Pentecost, and there are numerous recorded instances of Christians being filled with the Spirit after Pentecost. Therefore, I prefer the term "filled with the Spirit" over being "baptized with the Spirit."

BEING FILLED WITH THE HOLY SPIRIT

So the first incident of Christians being filled with the Holy Spirit occurred on the day of Pentecost. The Christians gathered together were all filled with the Holy Spirit. This experience, which frequently comes after salvation (by whatever name), is very real and is necessary for the Spirit-filled life. As I have said, I personally believe that "being filled with the Spirit" is the terminology the Scriptures use, and we will use it in this chapter. (I trust that my good brothers who use the term "being baptized with the Holy Spirit" will understand that I am referring to the same thing when I say "being filled with the Holy Spirit.")

When the Christians at Pentecost were filled with the Spirit, the Holy Spirit took control of them. He controlled their minds, their tongues, their feet, and their hands. In the Gospels we see Christ occasionally encountering somebody who is possessed by a demon, which causes him to do ungodly things. Being filled with the Spirit is the antithesis of that. In this case, the Holy Spirit totally controls a person, as long as that person is completely yielded to the Holy Spirit, causing him to do things that will glorify Christ and build up the body of Christ. This filling with the Spirit is dependent on our being completely yielded to God and *willing* for the Holy Spirit to control us. Unlike demon possession, where the individual cannot take back the control, when an individual is filled with (controlled by) the Holy Spirit, he *can* take back the control from the Holy Spirit. This shows that there is a willful, intelligent and cooperative relationship between the believer and the Holy Spirit.

In other instances in the New Testament, being filled with the Spirit is accompanied by a manifestation of supernatural power in the saints. For example, in Acts 4:31, the believers were filled with the Holy Spirit and began to speak the word of God with boldness. In Acts 7:55-60, Stephen, being full of the Spirit, saw the glory of God and Jesus standing at the right hand of God, and was able to glorify Christ while being stoned to death. Acts 13:9-11 tells how Paul, filled with the Spirit, was able to discern a spirit of the devil and cause a man to become blind by his words.

In the Scriptures we find that almost inevitably the filling with the Holy Spirit caused the individual Christians to exhibit some form of supernatural power (supernatural gift). This filling was also a freeing and exhilarating experience, that caused them to praise and worship God in a new and higher way. Acts 2 records that the onlookers thought these men were drunk. This must have been because they were so uninhibited, free and exuberant. This analogy to being drunk is carried further in Ephesians 5:

> **18 And do not get drunk with wine, for that is dissipation, but be filled with the Spirit,**
>
> **19 speaking to one another in psalms and hymns and spiritual songs, singing and making melody with your heart to the Lord;**
>
> **20 always giving thanks for all things in the name of our Lord Jesus Christ to God, even the Father;**
>
> **21 and be subject to one another in the fear of Christ.**

Verse 18 is in the imperative form: "Be filled with the Spirit." This is not a suggestion, but a command. Therefore, not to do so is sin. This filling is something that we can *choose* to allow to happen or not. It is up to us, whether or not we yield ourselves to the Holy Spirit, that He might take charge of our minds and bodies in order to glorify Christ in fullness.

In verse 20 of Ephesians 5 we see that the Holy Spirit causes us to always give thanks for everything, in the name of Jesus Christ, to God the Father. The Holy Spirit also chooses to give gifts to Christians who are filled with the Spirit. A gift of the Holy Spirit is not a state of being, or an office, but a God-led activity, used to build up the body of Christ, as we will now see.

GIFTS OF THE HOLY SPIRIT

The Holy Spirit gives various gifts for the building up of the body of our Lord Jesus Christ, and for equipping Christians to do the work that the Lord has for them to do. The following are two main passages of Scripture which list the gifts of the Spirit:

4 For just as we have many members in one body and all the members do not have the same function,

5 so we, who are many, are one body in Christ, and individually members of one another.

6 And since we have gifts that differ according to the grace given to us, *let each exercise them accordingly:* if prophecy, according to the proportion of his faith;

7 if service, in his serving; or he who teaches, in his teaching;

8 or he who exhorts, in his exhortation; he who gives, with liberality; he who leads, with diligence; he who shows mercy, with cheerfulness (Romans 12).

4 Now there are varieties of gifts, but the same Spirit.

5 And there are varieties of ministries, but the same Lord.

6 And there are varieites of effects, but the same God who works all things in all *persons.*

7 But to each one is given the manifestation of the Spirit for the common good.

8 For to one is given the word of wisdom through the Spirit, and to another the word of knowledge according to the same Spirit;

9 to another faith by the same Spirit, and to another gifts of healing by the one Spirit,

10 and to another the effecting of miracles, and to another prophecy, and to another the distinguishing of spirits, to another *various* kinds of tongues, and to another the interpretation of tongues.

11 but one and the same Spirit works all these things, distributing to each one individually just as He wills (1 Corinthians 12).

To take a closer look at the gifts mentioned in these two passages, I have listed them in tabular form:

ROMANS 12:4-8	1 CORINTHIANS 12:4-11
Prophecy	Wisdom
Service	Knowledge
Teaching	Faith
Exhortation	Healing
Giving	Effecting of miracles
Leading (ruling)	Prophecy
Showing mercy	Distinguishing of spirits
Hospitality	Tongues
	Interpretation of tongues

The Lord led me to eliminate the duplicates in the two lists, and to rewrite these gifts in a single list, putting all in a linguistic form that shows the actions that the Holy Spirit would cause:

1. Going as an apostle
2. Serving others
3. Teaching
4. Exhorting
5. Giving
6. Leading (ruling)
7. Showing mercy
8. Practicing hospitality
9. Speaking wisdom
10. Having knowledge
11. Having faith
12. Healing
13. Performing miracles
14. Distinguishing spirits
15. Speaking in tongues
16. Interpreting tongues

One question frequently asked is whether or not all of these gifts are for Christians today. Do you remember why they were given in the first place? They were given to build up the body of Christ. It is difficult for me to envisage that the Holy Spirit would give these types of actions earlier because they were necessary for the building up of believers and the body of Jesus Christ, and that these are no longer necessary for edification today. One time, while quizzing a minister on this subject, I presented him with this list and he concluded that items 2 to 9, and 11 are for today but items 1, 10, and 12 through 16 are not. It was incredible to me that a man could pick and choose, and sit as judge over the Holy Spirit. It seems to me that you must either throw out all of them or keep all of them.

I have been in services where all of these gifts were exercised to the glory of Jesus Christ. There was a power in the praise, and an awe in the worship; the power of God was manifest and life was breathed into the body of Christ that was assembled there.

I might just say a word or two about some of these gifts that are less well known in Christendom. Prophesying is speaking the word of God from the point of view of God. In this case, the Holy Spirit comes upon an individual and controls his tongue and mouth, causing him to speak the words that are on God's heart. The prophecy may sound something like this: "My little children, I love you. Turn from your wicked ways and enter into the Holy of Holies, says the Lord God Almighty." The individual is not talking *about* God, as one does in a sermon, but is speaking God's own words. Prophecies may or may not involve the future.

The word of knowledge or the gift of knowledge was what Christ was exercising when He knew beforehand that Peter would catch a fish with a gold coin in its mouth, that the disciples would encounter a man who had an upper room, that another man would give them his donkey, and that the woman at the well had had five husbands. This is a gift of knowing things without having had them revealed in any normal way.

When I hear of someone being "healed," I have mixed emotions as to whether to accept it as a miracle of God, because

I think that some of the "faith healers" are not being led by God. I *do* believe that God heals and that He can give an individual in the body of Christ a special gift of laying on of hands and praying for the sick.

Performing miracles refers to works other than healing, such as stopping the rain or causing it to rain, walking on water, turning water into wine, and raising the dead. As we will see later in this section, the effecting of miracles is something that Christians will be doing more of during the Tribulation.

Not all prophecies are of God, not all tongues are of God, not all teaching and preaching is of God. It is a precious gift to be able to distinguish the spirits and know when the Holy Spirit is truly using somebody, versus when that individual is moving in the flesh or is controlled by demonic spirits.

I realize that the gift of speaking in tongues has caused more dissension in the body of Christ than anything else in recent years. First we must realize that there are two distinct forms of this gift. The one that we are referring to here, the gift for building up the body of Christ, is always speaking in a language that has not been learned by the speaker. The Holy Spirit is doing the speaking as the Spirit-filled Christian yields himself, and the language is frequently a known one, although it is unknown to the speaker. There was a recent example of this. Into a particular group of believers came a Jewish man who spoke only a little English. Yiddish was his primary language. There was a girl from Oklahoma, who had never even heard Yiddish, who, under the anointing of the Holy Spirit, began to tell him the Good News about Jesus Christ, not only in Yiddish, but in his own peculiar dialect. He received Christ as his personal Savior. He then gave his testimony, in Yiddish, and this girl, with the supernatural power of the Holy Spirit, interpreted his testimony into English for the rest of the members of that body! That gift is still working today.

There is another type of speaking in tongues which is speaking in an unknown (or angelic) language. This gift is used normally for the building up of the individual Christian and is used in prayer, praise and worship. It can be used in a public meeting if there is one who can interpret by the Spirit, this unknown language. 1 Corinthians 14:27-28 says that this gift should at most be exercised by two or three in a meeting and they should speak in turn. Let's see what else Paul says about this gift in 1 Corinthians 14:

> 1 Pursue love, yet desire earnestly spiritual *gifts,* but especially that you may prophesy.
>
> 2 For one who speaks in a tongue does not speak to men, but to God; for no one understands, but in *his* spirit he speaks mysteries.
>
> 3 But one who prophesies speaks to men for edification and exhortation and consolation.
>
> 4 One who speaks in a tongue edifies himself; but one who prophesies edifies the church. . . .
>
> 13 Therefore let one who speaks in a tongue pray that he may interpret.
>
> 14 For if I pray in a tongue, my spirit prays, but my mind is unfruitful.

Here we see Paul urging that messages in the meetings of believers be spoken in the language known by the people, and not in an unknown tongue. Later in that chapter he admonishes that if there is no one to interpret, one should not speak out in tongues in church. He says that a person speaking in tongues edifies himself, but he does not edify the church. I know that there are many who will disagree with me, but even though speaking in tongues is common when a person is filled with the Holy Spirit, I do not think it is the only sign, or even a necessary sign that someone is filled with the Holy Spirit. However, some supernatural gift should accompany the filling. Remember that it is the Holy Spirit who is giving these various gifts, and He will give what is needed at the time to build up the individual Christian and the body of believers.

Some "tongues speaking" Christians are so hung up on tongues that they show no love to Christians who do not have this gift. On the other hand, some Christians who do not have this gift think that Christians who "speak in tongues" are demon controlled. I believe both are an abomination before the Lord. Paul says in 1 Corinthians 13:

> 1 If I speak with the tongues of men and of angels, but do not have love, I have become a noisy gong or a clanging cymbal.

2 And if I have *the gift* of prophecy, and know all mysteries and all knowledge; and if I have all faith, so as to remove mountains, but do not have love, I am nothing.

A person can have the gift of tongues, the gift of prophecy, the gift of knowledge and the gift of faith, but unless he has *love,* he is absolutely nothing. My heart goes out to "Spirit-filled Christians" I have seen who show so little love that they have driven their own children away from their homes. May God have mercy upon their souls!

The whole purpose of 1 Corinthians 13 is to point out that love is so much more important than any of these spiritual gifts. We are to love one another in the body of Christ, to build each other up, to bear one another's burdens, to rejoice together, to weep together, to work together—*all* for the glory of Christ.

Yet, although love is to be our greatest quest, we are also told to *earnestly desire* spiritual gifts (1 Corinthians 14:1). I hope that you will pray about the list of gifts that we presented earlier, and ask the Holy Spirit which ones He has for you. According to my understanding, these gifts are given only to those who have been filled with the Holy Spirit. So, the first thing to do is to ask God to totally control you and to fill you with His Holy Spirit. Ask, yield, and He *will* fill you.

Those who still might be having difficulty accepting the fact that these gifts are for today, I would encourage to pray over these four verses in Mark 16:

15 And He said to them, "Go into all the world and preach the gospel to all creation.

Is this verse for us today, as well as for those Christians in the first century? I think that we are in agreement that it is. The next verse says:

16 "He who has believed and has been baptized shall be saved; but he who has disbelieved shall be condemned.

Does this verse apply to us today? I believe that it does. Now let us consider the first half of the next verse:

17a And these signs will accompany those who have believed:

This verse is going to tell us something about those who, in verse 15 and 16, have believed in Christ, and "those who have believed" includes us, doesn't it? Let us then finish verses 17 and 18 to see what signs *will* accompany us:

17 "And these signs will accompany those who have believed: in My name they will cast out demons, they will speak with new tongues;

18 they will pick up serpents, and if they drink any deadly *poison,* it shall not hurt them; they will lay hands on the sick, and they will recover."

CALLINGS OF THE HOLY SPIRIT

Now let us turn to the callings of the Holy Spirit. The five-fold ministry is recorded in Ephesians 4:

11 And He gave some *as* apostles, and some *as* prophets, and some *as* evangelists, and some *as* pastors and teachers,

12 for the equipping of the saints for the work of service, to the building up of the body of Christ;

13 until we all attain to the unity of the faith, and of the knowledge of the Son of God, to a mature man, to the measure of the stature which belongs to the fulness of Christ.

Here we see these vocational callings, which the Holy Spirit can give:

Apostles

Prophets

Evangelists

Pastors

Teachers

Verse 12 says that these ministries are given for two reasons:

1. The equipping of the saints for service

2. The building up of the body of Christ

Verse 13 tells us how long these gifts will operate. It doesn't say that they are just for the first century, but that they will exist until:

1.   We all attain to the unity of the faith

2.   We all attain to the fulness of Christ

Since these two things have not yet occurred, these ministries must still be needed today, and will continue to be needed until we all have this unity and fulness.

It is interesting to note that Romans 11:29 says that these gifts and callings are irrevocable. Once given they remain, even if the Christian recipient turns to a life of sin. Perhaps this is why we sometimes see a scandalous individual being used of God. We can see this exemplified in the church of Corinth. They were committing such gross sins that the heathen didn't even have a word for it. Yet, Paul says that the Church at Corinth spoke in tongues more than any other church. Thus we see that the exercising of these gifts is not a "merit badge" to show that a Christian is living a righteous life.

Let me hasten to add that this is absolutely no reason to despise or not desire the gifts of the Spirit. God wants us to have both the gifts of the Spirit *and* to live a righteous life. We must have the power of the Holy Spirit both to exercise the gifts and to live a sanctified life.

Some Christians feel that once they have been filled (baptized) with the Holy Spirit, that is all there is. There is much more. This is just a step along the path. Galatians 5:25 tells us we should walk (moment by moment) by the Spirit. This path, if we will keep pressing forward, will take us to a sanctified life of righteousness and, as overcomers, on into the Holy of Holies. We cannot walk this road that Christ walked (take up your cross and follow me) in our own strength. The power of the Holy Spirit, promised in Acts 1:8, is necessary and—praise God— it is available to us, as we are filled with the Holy Spirit and learn to walk in His power.

I have very briefly discussed this vast subject of the Holy Spirit and His power and gifts. These will be discussed in detail in a forthcoming book of mine, *Going Through the Tribulation Victoriously*. In it will also be a detailed discussion of the overcomers, spiritual power, enduring persecution, hearing the voice of God, spiritual authority, spiritual covering, the body of

Christ, and much more. (Please pray for me as I undertake this work.)

THE POWER OF THE HOLY SPIRIT

Can you pray for someone and cause him to be healed? No. Can you command the rain to stop and it will stop? No. Can you know the name and home town of a stranger without him telling you? No. Can you walk through an apartment building in a communist country and stop before the door of the only Christian family in the building? No. However, if one were to ask if the Holy Spirit can do all of these things, the answer would be a very positive *YES*. The Holy Spirit has done these things, and much more, *through* people within the last couple of years.

The Holy Spirit has the power; we do not, of ourselves. He can achieve *anything,* even the moving of a mountain; we cannot. It is only as we are rightly related to Christ *and* the Holy Spirit that we can experience the power that will be necessary to be overcomers during the Tribulation. God alone can give us the victory. If we try to overcome in our own strength, we are dead. Yet, *we have available to us the same power that raised Jesus Christ from the dead.*

We should begin now to live filled with the Spirit, and to move towards the Holy of Holies and perfection in such a way that will glorify Jesus Christ. We should get accustomed to allowing the Holy Spirit use us in any way that He desires, and to having all of our needs met by the body of Christ. If we begin to do this now, our experience during the Tribulation will be much easier. If we wait until the Tribulation begins before attempting to move in this manner, we may be one of the many who will fall away. The power is available. The Holy Spirit *wants* to fill us, to control us, to use us to build up the body of Jesus Christ and to glorify the name of Christ. It is an act of the will to allow Him to do this. As we surrender all to Him, He will provide the power that we need to be overcomers.

14

PREPARING TO

LIVE SUPERNATURALLY

In our modern age of "enlightenment" and scientific analysis, many people, even Christians, tend to shy away from anything that cannot be understood with the mind. In plain terms, they have difficulty accepting the supernatural, or the events that transcend the laws of nature. The reason for the difficulty is that these events must be understood with the spirit and not with the mind. Our mind is simply a hindrance that tends to get in the way when it comes to understanding things of the Spirit.

If you have read this far in the book, you are most likely a born-again Christian and believe in the resurrection of Jesus Christ. You accept His resurrection, after He had been dead for three days, by *faith*—not because you intellectually comprehend it. We all know that after four to eight minutes of heart stoppage, irreversible brain damage sets in. After this, the body itself begins to decay. How was the brain damage in Christ's body reversed? How were decayed cells made whole and alive again? We cannot answer these questions with our mind, but our spirit perceives that God, in a miraculous way, caused these things to happen. We *understand,* but we understand with our spirit.

We could go through a similar exercise with the raising of Lazarus from the dead. We do not understand *how* it occurred, but our spirit tells us that it did. The same is true of the lame man that Peter and John healed as they were going into the temple. This man's legs had been crippled and twisted from birth. Peter said to him, "In the name of Jesus Christ of Nazareth rise up and walk" (Acts 3:6 *KJV*). Immediately his feet and ankles received strength and he lept up. We cannot understand with our mind how this happened, how the bones could grow and straighten and the muscles grow strong in that moment of time, but our spirit tells us that it is true and did occur.

Much of what goes on at a "faith healing meeting" could be explained, by the rationalists, as temporary recoveries from psychosomatic illnesses. However, the three events that we have just mentioned, and many others of modern times, cannot be attributed to this. The wife of a dear brother of mine, who is a minister, was examined by doctors and it was found that her body was literally riddled with cancer. They gave her very little time to live. The body of believers began to pray diligently for her healing. At her next visit, the doctors could not find a single trace of cancer! This occurred in 1976.

I could give many examples of such healings. One group in Detroit, Michigan, had a small church in a home. One of the members was a blind man. At one point he came to the elders and asked them to pray for his healing. With fear and trembling they searched the Scriptures in James and saw that not only were they to anoint him with oil and pray over him, but also they were to confess their faults and sins one to another. The elders and this blind member met and spent an entire morning confessing their faults and being cleansed by God. Then, as the Scriptures say to, they anointed him with oil and prayed. Yes! His sight was restored.

In the body of believers with whom I fellowshipped in Pasadena, there is a man who was raised from the dead. He was in the hospital, very seriously ill. His lungs filled up with fluid and his heart stopped. Five doctors pronounced him dead and the hearse was on its way. One of the elders entered the room, laid hands on this man, and in the name of Jesus and by the power of the Holy Spirit, commanded him to come back to life. The Holy Spirit raised him from the dead.

What is the power that will cure cancer, heal lameness, and can even raise the dead? As we saw in the last chapter, it is the power of the Holy Spirit, administered by a true Spirit-filled Christian in the name of Jesus Christ. This power is available to Christians today, but the trouble is that most Christians are afraid to reach out and take hold of it. They are afraid that someone will think them odd, fanatical or even crazy. Pride is the most frequent hindrance to having the supernatural power of God work in us and through us.

GOD MIRACULOUSLY PROVIDES

As we begin to look at God miraculously providing food for His children, we should remind ourselves about what we discussed earlier: God does not provide for us as long as we are able to provide for ourselves. He expects us to work and to make any preparations that He tells us to. If, after we have done all that He has guided us to do and are working hard, we are still unable to provide food for ourselves, He promises us in Matthew 6 that He will provide for our needs:

31 "Do not be anxious then, saying, 'What shall we eat?' or 'What shall we drink?' or 'With what shall we clothe ourselves?'

32 "For all these things the Gentiles eagerly seek; for your heavenly Father knows that you need all these things.

33 "But seek first His kingdom and His righteousness; and all these things shall be added to you.

We see numerous examples in the Old Testament of God miraculously providing food for His people. We are all familiar with the manna that rained from heaven while the children of Israel were wandering for forty years in the wilderness. They could not provide their own food at that time, so God miraculously created it and presented it to them. Just as miraculously, God provided grain during Joseph's time: through a miracle, He warned them to prepare ahead of time for a coming famine.

In the New Testament, on two different occasions we see Jesus talking to a large multitude out in the wilderness away from any restaurants or inns. When the people began to get hungry, He took what little food was available (fishes and loaves) and caused it to multiply so that several thousand people were fed on each occasion. Do you believe that that occurred?

I do! I do not understand with my mind how the pieces of bread could multiply, but my spirit tells me that it is true.

In Indonesia a miracle of God multiplying food was recorded in very recent years. Mel Tari, on pages 47-49 of *Like a Mighty Wind* (published by Creation House), relates this event:

"Another special miracle took place when the very first team went out to preach the Gospel. They came to a small village called Nikiniki about fifteen miles from our town of Soe. By this time, the Lord had used them to bring many people to the Lord Jesus.

"As is the custom, the team went to the pastor's house to stay with him. The pastor happened to be my uncle. That time my aunt, the pastor's wife, was embarrassed because so many people came and she had nothing to give them to eat. It was famine time in Timor. There were twenty on the team, and he went to my aunt, and said, 'Ma'am, the Lord told me that you have four tapioca roots in your cupboard and that you should take them and cook them. They will be sufficient for all of us.'

"'Lord,' she said, 'I don't know what to do. Please show me.'

"At the same time, the Lord spoke to the leader of the team, and he went to my aunt and said, 'Ma'am, the Lord told me that you have four tapioca roots in your cupboard and that you should take them and cook them. They will be sufficient for all of us.'

"'How do you know that I have four tapioca roots?' she asked.

"'I didn't know; the Lord told me,' he repeated.

"She went to the kitchen and found exactly four roots as the Lord had revealed to the team member.

"*If the Lord told him about the roots, I had better obey the Lord and cook them,* she thought.

"After she had cooked the tapioca, the team leader said, 'Please get water for tea.'

"My aunt had enough sugar and tea for only two or three cups, but she obeyed.

"'Put the water, tea and sugar in the pitcher and mix it up for the people to drink as they eat the tapioca,' the leader said. She did as he told her. Then she made a small flat loaf of bread out of the tapioca, put it on a plate, and prayed over it. The team leader also prayed. After they prayed, the Lord told them to give each of the guests a plate, which they did. They also handed out cups.

"Then the Lord said to the team member, 'Now tell the pastor's wife that she is to break the tapioca into pieces and give it to the people until their plates are full.'

"Even though she thought, *This is impossible to do, because there isn't even enough to fill one plate,* she obeyed the Lord.

"The first man who came for food was pretty glad. *If I am the first of the line, I'll be sure to eat,* he thought. But the man who was last in the line, who was a real good friend of mine, was quite upset because he liked to eat a lot. He was a big guy. I asked him later, 'What did you feel that time?' He said, 'I was really scared. I prayed real hard and said, 'Lord, I'm the last one in the line. There is only one tapioca loaf. Only three or four will have any. So, Lord Jesus, you had better perform a miracle, and please remember me, who's the last one in the line, because I'm really hungry.'

"My aunt then took the bread and broke it. Usually mathematics will tell you when you break one in half, you get two halves. That is not necessarily so in God's counting. My aunt broke one, and then the half in her right hand became whole again. The Lord told her to put the one that was in her left hand on the plate. She broke the one in her right hand again, and, as she did this, it made her cry because she realized that a miracle was taking place in her hand. So she just praised the Lord and cried and broke the bread and broke it.

"The first man had a plateful and the second one, and the third one. Now everyone realized that a miracle was taking place. Even my friend who was the last one in line got a plateful. He too thanked the Lord and said, 'Oh, Lord, You've done a miracle.'

"All of them, after they had eaten some tapioca bread, came for tea at the same time. When you eat tapioca it is so dry, if you don't get something to drink you feel terrible. My aunt wanted to put only a little bit in the cups, but the Lord said, 'Just fill the cups up.' She obeyed again, and the tea just kept coming until all of them had something to drink. Many of them had two or three glasses of tea. So all of the team ate until they were completely full.

"As a matter of fact, there was food left over they couldn't eat. So even the dogs were satisfied; the Lord even took care of the animals."

Isn't it precious and wonderful the way that God took care of them when they were helpless to take care of themselves? God does not love you less than he loved the multitudes who were sitting at Jesus' feet or these precious brothers and sisters in Indonesia. When the time comes, and you have done all that He has told you to and can no longer provide for yourself, He will miraculously provide for you, if you exercise faith.

HEARING AND FOLLOWING GOD'S VOICE

I believe that almost all Christians want to hear the voice of God and be personally directed by Him. It is a tragedy that so many Christians are looking for an easy way out; they want some pastor, elder or minister to find out God's direction for their life. This is not God's way. He wants to speak to you personally and to guide you.

In Proverbs 3, we find that in order for Him to guide our paths we must not "lean on our own understanding." Trying to figure things out and having to understand everything is a tremendous hindrance when it comes to hearing and obeying God's voice.

Jesus said, "My sheep hear My voice, and I know them, and they follow Me;" (John 10:27). Are you one of Jesus' sheep? If so, He says that you will hear His voice. Surely no one would claim that this is only for the first century. If you are not hearing His voice, you might ask Him in prayer, *why not?* I believe that if you sincerely ask Him that question, He will answer you. He may tell many people that it is because they are too busy; He may tell others that it is because the last time He spoke, they didn't obey. Whatever the reason is, clear it up so that you can hear His voice.

There may be a day when you need to hear Him in order that He might direct you to another Christian. (This would be particularly true during a time of persecution.) Pat Boone, in his new book, *A Miracle A Day Keeps The Devil Away,* relates 31 specific miracles that have happened to him and his family. One occurred when his daughter Lindy, then eighteen years old, drove into a filling station and had a young man walk over to the car and say, "I sure love Jesus!" Lindy had no "Jesus stickers" on her car, and had never seen this young man before. She replied, "So do I." The young man replied, "Yes, I know." When asked "how" by Lindy, he said, with a warm smile, "We have the same Spirit."

A miraculous leading of God was experienced by John Chamberlin who works with an Eastern European mission. He had just taken 2,000 Christian books behind the Iron Curtain.

He writes to Barney Coombs, Pastor of St. Margaret's Church in Vancouver, B.C., saying:

"In a small town quite close to the Russian border, our last literature contact lived. My instructions were to turn left on one of the first streets after passing a certain road sign and 'there it is.' One thing I have learned about Eastern Europe is never to trust a map. Something always changes. We arrived at night, for our car would attract attention. We discovered that all the streets went only in one direction—left. Besides that, there were no names on the streets. The first three streets led into groups of apartments. Usually there is a list at the entrance of each apartment indicating the people who live there and their flat numbers, but not in this case. After walking around for what seemed an hour, I found myself in a long building complex with many military personnel running about. My mind was telling me to go back to the car, but my heart and spirit said, 'Lord, I'm in your will, sent by your word and covered by your love. For the sake of your children, show yourself.' At once I heard a voice inside that said, 'Are you willing to walk in faith?' 'Yes,' I said. He then led me down several streets to an apartment block and a door marked number 13. Then He simply said, 'Knock.' Hesitation flooded my mind with thoughts like 'What will you say if they're not the right people?' or 'The mission would not tell you to do this. How can you believe that God works in such slapshot ways?' But I knew I was walking in faith. Once again I said, 'Yes Lord' and knocked. A woman answered the door. 'Does Pezaid live here?' I asked. She looked for a moment and said, 'Come in John, we've been praying for you.' Previously that day, many miles south, a pastor had passed our car and the Lord told him, 'Pray for the occupants, for they will come to see you.' And that night we did. We had a time of fellowship and praise. God provides if we have the faith to walk."

It would be easy after reading such a letter for us to get excited about God leading, and miss God Himself. The important thing is that God loves John Chamberlin and each of us, and yearns to guide us and speak to us. He often speaks in a still, small voice and therefore we have to be sensitive to hear Him when He speaks. As times progressively worsen, being able to hear the voice of God could mean our survival. We must begin to walk with a sensitive ear *now,* so that we are already accustomed to doing so when we *need* to depend on God alone.

POWER OVER NATURE

All through the Old Testament we see examples of men of God, in the power of the Holy Spirit, exercising control over nature. There is the example of Elijah stopping the rain for three years and then causing it to rain again. There is the situation where Elijah called down lightning (fire from heaven) to consume the sacrifice. Daniel prayed and the lions' mouths were closed. Shadrach, Meshach and Abed-nego said that God would deliver them, and they were not harmed by the flames when they were thrown into a fiery furnace. These are but a few examples. I believe these all relate back to God's initial command to Adam: conquer and subdue nature.

The two witnesses, spoken of in Revelation, will have the power (of the Holy Spirit in the name of Jesus Christ) to do many amazing things. In Revelation 11 we read:

> 3 "And I will grant *authority* to my two witnesses, and they will prophesy for twelve hundred and sixty days, clothed in sackcloth."
> 4 These are the two olive trees and the two lampstands that stand before the Lord of the earth.
> 5 And if any one desires to harm them, fire proceeds out of their mouth and devours their enemies; and if any one would desire to harm them, in this manner he must be killed.
> 6 These have the power to shut up the sky, in order that rain may not fall during the days of their prophesying; and they have power over the waters to turn them into blood, and to smite the earth with every plague, as often as they desire.

Here we see that the two witnesses during the Tribulation will not only have the power to shut up the sky, but will also have power over the water and over plagues. Once again we can see that this kind of miraculous power was not just for the Old Testament, and the first century, but that it is for *all* ages.

Our authority over nature includes authority over the animals. Mel Tari, in *Like a Mighty Wind,* has this to say (pages 40-42):

> "In Mark 16:18 we read, 'They shall take up serpents.' This shows the Christian's power over the animal kingdom. When the Lord created

Adam and Eve, he said to them, 'You have the power over the animal kingdom. You rule over them.' But when man fell into sin he lost authority over the animals. Sometimes a dog will bite you because the dog doesn't honor you as the highest creation of God.

"I praise God that, by confidence in the Lord Jesus Christ, we have had this authority restored to us. Maybe you in America don't need this authority. You have your cars, trains and planes. But we live in the jungle so we really need authority over the animals.

"Sometimes we meet with crocodiles, tigers or poisonous snakes. Many times we have said, 'Snake, you stop there, because I want to pass by.' And that snake just stops. We pass by, and the snake never bothers us. Why? Because God has given us power over the animal kingdom.

"In my country, there are many scorpions. If one bites you, you really get into trouble. But I tell you, we have power over the animal kingdom. If the scorpion bites us, we just pray in the name of Jesus and the pain disappears. The scorpion and the animal are not supposed to bother us, because we are the highest creation of God. They are supposed to honor us, as we are supposed to honor God. I praise God that he brought us back to this place of authority over the animal kingdom.

"My sister and a brother in the Lord work for the Lord in the jungles of Sumatra. Many times they must cross rivers. One day this brother went to cross the river. He could not swim, and the water came to his waist as it was flood time. The Moslems and pagans stood on the bank and laughed.

"'Ha, ha,' they said, 'This is the day for him to die.'

"As he was struggling to get across the river, crocodiles came toward him to swallow him. When they were three or four feet from him, they were ready to use their tails to crush him. When crocodiles hit with their tails they can knock canoes in half. So when they come at a man, he has absolutely no power to protect himself.

"Suddenly this brother remembered Mark 16:18. As he stood there in the river, he said, 'Crocodiles, in the name of Jesus I command you to leave.'

"The crocodiles came another foot closer, then, swish, they turned around and swam away. The Moslems and the pagans stood on the bank of the river and said, 'We've never seen anything like this. The crocodiles obeyed that man.'

"The crocodile is one of the most stupid animals in the world. It has a very small brain. It is easier to make a dog or cat obey than a crocodile. But I tell you, when Jesus spoke to the crocodiles, they understood Him and went away. Once again the pagans saw the power of God performed before their very eyes.

"Those that saw this came to Jesus."

Today in the United States also, Christians—at the command of God—are taking dominion over nature. One example occurred in Illinois: a tornado was racing toward a small town. Everyone in the town had rushed into his storm cellar. A group of Christians gathered on a front lawn and said to the tornado, "In the name of Jesus Christ we command you not to strike our town."

What do you think happened? The tornado lifted on the outskirts of the town, crossed high over, and hit the earth again, right past the town.

A similar thing happened to me. On June 30, 1976, my wife and I were having a wedding dedication service outside at her parents' home in Penticton, B. C. We were doing this purely for the glory of God, desiring to give a witness for Christ to her friends. Normally this was the dry season, but it had been raining almost solid for two days. We had all been praying that the rain would stop, but it continued. The dedication was to start at 3:30 and about 2 o'clock I went outside in the rain, and walked around praying. As I was praying that the rain would stop, God said to me, "Prayer is not enough. I want you to take dominion over the rain." My reaction was, "Who—me?". It took me about fifteen minutes of confessing my sins and drawing close to God in the Holy Spirit, before I felt under His control and power enough to say, "Rain, in the name of Jesus Christ I command you to stop until after this wedding dedication is over." Praise God! Within an hour there was the most beautiful blue sky and sunshine, which remained all through the dedication and the dinner that followed (all of which was out-of-doors). Then, just as we were taking up the tablecloths, a few raindrops began to fall.

Now, I don't think that I could go out just any old time and take dominion over the rain. It has to be when God tells us to, and we have to do it under *His* control. However, when He speaks to us, He expects us to obey and follow. The end result will always glorify Him!

GOD'S MIRACULOUS PROTECTION

God protects His children, even more than we protect our children. If necessary He will use miraculous, supernatural power to do this. We are all familiar with the exciting deliverance of the children of Israel from bondage in Egypt. As Pharoah was chasing them, they were backed up against the Red Sea. God miraculously dried up the sea bed so that they could cross en masse. Once they arrived on the other side, the waters filled in and drowned Pharoah's army. This is certainly an example of God, by miraculous power, protecting His people.

However, there is an even more wondrous way in which He protects His children. God can and does send spiritual beings to do battle for us. I am so glad that this is the case, because the spiritual conflict will grow hotter and heavier as the Tribulation apporaches and occurs. We will need these angelic warriors from God to defend us. We will look closely at them in the next chapter.

15

PREPARING FOR

SUPERNATURAL WARFARE

I would like to begin with one of the many instances in the Old Testament of supernatural warfare. In this case, Elisha, a prophet of God, single-handedly defeated a great army, as told in II Kings 6:

8 Now the King of Syria was warring against Israel; and he counseled with his servants saying, "In such and such a place shall be my camp."

9 And the man of God sent *word* to the king of Israel saying, "Beware that you do not pass this place, for the Syrians are coming down there."

10 And the king of Israel sent to the place about which the man of God had told him; thus he warned him, so that he guarded himself there, more than once or twice.

11 Now the heart of the king of Syria was enraged over this thing; and he called his servants and said to them, "Will you tell me which of us is for the king of Israel?"

12 And one of his servants said, "No, my lord, O king; but Elisha, the prophet who is in Israel, tells the king of Israel the words that you speak in your bedroom."

13 So he said, "Go and see where he is, that I may send and take him." And it was told him, saying, "Behold, he is in Dothan."

14 And he sent horses and chariots and a great army there, and they came by night and surrounded the city.

15 Now when the attendant of the man of God had risen early and gone out, behold, an army with horses and chariots was circling

the city. And his servant said to him. "Alas, my master! What shall we do?"

16 So he answered, "Do not fear, for those who are with us are more than those who are with them."

17 Then Elisha prayed and said, "O LORD, I pray, open his eyes that he may see." And the LORD opened the servant's eyes, and he saw; and behold, the mountain was full of horses and chariots of fire all around Elisha.

18 And when they came down to him, Elisha prayed to the LORD and said, "Strike this people with blindness, I pray." So He struck them with blindness according to the word of Elisha.

19 Then Elisha said to them, "This is not the way, nor is this the city; follow me and I will bring you to the man whom you seek." And he brought them to Samaria.

20 And it came about when they had come into Samaria, that Elisha said, "O Lord, open the eyes of these *men,* that they may see." So the LORD opened their eyes, and they saw; and behold, they were in the midst of Samaria.

21 Then the king of Israel when he saw them, said to Elisha, "My father, shall I kill them? Shall I kill them?"

22 And he answered, "You shall not kill *them.* Would you kill those you have taken captive with your sword and with your bow? Set bread and water before them, that they may eat and drink and go to their master."

23 So he prepared a great feast for them; and when they had eaten and drunk he sent them away, and they went to their master. And the marauding bands of Syria did not come again into the land of Israel.

Here we see Elisha, the man of God, defeat the entire Syrian army by the power of God. Until Elisha's servant's eyes were opened spiritually, he could not see that the mountain was full of the Lord's army of heavenly hosts. I believe that same heavenly army is with us now; we need only become aware of it and learn to utilize the power that God has given to us.

I am certain that you can think of many more examples of supernatural warfare in the Old Testament. There was Samson killing 3,000 Philistines by pulling the house down on them; Joshua taking the city of Jericho by marching around it; Gideon, with his tiny army of men with pitchers, torches and trumpets, defeating the army of Midian; and armies who were opposing the children of Israel, defeated by a rain of large stones and, in another situation, by an attack of dysentery.

One notable example is the case where Amalek came out to fight against Israel. Joshua and some of his men went to fight Amalek in the valley, while Moses went up to the top of the hill. When Moses held his hands up Israel prevailed, and when he let his hands down Amalek prevailed. Eventually Aaron and Hur had to support Moses' hands and hold them steady until sunset. Thus Joshua overwhelmed Amalek and his people with the sword (Exodus 17:8-13).

Where was the battle won? Did Joshua or Moses win the battle? I believe that it was actually won in the heavenlies, although the physical manifestations of it had to occur on the earth.

It is this type of war and warfare, involving a combination of natural and supernatural, that we are dealing with in this chapter. The battles are actually being fought in the heavenlies, but there are very real manifestations on the earth. In this warfare, you—as a born-again believer in Jesus Christ—are either an asset or a liability to God.

If a group of rioters or looters were coming up your driveway to attack you and your family, or to steal your food and leave you to starve to death, and if you felt before the Lord you should fight them, would you rather fight them in the natural or supernatural? I am sure that your answer is the same as mine. I would much rather fight them in the supernatural. However, the time when rioters are walking up your driveway is too late to *begin* to move in the supernatural realm. We must now begin walking close to God—sensitive to, and empowered by, His Spirit—so that when the time comes, we will be able to use supernatural force, of course under His direction and control, and use it effectively.

A LOOK AT THE ENEMY

Let me first ask a question. Let's suppose that you and I got into a fight and you hit me with a baseball bat, and then I took my baseball bat and hit your shadow. Again you hit me, and again I hit your shadow. After we did this a number of times, you would think that I was quite foolish, because I was not fighting the real thing, but only your shadow. Is it possible that in this spiritual warfare we tend to fight shadows rather than the actual enemy? Let's look in Ephesians 6:

> 10 Finally, be strong in the Lord, and in the strength of His might.
>
> 11 Put on the full armor of God, that you may be able to stand firm against the schemes of the devil.
>
> 12 For our struggle is not against flesh and blood, but against the rulers, against the powers, against the world forces of this darkness, against the spiritual *forces* of wickedness in the heavenly *places*.
>
> 13 Therefore, take up the full armor of God, that you may be able to resist in the evil day, and having done everything, to stand firm.

Here we see that we are not wrestling against flesh and blood. Flesh and blood constitute the shadow. How often do we pray about someone at work who is irritating us, our neighbors who are causing us turmoil, our children who know how to drive us up the wall, or someone in our fellowship or church group who perturbs us by his behavior? If we are struggling to change the behavior of these people, we are wrestling against flesh and blood. Right?

But the Bible says that our struggle is not against flesh and blood, but against Satan and his demonic organization. Rather than wrestling with people, we should be coming against the evil spirits that are causing these people to act as they do. In that way we would be attacking the real cause of the problem, and not just the shadow.

I happen to be a football fan. When a football team is going to play another team, they send out scouts several weeks ahead of time to watch the games of the opponents. These scouts take movies, and draw diagrams. Before the team plays this particular opponent, the scout thoroughly briefs them, and they usually even have a special "opponents squad" that actually runs the plays that the opponent is likely to run. All of this effort is made so that the team can "know their opponent" and not be caught unaware.

The reason that many Christians lose significant battles to Satan is because they do not "know the opponent." I would therefore like us to briefly take a look at our opponent.

We all know that Satan is a fallen angel. As such he can only be in one place at a time and, therefore, he has to have an organization, with—I'm sure—an excellent communication system to keep him and his cohorts informed as to what is going on. In reading Daniel 10, it appears that Satan has a number of "generals," also fallen angels, in charge of various geographic areas. Under these fallen-angel generals are colonels, lieutenants, sergeants, and so forth, of evil angels (evil spirits). These are all part of the kingdom of Satan. Thus, when we feel that we are being attacked in the spiritual realm, more often than not it is one of Satan's demons harassing us, rather than Satan himself. Yes, Satan has a kingdom, according to Matthew 12:

> 24 But when the Pharisees heard it, they said, "This man casts out demons only by Beelzebul the ruler of the demons."
>
> 25 And knowing their thoughts He said to them, "Any kingdom divided against itself is laid waste; and any city or house divided against itself shall not stand.
>
> 26 "And if Satan casts out Satan, he is divided against himself; how then shall his kingdom stand?

What most people don't realize is that all non-Christians are part of Satan's kingdom. In 1 John 3 we read:

> 7 Little children, let no one deceive you; the one who practices righteousness is righteous, just as He is righteous;
>
> 8 the one who practices sin is of the devil; for the devil has sinned from the beginning. The Son of God appeared for this purpose, that He might destroy the works of the devil.

A simple definition of sin is *living independent of God.* With this in mind, we see that it is not only the "bad" non-Christians who belong to Satan, but also all non-Christians, even the "good" religious leaders who do not know Jesus Christ as their personal Savior. In John 8 we read:

> 13 The Pharisees therefore said to Him, "You are bearing witness of Yourself; Your witness is not true." . . .
>
> 44 "You are of *your* father the devil, and you want to do the desires of your father. He was a murderer from the beginning, and does

not stand in the truth, because there is no truth in him. Whenever he speaks a lie, he speaks from his own *nature;* **for he is a liar, and the father of lies.**

No matter how good, wonderful or moral someone may be, if they do not *know Jesus Christ* as their Savior, they are part of Satan's kingdom and they are our blood enemies. This is why God commands us to not be unequally yoked together with unbelievers (2 Corinthians 6:14). If you are considering marrying a non-Christian, you are considering marrying someone who belongs to a kingdom that is completely opposed to Jesus Christ, Whom we love. If you are considering going into business with somebody who does not know Jesus Christ, you are considering something far worse than going into business with a Communist or a Nazi. This is not peace time—we are at war! This is not to say that we shouldn't love these people and do anything we can to help them. The thing that is wrong is to enter into relationships wherein their decisions (influenced by Satan) can affect our future.

Wherever you are sitting reading this book—in your home, at your office, or maybe in an airport—I would like to ask you what you would do if a 1,000-pound hungry lion were to come charging into the room where you are, roaring, licking his chops, viciously looking for someone to devour? I am sure that you would either run or do something to protect yourself. You certainly would not placidly sit there. 1 Peter 5:8-9 tells us that Satan *is* a roaring lion, prowling about looking for someone to devour. And that someone that he is after is you or me, dear Christian brother. He will use anything in his kingdom to help him in his effort to defeat us. "Wherefore come out from among them and be ye separate, saith the Lord" (2 Corinthians 6:17a *KJV*).

LET'S LOOK AT *OUR* ARMY!

Jesus Christ, the Son of God, is the head of our army. Christ also has His "angel generals," which are called archangels. But like us, they use the power of the Lord, and not their own strength, in this battle. We see in the book of Jude:

> 9 But Michael the archangel, when he disputed with the devil and argued about the body of Moses, did not dare pronounce against him a railing judgment, but said, "THE LORD REBUKE YOU."

Here "General" Michael fought against Satan, but rebuked him in the name of the Lord. To me it is exciting that our angel generals can effectually battle against Satan by utilizing the power of our Commander in Chief. Still more exciting is the fact that you and I can also battle effectively against Satan, utilizing the same power.

In addition to angel generals, God's army also has a rank of angels assigned to protect Christians. I used to think that the concept of "guardian angels" was a nice thing to tell little kids, but that it did not have any reality. However, Jesus Christ straightened me out. We see His statement of the facts in Matthew 18:

> 10 "See that you do not despise one of these little ones, for I say to you, that their angels in heaven continually behold the face of My Father who is in heaven.

Here Jesus says that each of the little children has an angel in heaven. Psalm 91, one of my favorite Psalms, also beautifully says that God delegates angels to watch over us and protect us:

> 1 He who dwells in the shelter of the Most High
>   Will abide in the shadow of the Almighty.
> 2 I will say to the LORD, "My refuge and my fortress,
>   My God, in whom I trust!"
> 3 For it is He who delivers you from the snare of the trapper,
>   And from the deadly pestilence.
> 4 He will cover you with His pinions,
>   And under His wings you may seek refuge;
>   His faithfulness is a shield and bulwark.
> 5 You will not be afraid of the terror by night,
>   Or of the arrow that flies by day;
> 6 Of the pestilence that stalks in darkness,
>   Or of the destruction that lays waste at noon.
> 7 A thousand may fall at your side,
>   And ten thousand at your right hand;
>   But it shall not approach you.

8   You will only look on with your eyes,
    And see the recompense of the wicked.
9   For you have made the LORD, my refuge,
    Even the Most High, your dwelling place.
10 No evil will befall you,
    Nor will any plague come near your tent.
11 For He will give his angels charge concerning you,
    To guard you in all your ways.
12 They will bear you up in their hands,
    Lest you strike your foot against a stone.
13 You will tread upon the lion and cobra,
    The young lion and the serpent you will trample down.
14 "Because he has loved Me, therefore I will deliver him;
    I will set him *securely* on high, because he has known My name.

Verse 11 states that He will give His angels charge over us to guard us in all of our ways, because we have known His name.

Unfortuantely, not very much is written about angels. This is why Billy Graham recently wrote the book entitled *Angels: God's Secret Agents* (published by Pocket Books). It is an excellent book and I would recommend it. In introducing the subject, he says (pages 14 and 15):

"Dr. S. W. Mitchell, a celebrated Philadelphia neurologist, had gone to bed after an exceptionally tiring day. Suddenly he was awakened by someone knocking on his door. Opening it he found a little girl, poorly dressed and deeply upset. She told him her mother was very sick and asked him if he would please come with her. It was a bitterly cold, snowy night, but though he was bone tired, Dr. Mitchell dressed and followed the girl.

"As *Reader's Digest* reports the story, he found the mother desperately ill with pneumonia. After arranging for medical care, he complimented the sick woman on the intelligence and persistence of her little daughter. The woman looked at him strangely and then said, 'My daughter died a month ago.' She added, 'Her shoes and coat are in the clothes closet there.' Dr. Mitchell, amazed and perplexed, went to the closet and opened the door. There hung the very coat worn by the little girl who had brought him to tend to her mother. It was warm and dry and could not possibly have been out in the wintry night.

"Could the doctor have been called in the hour of desperate need by an angel who appeared as this woman's young daughter? Was this the work of God's angels on behalf of the sick woman?

"The Reverend John G. Patton, a missionary in the New Hebrides Islands, tells a thrilling story involving the protective care of angels. Hostile natives surrounded his mission headquarters one night, intent on burning the Pattons out and killing them. John Patton and his wife prayed all during that terror-filled night that God would deliver them. When daylight came they were amazed to see the attackers unaccountably leave. They thanked God for delivering them.

"A year later, the chief of the tribe was converted to Jesus Christ, and Mr. Patton, remembering what had happened, asked the chief what had kept him and his men from burning down the house and killing them. The chief replied in surprise, 'Who were all those men you had with you there?' The missionary answered, 'There were no men there; just my wife and I.' The chief argued that they had seen many men standing guard— hundreds of big men in shining garments with drawn swords in their hands. They seemed to circle the mission station so that the natives were afraid to attack. Only then did Mr. Patton realize that God had sent His angels to protect them. The chief agreed that there was no other explanation. Could it be that God had sent a legion of angels to protect His servants, whose lives were being endangered?"

In the last two verses of the first chapter of Hebrews, the writer points out that angels are ministering spirits (serving spirits) "sent out to render service for the sake of those who will inherit salvation." The angels are sent out to be *our* servants! Do you believe this? If so, when was the last time you thanked God for having an angel do something for you?

I certainly am not advocating worshipping angels or becoming overly concerned about them. Our emphasis and focus must be on Jesus Christ. Yet God has created angels and given them to us for a real purpose. We should be utilizing them properly in our spiritual warfare.

As well as all of the angels being a part of God's army, all born-again Christians are part of Christ's kingdom and army. Unfortunately, many Christians do not even realize that we are at war, or that they are needed for the battle. Spiritually they are AWOL (Absent WithOut Leave). They need to be awakened and to become cognizant that a battle is going on, and that it is urgent for them to get involved. These dear Christians tend to sing "Onward Christian Soldiers," while sitting around in spiritual civilian clothes polishing their spiritual fingernails. I yearn that all Christians would heed God's call, join the fight and utilize the power that God has given to us through Jesus Christ.

THE INTENSITY OF THE BATTLE
WILL INCREASE

We are in a battle now which has been going on for a long time. In writing to Christians during the first century, James had this to say in the fourth chapter of his letter:

> 2 You lust and do not have; *so* you commit murder. And you are envious and cannot obtain; *so* you fight and quarrel. You do not have because you do not ask.
>
> 3 You ask and do not receive, because you ask with wrong motives, so that you may spend *it* on your pleasures.
>
> 4 You adulteresses, do you not know that friendship with the world is hostility toward God? Therefore whoever wishes to be a friend of the world makes himself an enemy of God.
>
> 5 Or do you think that the Scripture speaks to no purpose: "He jealously desires the Spirit which He has made to dwell in us"?
>
> 6 But He gives a greater grace. Therefore *it* says, "GOD IS OPPOSED TO THE PROUD, BUT GIVES GRACE TO THE HUMBLE."
>
> 7 Submit therefore to God. Resist the devil and he will flee from you.
>
> 8 Draw near to God and He will draw near to you. Cleanse your hands, you sinners; and purify your hearts, you double-minded.

It says here very clearly that whoever is a friend of the world is an enemy of God. Are you a friend of the world? Only you can answer that. I hope that you ask yourself this question very seriously and honestly, and ask God whether or not *He* thinks you are a friend of the world. If you are, then even as a Christian, you are a traitor to God. You have switched over to the side of the enemy. Verses 7 and 8 tell us what to do if we find ourselves in this condition: submit to God and draw close to Him, cleanse our hands, purify our hearts and resist the devil. After we have done this, the devil will flee from us.

These verses also point out that fighting and quarreling among Christians is of Satan. Unfortunately, much of what many of us do aids Satan in this war. It behooves us to hold these things before God to be sure that we are solidly, 100 percent in the Lord's army, hating the enemy and evil and serving the Lord with all of our heart.

In this warfare, another trick that Satan has is to come in and try to steal what rightfully belongs to Christians. Many of us have memorized John 10:10b as part of the Four Spiritual Laws of Campus Crusade. We tend to neglect John 10:10a. In this verse Christ is contrasting Himself to Satan. In the first part of the verse Christ compares Satan to a thief:

> 10 "The thief comes only to steal, and kill, and destroy; I came that they might have life, and might have *it* abundantly."

Satan is the thief, and what is it that he steals from Christians? Their peace, their joy, their victory, their power. After appropriating these things, Satan takes them into his house. In Matthew 12 Christ tells us how to get our rightful possessions back out of Satan's house (the strong man):

> 25 And knowing their thoughts He said to them, "Any kingdom divided against itself is laid waste; and any city or house divided against itself shall not stand.
>
> 26 "And if Satan casts out Satan, he is divided against himself; how then shall his kingdom stand?
>
> 27 "And if I by Beelzebul cast out demons, by whom do your sons cast them out? Consequently they shall be your judges.
>
> 28 "But if I cast out demons by the Spirit of God, then the kingdom of God has come upon you.
>
> 29 "Or how can anyone enter the strong man's house and carry off his property, unless he first binds the strong *man*? And then he will plunder his house.

Here we see that before we can get these things back, we must bind the strong man. Satan can be bound by prayer, in the name of our Lord Jesus Christ. After realizing this, a verse that had confused me most of my Christian life began to make sense for the first time. It is found in Matthew 18:

> 18 "Truly I say to you, whatever you shall bind on earth shall have been bound in heaven; and whatever you loose on earth shall have been loosed in heaven.

What this is saying is that whatever we bind here on earth on our knees, will be bound in the heavenlies where the war is actually going on. If we bind Satan on our knees, the Bible promises that he will be bound in heavenly places. Similarly, if in prayer we loose our peace or our joy from his house, it will be loosed in the heavenlies and returned to us. Satan would love to have every Christian live a defeated tumultuous, unjoyful life. The things that he would steal from us *belong* to us as our inheritance in Christ Jesus. In this spiritual warfare *we need* to bind Satan and take back these possessions that are ours by right.

During the Tribulation, when Satan is cast out of heaven, this war will become unbelievably intense. In Revelation 12 we read:

> 9 And the great dragon was thrown down, the serpent of old who is called the devil and Satan, who deceives the whole world; he was thrown down to the earth, and his angels were thrown down with him. . . .
>
> 12 "For this reason, rejoice, O heavens and you who dwell in them. Woe to the earth and the sea; because the devil has come down to you, having great wrath, knowing that he has *only* a short time."
>
> 13 And when the dragon saw that he was thrown down to the earth, he persecuted the woman who gave birth to the male *child.*
>
> 14 And the two wings of the great eagle were given to the woman, in order that she might fly into the wilderness to her place, where she was nourished for a time and times and half a time, from the presence of the serpent.
>
> 15 And the serpent poured water like a river out of his mouth after the woman, so that he might cause her to be swept away with the flood.
>
> 16 And the earth helped the woman, and the earth opened its mouth and drank up the river which the dragon poured out of his mouth.
>
> 17 And the dragon was enraged with the woman, and went off to make war with the rest of her offspring, who keep the commandments of God and hold to the testimony of Jesus.

There is much I would like to share about the woman and the man child, but I do not have the space to adequately deal with this. Suffice it to say that they represent groups of Christians. Here we see Satan thrown down to the earth, enraged and making such impassioned war on these Christians that some of them (the woman) have to flee into the wilderness. We can see that the intensity of the war will continually increase. Many of us who have wrestled against evil spirits and Satan himself already know a little about the power that the enemy has. And yet I am convinced that we have seen nothing, compared to what we will see when his full fury is unleashed against us.

When we get into this vigorous warfare, moving in the supernatural realm will be absolutely essential. In reading about the two witnesses in Revelation 11, we see that when anyone desires to harm them, fire proceeds out of their mouth and devours their enemies:

> 3 "And I will grant *authority* to my two witnesses, and they will prophesy for twelve hundred and sixty days, clothed in sackcloth."
>
> 4 These are the two olive trees and the two lampstands that stand before the Lord of the earth.
>
> 5 And if any one desires to harm them, fire proceeds out of their mouth and devours their enemies; and if any one would desire to harm them, in this manner he must be killed.

If you think that calling down fire to devour enemies is a new thing, or is just symbolic, you should be aware of what Elijah did, as recorded in 2 Kings 1:

> 9 Then *the king* sent to him a captain of fifty with his fifty. And he went up to him, and behold, he was sitting on the top of the hill. And he said to him, "O man of God, the king says, 'Come down.'"
>
> 10 And Elijah answered and said to the captain of fifty, "If I am a man of God, let fire come down from heaven and consume you and your fifty." Then fire came down from heaven and consumed him and his fifty.
>
> 11 So he again sent to him another captain of fifty with his fifty. And he answered and said to him, "O man of God, thus says the king, 'Come down quickly.'"
>
> 12 And Elijah answered and said to them, "If I am a man of God, let fire come down from heaven and consume you and your fifty." Then the fire of God came down from heaven and consumed him and his fifty.
>
> 13 So he again sent the captain of a third fifty with his fifty. When the third captain of fifty went up, he came and bowed down on his knees before Elijah, and begged him and said to him, "O man of God, please let my life and the lives of these fifty servants of yours be precious in your sight.

14 "Behold fire came down from heaven, and consumed the first two captains of fifty with their fifties; but now let my life be precious in your sight."

15 And the angel of the LORD said to Elijah, "Go down with him; do not be afraid of him." So he arose and went down with him to the king.

Here we see Elijah calling down fire to kill those who would capture him. It is significant that a prerequisite appears to be that he was a man of God. One characteristic of a man of God is that he *listens* to God on every occasion. Many of us would *assume* that after God sent fire on two occasions, this would be His will for the third as well. When God redirects us, we must be careful to change direction quickly in order to remain in His will, and thus have access to His power.

BE WILLING TO DIE FOR CHRIST

What we have looked at so far is powerful and wonderful. We have just seen that no one could kill the two witnesses. Later in Revelation 11, however, when they have finished their testimony, we see that the beast that comes up out of the abyss will make war with them, overcome them, and kill them (verse 7). This is purely conjecture on my part, but I get the feeling that the two witnesses, like Christ, were willing to voluntarily lay down their lives that God might be glorified in an even greater way. (And God was glorified because after three and a half days they came back to life and great fear fell upon all those who beheld them—Revelation 11:11-12).

A time of real persecution lies ahead for Christians, if not *before* the Tribulation, certainly during it. We have already seen that Christians will not be able to buy or sell anything, they will be criminals and many of them will be beheaded (executed) because of their faith in Christ. One of the five major calamities that David Wilkerson sees coming to America—as told in his book, *The Vision,* is severe persecution of Christians.

God layed his hands on me as a small child and called me to do His work. Even in my young years I felt in my spirit that I would see Christians persecuted and meeting in caves and aban-

doned basements before I died. We have seen Christians persecuted in our lifetime in Korea, China, Russia, Hungary, Romania
and so on. What makes us think that the Christians in America
will be spared?

If God does allow persecution to come to Christians in the
western world, there will be a definite purpose for it. Persecution invariably purifies the church and deepens the dedication
of those who remain true to Christ.

I believe that Jesus Christ foresaw not only the persecution
of the Christians in the first two centuries, but the periodic persecution of them all the way to the end of the age. Therefore,
He had some strong things to say in relation to this, such as what
we read in Matthew 16:

> 24 Then Jesus said to His disciples, "If any one wishes to come
> after Me, let him deny himself, and take up his cross, and follow Me.
> 25 "For whoever wishes to save his life shall lose it; but whoever
> loses his life for My sake shall find it.

Twice more he addresses this subject:

> 38 "And he who does not take his cross and follow after Me is
> not worthy of Me.
> 39 "He who has found his life shall lose it, and he who has lost
> his life for my sake shall find it (Matthew 10).

> 24 "Truly, truly, I say to you, unless a grain of wheat falls into
> the earth and dies, it remains by itself alone; but if it dies, it bears
> much fruit.
> 25 "He who loves his life loses it; and he who hates his life in this
> world shall keep it to life eternal (John 12).

When Christ talks about taking up your cross and following Him, we must remember that the cross was an instrument
of torture and execution. Today it would be equivalent to Him
saying, "Take up your electric chair or guillotine and follow
Me." And then to make sure that the people understood what
He was saying, in every case He goes on to emphasize the fact
that we should be willing to die (physically) for Him.

In laying down our life, we are still very close to Christ
and in His love, as told in Romans 8:

35 Who shall separate us from the love of Christ? Shall tribulation, or distress, or persecution, or famine, or nakedness, or peril, or sword?

36 Just as it is written,

> "FOR THY SAKE WE ARE BEING PUT TO DEATH ALL DAY LONG;
> WE WERE CONSIDERED AS SHEEP TO BE SLAUGHTERED."

37 But in all these things we overwhelmingly conquer through Him who loved us.

38 For I am convinced that neither death, nor life, nor angels, nor principalities, nor things present, nor things to come, nor powers,

39 nor height, nor depth, nor any other created thing, shall be able to separate us from the love of God, which is in Christ Jesus our Lord.

This passage is so beautiful. As a Christian is dying for the sake of Christ, he can be assured that God is loving him and appreciating the sacrifice of his life at that moment.

Most Christians fear death, which is very strange. I believe that what Red Harper said, right after the first atomic bomb was dropped, epitomizes what we should feel. I heard him say: "This here atomic bomb don't bother me at all. It would just be BOOM, hello Lord!" Death is simply stepping out of this messed up world into a beautiful eternity with our Lord.

Nevertheless, there is a time ahead when Christians, maybe you and I, will be called upon to go to jail, be tortured and perhaps even die for the sake of our faith in Jesus Christ. God *can* and *will* give us the strength at the time so that, like the Christians in the early Colosseum, we could go singing and praising God to our deaths and we, like them, would gladly lay down our lives for the sake of Him who died for us.

As this time draws closer, there are things that you may want to prayerfully consider, such as memorizing many of the verses in the Bible that give comfort to Christians who are being persecuted and who are suffering. I believe that in the heat of the battle, the Holy Spirit can use those verses you have memorized to beautifully encourage and strengthen your soul.

BALANCE OF POWER

The exciting thing is that though we are presently in the war, we know the eventual outcome—Jesus Christ will win! In fact, this is the reason that Christ came:

8 . . . The Son of God appeared for this purpose, that He might destroy the works of the devil (1 John 3).

In Chapter 4 of 1 John, we read:

4 You are from God, little children, and have overcome them; because greater is He who is in you than he who is in the world.

Isn't that tremendous? We know that Jesus Christ is greater than Satan and that in the end He will totally destroy the works of Satan.

In II Corinthians 2 we read:

14 But thanks be to God, who always leads us in His triumph in Christ, and manifests through us the sweet aroma of the knowledge of Him in every place.

Here Paul is thanking God because Jesus Christ always leads us in the triumphal parade. We are more than conquerors through Him who loved us (Romans 8:37).

As the final battle for this war begins we see our Commander in Chief appearing, in Revelation 19, as follows:

11 And I saw heaven opened; and behold, a white horse, and He who sat upon it *is* called Faithful and True; and in righteousness He judges and wages war.

12 And His eyes *are* a flame of fire, and upon His head *are* many diadems; and He has a name written *upon Him* which no one knows except Himself.

13 And *He is* clothed with a robe dipped in blood; and His name is called the Word of God.

14 And the armies which are in heaven, clothed in fine linen, white *and* clean, were following Him on white horses.

This is the point in time at which I believe the Scriptures teach that the Rapture will occur. We will be caught up into heaven to meet the Lord in the air and become part of His army to follow Him back to the earth. With Him from above, we will see the great climactic battle in this warfare. If we continue to read in Revelation 19, we see what He is like and what the last battle will be like:

> 15 And from His mouth comes a sharp sword, so that with it He may smite the nations; and He will rule them with a rod of iron; and He treads the wine press of the fierce wrath of God, the Almighty.
>
> 16 And on His robe and on His thigh He has a name written, "KING OF KINGS, AND LORD OF LORDS."
>
> 17 And I saw an angel standing in the sun; and he cried out with a loud voice, saying to all the birds which fly in midheaven, "Come, assemble for the great supper of God;
>
> 18 in order that you may eat the flesh of kings and the flesh of commanders and the flesh of mighty men and the flesh of horses and of those who sit on them and the flesh of all men, both free men and slaves, and small and great."
>
> 19 And I saw the beast and the kings of the earth and their armies, assembled to make war against Him who sat upon the horse, and against His army.
>
> 20 And the beast was seized, and with him the false prophet who performed the signs in his presence, by which he deceived those who had received the mark of the beast and those who worshipped his image; these two were thrown alive into the lake of fire which burns with brimstone.
>
> 21 And the rest were killed with the sword which came from the mouth of Him who sat upon the horse, and all the birds were filled with their flesh.

When this great and final battle (Armageddon) is fought, Jesus Christ is clearly going to be the victor. And with this victory, all that is evil will have been removed from the earth, and Satan will be bound for a thousand years. God will have finished with the task of plowing up the earth, purifying it and renewing it. He will then have achieved all that He set out to do at the beginning of the Tribulation. Jesus Christ will be back on this renewed earth, with His saints, ready to begin an exciting reign of one thousand years.

16

REIGNING WITH CHRIST

FOR ONE THOUSAND YEARS!

Now that the battle of Armageddon is over, the beast-dictator and the beast-prophet have been cast into the lake of fire, and Satan has been captured, we need to look at the Millennium —the one thousand years during which Christ will reign on the earth. Actually, very little is said in the New Testament about this thousand-year period. There are only four verses on it, all of which are found in Revelation 20:

1 And I saw an angel coming down from heaven, having the key of the abyss and a great chain in his hand.

2 And he laid hold of the dragon, the serpent of old, who is the devil and Satan, and bound him for a thousand years,

3 and threw him into the abyss, and shut *it* and sealed *it* over him, so that he should not deceive the nations any longer, until the thousand years were completed; after these things he must be released for a short time.

4 And I saw thrones, and they sat upon them, and judgment was given to them. And I *saw* the souls of those who had been beheaded because of their testimony of Jesus and because of the word of God, and those who had not worshiped the beast or his image, and had not received the mark upon their forehead and upon their hand; and they came to life and reigned with Christ for a thousand years.

From these few verses we see that Satan will not be on the earth during this one thousand years, and that the Christians who come back to life will reign with Christ. We also see that there is a special group of Christians who will sit on thrones and act as judges for Christ.

Almost everything else that we know about the Millennium has to be gleaned from the Old Testament. Let me be the first to admit that there are real difficulties with pulling prophecies out of the Old Testament and applying them to the Millennium. For example, one of the key passages in the Old Testament attributed to Christ's reign of a thousand years, is in Isaiah 11. But if you go back to the beginning of that prophecy (Isaiah 10: 24), you can see that it is a specific prophecy about a period of time in Israel's history. Thus, one could legitimately argue that this should not necessarily be applied to the Millennium. I would have to agree to a certain extent. The only reason that I would tend to apply Isaiah 11 to the Millennium is that, to my knowledge, this prophecy has not yet been fulfilled, and the only place wherein it appears that it will be fulfilled is during Christ's reign on earth. However, if one wishes to exclude all of the Old Testament passages, we would know very little about the Millennium.

What we would like to do in looking at the Millennium, is to utilize the passages that Biblical scholars normally attribute to this period. Many Bible scholars feel that the Old Testament references to "the day of the Lord" refer to the Millennium. Realizing that a thousand years in the eyes of the Lord is like a day (Psalm 90:4) and that the prophesied "day of the Lord" is yet to come, this seems like a reasonable assumption. If we err by incorrectly applying verses to the Millennium, or if we exclude other prophecies that should be applied, I trust that the Lord will forgive and make real to your hearts what is truth.

NATURE IS RESTORED

Nature, which has been under a curse since Adam's fall, is restored to its initial freedom and glory at this point in time. I believe the best passage to show this is found in Romans 8:

19 For the anxious longing of the creation waits eagerly for the revealing of the sons of God.

20 For the creation was subjected to futility, not of its own will, but because of Him who subjected it, in hope

21 that the creation itself also will be set free from its slavery to corruption into the freedom of the glory of the children of God.

22 For we know that the whole creation groans and suffers the pains of childbirth together until now.

23 And not only this, but we ourselves, having the first fruits of the Spirit, even we ourselves groan within ourselves, waiting eagerly for *our* adoption as sons, the redemption of our body.

I place the restoration of nature at the beginning of the Millennium for a number of reasons. First, it is obvious that during the Tribulation nature is not set free. Rather, it is in tremendous agony at that time. Secondly, verse 23 says that the bodies of the sons of God will be redeemed. This redemption of our bodies occurs at the Rapture—at the climax of the Tribulation when, in the twinkling of an eye, we will all be changed as we meet our Lord in the air. It is at this point—when the sons of God are made manifest—that creation is set free. I do not see how nature can be set free and our bodies redeemed until after the Tribulation.

Once nature has been set free, some of the things that we have read about in the Old Testament can occur. Let's look at the passage in Isaiah 11:

6 And the wolf will dwell with the lamb,
And the leopard will lie down with the kid,
And the calf and the young lion and the fatling together;
And a little boy will lead them.

7 Also the cow and the bear will graze;
Their young will lie down together;
And the lion will eat straw like the ox.

8 And the nursing child will play by the hole of the cobra
And the weaned child will put his hand on the viper's den.

9 They will not hurt or destroy in all My holy mountain,
For the earth will be full of the knowledge of the LORD
As the waters cover the sea.

10 Then it will come about in that day
That the nations will resort to the root of Jesse,
Who will stand as a signal for the peoples;
And His resting place will be glorious.

Here we see the wolf living in tranquility with the lamb and the leopard lying down with the kid. It is interesting to note that the lion lies down with the calf and the fatling, not with the lamb. I can not find any place in the Scriptures that talks about the lion and the lamb lying down together. I think that this commonly-referred-to combination is another one of our many misconceptions about what the Scriptures actually say. We see further that the lions no longer are meat eaters, but that they eat grass like the oxen. This means that they are no longer killers. A little baby, who still nurses, is able to play with a cobra without being harmed in any way. What a wonderful time it will be when all of nature is in loving harmony and peaceful coexistence!

Looking at the land itself, Ezekiel 36 portrays the renewal of the land to follow the purging and purification accomplished during the Tribulation.

> 33 'Thus says the Lord GOD, "On the day that I cleanse you from all your iniquities, I will cause the cities to be inhabited, and the waste places will be rebuilt.
> 34 "And the desolate land will be cultivated instead of being a desolation in the sight of everyone who passed by.
> 35 "And they will say, 'This desolate land has become like the garden of Eden; and the waste, desolate, and ruined cities are forti-fied *and* inhabited.'
> 36 "Then the nations that are left round about you will know that I, the LORD, have rebuilt the ruined places *and* planted that which is desolate; I, the LORD, have spoken and will do it."

The desolate lands (deserts, rocky places) will become like the garden of Eden. Isn't that wonderful! There are very few books about the Millennium, but there is one that I believe is head and shoulders above any of the others. It is entitled:

Millennium Man
by George Otis
Published by Bible Voice, Inc.
P. O. Box 7491, Van Nuys, CA 91409

Concerning the physical revamping of the earth during the Tribulation (in preparation for its "rebirth"), and the renewed planet earth of the Millennium, George Otis has this to say (pages 49-50):

"From all those bursts of earthquake-energy, not only will earth receive a facelift, but also newly increased land surface to provide more living area. 'Every valley shall be exalted, and every mountain and hill shall be made low: and the crooked shall be made straight, and the rough places plain' Isa. 40.

"Today it's fashionable to undertake urban renewal projects. Have you ever watched the rebuilding process? First the wrecking crews: Swarms of bulldozers, wrecking balls and dynamite reduce old, decaying structures to rubble. Along come the builders who 'magically' erect handsome, new facilities. Presto! The area is 'born again.'

"So it will be with this tired and abused planet. Physical earth also needs to be 'born again.' But before it can, there must be a clearing away of everything decadent. Our all-wise Heavenly Father knows He must 'PLOW UP THE EARTH,' root out and eliminate everything that won't harmonize with His Millennial-life blueprint.

"Through those earthquakes He will redistribute the waters and the lands—all within days. 'And there were voices, and thunders, and lightenings; and there was a great earthquake. . . . And every island fled away, and the mountains were not found' Rev. 16. Great firmament rearrangements which will both enhance the cosmetics of the planet and provide vast, new habitable land area. There is, presently, an enormous 140-million-square-mile land area hiding under our oceans. These 'land masses' include mountains higher than Everest and chasms deeper than the Grand Canyon. Realms to provide the most pleasant scenery.

"All present faults and strains will be relieved during that series of exploding quakes. When the dust settles, our planet will be entirely earthquake-free. 'Behold, the Lord maketh the earth empty, and maketh it waste, and turneth it upside down, and scattereth abroad the inhabitants thereof' Isa. 24.

"It may also be that the 22° tilt and the earth's wobble will be corrected by the finger of God at the same time. These may have been caused by the violence in Lucifer's rebellion. Meteorologists say these irregularities contribute to the climate extremes: hurricanes, floods, blizzards, droughts, etc.

"When her tilt and wobble are corrected, we will see an idealizing of the earth's climate. 'And I will cause the shower to come down in his season; there shall be showers of blessing. And the tree of the field shall yield her fruit' Ezek. 34. And through Isaiah, 'And the parched ground

shall become a pool, and thirsty land springs of water; in the habitation of
dragons, where each lay, shall be grass with reeds and rushes' Chapt. 35. . . .

"First, Armageddon, then: TO WORK! There will be limited time
for 'harping,'—Praise God! Earth will be plowed and ready for our loving
attention. Ready to be replanted, rebuilt and reorganized."

THE GOVERNMENT
DURING THE MILLENNIUM

We all know that during this era Christ will be the King of
the earth. ". . . the government shall be upon His shoulder . . ."
(Isaiah 9:6 *KJV*). I believe that many of His parables and analogies concerning the kingdom of God were referring to this period in time.

In trying to help people to understand what this kingdom
would be like, He gave the parable found in Luke 19:

11 And while they were listening to these things, He went on to
tell a parable, because He was near Jerusalem, and they supposed
that the kingdom of God was going to appear immediately.

12 He said therefore, "A certain nobleman went to a distant country to receive a kingdom for himself, and *then* return.

13 "And he called ten of his slaves, and gave them ten minas, and
said to them, 'Do business *with this* until I come *back.*'

14 "But his citizens hated him, and sent a delegation after him,
saying, 'We do not want this man to reign over us.'

15 "And it came about that when he returned, after receiving the
kingdom, he ordered that these slaves, to whom he had given the
money, be called to him in order that he might know what business
they had done.

16 "And the first appeared, saying, 'Master, your mina has made
ten minas more.'

17 "And he said to him, 'Well done, good slave, because you have
been faithful in a very little thing, be in authority over ten cities.'

18 "And the second came, saying, 'Your mina, master has made
five minas.'

19 "And he said to him also, 'And you are to be over five cities.'

20 "And another came, saying, 'Master, behold your mina, which
I kept put away in a handkerchief;

21 for I was afraid of you, because you are an exacting man; you
take up what you did not lay down, and reap what you did not sow.'

22 "He said to him, 'By your own words I will judge you, you worthless slave. Did you know that I am an exacting man, taking up what I did not lay down, and reaping what I did not sow?

23 'Then why did you not put the money in the bank, and having come, I would have collected it with interest?'

24 "And he said to the bystanders, 'Take the mina away, from him, and give it to the one who has the ten minas.'

25 "And they said to him, 'Master, he has ten minas *already.'*

26 "I tell you, that to everyone who has shall *more* be given, but from the one who does not have, even what he does have shall be taken away.

27 "But these enemies of mine, who did not want me to reign over them, bring them here, and slay them in my presence."

Here we see that to the overcomers—those Christians to whom Christ can say, "Well done"—He will give authority over ten cities. To other Christians who have followed Him less closely, He will give authority over five cities. And to some Christians, who had as much *potential* as the others, but did nothing, He will give no authority at all. We see that all Christians will not have the same level of authority during the Millennium. There will be a hierarchial structure, and our reward and our authority will depend on how we have served Him.

The citizenry of this Millennial kingdom of God will include all of the saints, as well as the unsaved people still alive at the conclusion of Armageddon. In addition to this, children will likely be born to the people without resurrection bodies. This entire social structure will be directed by King Jesus from Zion, at the edge of Jerusalem. He will delegate authority and power to the saints, who will reign over various designated areas. Without all of the strife of today, it should be a highly efficient system for managing the replanting and rebuilding on the renewed earth.

OUR BODIES DURING THE MILLENNIUM

We have already seen in Romans 8 that our bodies will be redeemed at the beginning of this new age. Philippians 3 tells us a little more about our new bodies:

> 20 For our citizenship is in heaven, from which also we eagerly wait for a Savior, the Lord Jesus Christ;
>
> 21 who will transform the body of our humble state into conformity with the body of His glory, by the exertion of the power that He has even to subject all things to Himself.

Our bodies will be changed into the likeness of His glorious body! If we look at the resurrection body of Christ, we see that time and space became irrelevant. He could walk through doors that were locked. He could go from point "A" to point "B" faster than by any means of transportation known in the first century. Like His, our bodies will be without spot or blemish. Our health will be perfect. This is fantastically presented in 1 Corinthians 15:

> 35 But some one will say, "How are the dead raised? And with what kind of body do they come?"
>
> 36 You fool! That which you sow does not come to life unless it dies;
>
> 37 and that which you sow, you do not sow the body which is to be, but a bare grain, perhaps of wheat or of something else.
>
> 38 But God gives it a body just as He wished, and to each of the seeds a body of its own. . . .
>
> 40 There are also heavenly bodies and earthly bodies, but the glory of the heavenly is one, and the *glory* of the earthly is another.
>
> 41 There is one glory of the sun, and another glory of the moon, and another glory of the stars; for star differs from star in glory.
>
> 42 So also is the resurrection of the dead. It is sown a perishable *body,* it is raised an imperishable *body;*
>
> 43 it is sown in dishonor, it is raised in glory; it is sown in weakness, it is raised in power;
>
> 44 it is sown a natural body, it is raised a spiritual body. If there is a natural body, there is also a spiritual *body.*

These new bodies will not have weakness, but *power.* They will be imperishable. Our new bodies will be recognizable to our friends. On the Mount of Transfiguration, Peter, James and John recognized Elijah and Moses who were talking to Jesus. After Jesus was resurrected and came to the disciples in the closed room, they recognized Him.

Our heavenly bodies are not going to be *just* spiritual without substance. Remember that the resurrected Jesus invited

Thomas to touch Him and He also participated in a fish fry in Galilee.

Gravity does not have a limiting effect on the resurrected body. As the disciples of Jesus watched in Acts 1, Jesus ascended into the clouds. Won't it be great to be able to move as the angels do? What a joy it will be to be able to fly (without wings) at any moment to the feet of King Jesus.

George Otis, in *Millennium Man,* views our new bodies this way (page 78):

"Have you ever looked at a group of senior citizens and tried to imagine what they looked like when they were younger? Won't it be fun, after translation, to see some of the lovely 'young women' we've always thought of as old ladies?

"Yes, Millennium saints will be vivacious and handsome! And this startling event will occur sometime soon: When He comes back He will take these dying bodies of ours and change them into GLORIOUS bodies like His own' Phil. 3, L.B. It seems almost too good to be true, doesn't it? Since this is now approaching 'Current Event' status, it might be profitable to look at it a bit closer.

"At some coming microsecond of time (in the twinkling of an eye) glorified saints will find themselves far better than in their finest prime years—with throbbing beauty, vitality and freshness! We will, however, still carry into glorification, the accumulation of character values which we developed;—but not the painful negatives from this life."

Our minds, being part of our bodies, will be made new and totally usable. Today scientists tell us that we use less than 10 percent of our brain. In our resurrected body, we should be able to use 100 percent of our brain. It is exciting to anticipate the wonderful things that will be invented and created during the Millennium. We could create ways to generate all the energy we need without any pollution whatsoever. We could create ways to feed the population with fantastic delicacies, without killing any of the animals. What an incredible life that is going to be!

PEACE FOR ONE THOUSAND YEARS

People today yearn for peace, which doesn't come. The Bible says that it will not come—that there will continually be wars and rumors of wars. It is only during the Millennium that we will have real peace. We read about this in Isaiah 2:

1 The word which Isaiah the son of Amoz saw concerning Judah and Jerusalem. Now it will come about that

2 In the last days,
The mountain of the house of the LORD
Will be established as the chief of the mountains,
And will be raised above the hills;
And all the nations will stream to it.

3 And many peoples will come and say,
"Come, let us go up to the mountain of the LORD,
To the house of the God of Jacob;
That He may teach us concerning His ways,
And that we may walk in His paths."
For the law will go forth from Zion,
And the word of the LORD from Jerusalem.

4 And He will judge between the nations,
And will render decisions for many peoples;
And they will hammer their swords into plowshares, and their
    spears into pruning hooks.
Nation will not lift up sword against nation,
And never again will they learn war.

Here we see the hammering of swords into plowshares and spears into pruning hooks. It is interesting that this not only implies peace, but also farming. There will be ground to plow and plant, and harvests to take in.

Can you imagine a thousand years without any violence? No killing, no murders, no maimings, no wars, no bloodshed? The Prince of Peace will reign supreme and His peace will be upon all of the earth!

A VIEW OF THE KINGDOM

John F. Walvoord, President of Dallas Theological Seminary has written a book entitled *The Millennial Kingdom* (Zondervan Publishing House). The following is his overview of the social, economic and physical aspects of the Millennium (pages 316-319):

"The fact that wars will cease during the millennium will have a beneficial effect upon both the social and economic life of the world. Instead of large expenditure for armaments, attention no doubt will be directed to improving the world in various ways. Even under present world conditions, a relief from taxation due to military expenditure would have a great effect upon the economy. This coupled with absolute justice, assuring minority people of government protection and greatly reduced crime, will establish a social and economic order far different from anything the world has ever experienced prior to the millennium. Many of the prophetic Scriptures such as Psalm 72 and Isaiah 11 testify to these unusual millennial conditions. . . .

"Another important factor in the millennium is the fact that the curse which descended upon the physical world because of Adam's sin apparently is lifted during the millennium. According to the prophet Isaiah: 'The wilderness and the dry land shall be glad; and the desert shall rejoice, and blossom as the rose. It shall blossom abundantly, and rejoice even with joy and singing; the glory of Lebanon shall be given unto it, the excellency of Carmel and Sharon; they shall see the glory of Jehovah, the excellency of our God' (Isa. 35:1-2). The rest of the thirty-fifth chapter of Isaiah continues in the same theme. Abundant rainfall characterizes the period (Isa. 30:23; 35:7) and the abundance of food and cattle are pictured (Isa. 30:23-24). Though the curse on the earth is only partly lifted as indicated by the continuance of death, and will remain in some measure until the new heaven and the new earth are brought in (Rev. 22:3), the land of Palestine will once again be a garden. The world in general will be delivered from the unproductiveness which characterized great portions of the globe in prior dispensations. . . .

"Widespread peace and justice, spiritual blessing, and abundance of food will result in a general era of prosperity such as the world has never known (Jer. 31:12; Ezek. 35:25-27; Joel 2:21-27; Amos 9:13-14). The many factors which produce poverty, distress, and unequal distribution of goods will to a great extent be nonexistent in the millennium. Labor problems which now characterize the world will be solved, and everyone will receive just compensation for his labors (Isa. 65:21-25; Jer. 31:5). Thus the curse which creation has endured since Adam's sin (Gen. 3:17-19) will be in part suspended as even animal creation will be changed (Isa. 11: 6-9; 65:26). . . .

"One of the predictions regarding the coming of the Messiah was that healing from sickness would characterize His reign. Though Christ healed many in His first advent, most of the prophecies seem to point to the millennial situation. Thus Isaiah writes: 'And the inhabitant shall not say, I am sick: the people that dwell therein shall be forgiven their iniquity' (Isa. 33:24). Those who have physical disability shall be healed of blindness and deafness (Isa. 29:18) and healing will be experienced in a similar way by others. Again Isaiah states: 'Then the eyes of the blind shall be opened, and the ears of the deaf shall be unstopped. Then shall the lame man leap as a hart, and the tongue of the dumb shall sing: for in the wilderness shall water break out, and streams in the desert' (Isa. 35: 5-6). The brokenhearted will be comforted and joy will replace mourning (Isa. 61:1-3). Longevity will apparently characterize the human race for Isaiah speaks of the death of a person one hundred years old as the death of a child (Isa. 65:20). The freedom from these human ills so common in the present world is in keeping with the lifting of many other aspects of the curse upon nature. Not only will people live much longer, but there will be also a tremendous increase in birth rate as children are born to those who survive the tribulation. Of this Jeremiah says: 'I will multiply them, and they shall not be a few; I will also glorify them, and they shall not be small. Their children also shall be as aforetime, and their congregation shall be established before me' (30:19-20). This blessing will not only characterize Israel, but also the Gentile in the millennial kingdom (Ezek. 47:22).

"Taken as a whole, the social and economic conditions of the millennium indicate a golden age in which the dreams of social reformists through the centuries will be realized, not through human effort but by the immediate presence and power of God and the righteous government of Christ. That mankind should again fall under such ideal circumstances and be ready to rebel against Christ at the close of the millennium is the answer to those who would put faith in the inherent goodness of man."

JERUSALEM AND ZION

Mount Zion is a hill right at the edge of Jerusalem. It overlooks the city. David never actually conquered Jerusalem, but ruled and reigned from Mount Zion, with Jerusalem at his feet. It is from Mount Zion that Christ, with us, will rule the world. When we sing songs such as "We're Marching to Zion," we should be looking forward to the time when we will be there on Zion with Christ, reigning over the entire earth. Isaiah, Jeremiah and Zechariah said the following of Zion:

> 5 then the LORD will create over the whole area of Mount Zion and over her assemblies a cloud by day, even smoke, and the brightness of a flaming fire by night; for over all the glory will be a canopy (Isaiah 4).

6 "For there shall be a day when watchmen
On the hills of Ephraim shall call out,
'Arise, and let us go up *to* Zion,
To the LORD our God.'" (Jeremiah 31).

2 "Thus says the LORD of hosts, 'I am exceedingly jealous for Zion, yes, with great wrath I am jealous for her.'
3 "Thus says the LORD, 'I will return to Zion and will dwell in the midst of Jerusalem. Then Jerusalem will be called the City of Truth, and the mountain of the LORD of hosts *will be called* the Holy Mountain' (Zechariah 8).

Mount Zion is the mountain of the Lord, the holy mountain, and the place where the cornerstone is set (Isaiah 28:16). To be sure, there is a spiritual Zion and a spiritual kingdom. The spiritual kingdom is within us, as Christ reigns within our hearts. Since many books have been written about the spiritual kingdom and the spiritual Zion, we will not elaborate on these here. However, it is important to realize that there is also a physical Zion from which we, as Christ's princes and lieutenants, will help Christ rule the earth for a thousand years.

17

THE HAPPY UN-ENDING

This book doesn't have a happy ending; it has something infinitely superior—a "happy un-ending." The happiness that we will be describing in this chapter, we will enjoy for time without end.

A QUICK REVIEW

Before we look at this "happy un-ending," let's pause for a moment and see where we have come thus far. We began by examining *when* the Rapture would occur, and saw that the historical view of the church was that the Rapture would occur at the end of the Tribulation. The pre-Tribulation Rapture theory, which is of recent origin, began with the visions of a young girl, Margaret McDonald, in 1830. This theory was picked up by Edward Irving, and was later really popularized by C. I. Scofield, editor of the *Scofield Reference Bible,* and by Dallas Theological Seminary. We examined a number of problems with the pre-Tribulation Rapture theory. I have found that many laymen and clergy alike, who today subscribe to this theory, have never really examined the Scriptures with an open mind as to the possibility that the Rapture will occur at the end of the Tribulation. Instead they have taken the word of the present day "authorities" on the subject that it will occur prior to the Tribulation.

Even after talking with a number of men who are accepted authorities on the pre-Tribulation position, I have not found adequate answers within that theory to some fundamental Biblical questions. After all the arguments have been made, and the dust has settled, there remain two items that stand like the Rock of Gibraltar. 1 Corinthians 15 states that Christians who have died will be raised imperishable, and Christians who are alive will be changed, *at the last trumpet.* This means that these events occur either at the seventh trumpet in Revelation, or after that. Thus, the Bible itself places the Rapture, which takes place *at the last trumpet,* at the end of the Tribulation. The other thing that stands irrefutable is that the resurrection in Revelation 20 is the "first resurrection" (verse 5). If it is the *first,* there could not be a resurrection seven years earlier, at the beginning of the Tribulation. To me the Scriptures are very clear that the Rapture will occur at the end of the Tribulation—which means that Christians will go through the Tribulation.

Let me hasten to add that I am not trying to ridicule those who hold a different position. I simply cannot reconcile their position to the Scriptures.

We next looked at the question of whether or not we are living in the end times—the end times being the last seven years of this present age, plus some period of time prior to them. Thus, the real question is: is the Tribulation getting near? We saw that no one can give a definitive answer to this, because *no one* knows the day and the hour of our Lord's return, except the Father Himself (Matthew 24:36). However, the Holy Spirit, on a worldwide basis, appears to be giving a sense of urgency to Christians and a sense that we are indeed living in the last days of this present age. God is raising up many prophets and spokesmen who are proclaiming that these are the end times.

If one believes, first, that Christians will go through the Tribulation, and second, that we are living in the end times, this will change his entire life. It will change his value system, his dedication to God, and the amount of physical and spiritual preparation that he is making for the events of the Tribulation.

Physical Preparation

I was severely tempted to remove the chapters on physical preparation from this book and to put them in a separate book.

Yet the Lord would not allow me to do this. He showed me afresh that you cannot separate the physical and spiritual aspects of a man or of his life. These two aspects are intricately interrelated and intertwined. Christ spent as much time healing people's physical bodies and providing them food and wine, as He did ministering to their souls. It is evident that our Master felt both physical and spiritual needs were very important. The reason that I debated leaving out that section was that I felt some of the "spiritual" leaders in America would object to it and therefore not recommend this book to their followers. Leaving those chapters in may mean that I will sell fewer copies, and yet I am sure that God had me to write the book in this fashion, because of His love for His precious children and His concern for both our physical and spiritual needs.

If one becomes truly concerned about the physical well-being of his family, loved ones, friends, and brothers and sisters in Christ during a time of disaster, there may be some things that God would lead him to do in preparation for such a time. God is not going to lead everyone to do the same thing and therefore each of us must seek God's face and do only those things that He directs us to do. (However, we must be very careful to do *everything* that God does direct us to do.)

Since there is a nuclear war on the horizon, one of the things God might lead us to do is to make some preparation for this war, *before* it occurs. There are things that can be done with no cost at all, such as having an emergency plan for the family, or having big plastic garbage sacks in a desk drawer at the office. Further, for this and some of the other catastrophes that will occur, it is very important to have some water stored, since water lines are likely to be inoperative. Water can be stored by using Sparkletts bottles, filling up empty bleach bottles, or empty milk containers and so on. The storage of some food is also highly desirable, but less important than the water. If you want to store food, you can simply have a few weeks' supply of regular grocery store food on hand. This extra stock can be built up gradually by buying eight days' food each week. Specifically for the event of a nuclear war, something that could be done, in most cases, is to make some type of a shelter for protection from radiation. This may be cement blocks piled up in the corner of a garage, a "root cellar" dug in one corner of the backyard, or some such thing. The digging of a root cellar costs no money. You could cover it with boards or scrap lumber and pile the dirt that has been dug out back over the top. I realize that many people will respond, "But the neighbors would laugh at me." What makes you think you are better than Noah? If they do laugh at you, or inquire, it might be a good chance to witness to them about the wonderful saving love of Jesus.

Concerning preparation for the famines that are coming, God can lead individuals differently. Some He may lead to store up a large amount of dehydrated food, others He might lead to begin a garden, and others to develop a hydroponics food factory. Again I must emphasize that any food that He may lead you to store or to produce belongs to Him. He may lead you to give it all away, to share some of it, or to keep all of it for your family. Do not greedily clutch onto it, but be obedient to whatever He tells you to do with it.

Preparations made in order to survive a nuclear war and famines are also valuable provisions for the inevitable earth upheavals. In addition, we saw that there are some things you can do specifically to help endure an earthquake in a much better manner. Again, having some water stored would be most important, but also having fire extinguishers on hand, strapping the hot water heater to the wall, and wiring any tall heavy objects of furniture to the walls would make life much easier when an earthquake hits.

I believe that the roughest time of all will come when Christians can no longer buy or sell. At that point they will not be able to buy electricity, sewerage usage, garbage collection, food, clothes, or water; neither will they be able to rent a house or apartment. When that day comes, I believe that unfortunately many Christians will weaken and accept the mark of the beast, so that they and their loved ones can survive. God strongly warns us against accepting the mark of the beast and His Word tells us that it is far better to die for Christ. Provisions need to be made in order to be able to live in that environment of not being able to buy or sell. God may lead some to move to a farm. Others He may lead to stay right in the middle of the city, giving them the assurance that He will provide their necessities by miraculous intervention in times of crisis. The important thing is to *do* what God tells you to, and to *be* where He wants you to be.

In the final chapter on physical survival, we talked about the "tyranny of the urgent." After reading this book many people will feel that God wants them to do some of these things, but the tendency is to never get around to doing them. If God tells you to do any of these things, *do not delay*. Make a schedule, have a plan, and actually begin to do what God is directing you to do. Once you have been obedient in making the preparations that He has laid on your heart, rest in His hands and in His care. Anything else that you need He will provide, even if in a supernatural, miraculous way. (Continue to bring your state of preparedness before the Lord in prayer, in case He ever wants you to add to, or to revise, your preparations.)

Spiritual Preparation

Although it is important to obey God by making any physical preparations that He leads us to make, we saw that preparing spiritually for great tribulation and persecution is even more crucial. God has clearly said that there is going to be an outpouring of His Spirit in the last days. I believe that we are seeing that outpouring today. Within the last few years we have witnessed many miraculous events. Those Christian leaders who are putting down the recent charismatic revival, and are trying to convince people that the gifts of the Holy Spirit were only for the first generation, I believe are misleading Christians today. There is no way that we could refuse to receive the mark of the beast and survive the Tribulation, without the supernatural power of the Holy Spirit.

If you have not been filled with the Holy Spirit, and had the excitement and joy of the Holy Spirit totally taking over your body, mind, tongue, and heart, I would encourage you to ask God for this experience and I know that He will give it to you. He commanded us to "be filled with the Spirit" (Ephesians 5:18). He certainly would not command us to do something, and then withhold that very thing from us, would He? Ask and you *will* receive (Matthew 7:7)!

Being filled with the Spirit is not enough. God wants us to go on to the Holy of Holies and be overcomers. Not only will we need to live supernaturally, even commanding nature when necessary, but we are going to be more directly involved in a spiritual warfare. When Satan unleashes his full fury on the inhabitants of the earth, we will not be able to stand against him in our own strength. We *must* have God's supernatural power flowing through us in order to combat the enemy, and we also need to be aware that there are supernatural beings in God's army (angels) warring side by side with us. Remember that one man *can* conquer (and *has* conquered) an entire army! If a mere handful of soldiers or looters were to come against you, you could easily control them by God's supernatural power, if He so led you.

The Tribulation will end with the Rapture of the saints, who will be caught up to meet Christ in the air as He is coming back to destroy the forces of evil in the battle of Armageddon. After this final battle, in which the beast and the false prophet will be cast into the lake of fire and Satan will be bound, the saints will reign with Christ for a thousand years on this earth. Through the events of the Tribulation, God will have purged this planet earth and made it ready for the glorious reign of our Lord, Jesus Christ. Now let's take a look at what will happen at the end of this wonderful, peaceful Millennium.

TIME-OUT FOR JUDGMENT

By the end of the thousand years (the Millennium) there will be many people born on the earth, who will be the descendants of those who were alive at the end of the Tribulation. These people will never have been tempted by Satan. For some reason, unknown to us, at the end of a thousand years Satan will be released and allowed to tempt them. Once again Satan will gather an army and attack Jerusalem, the camp of the saints.

Fire will come down from heaven and devour Satan and this army. We find this recorded in Revelation 20:

> 7 And when the thousand years are completed, Satan will be released from his prison,
>
> 8 and will come out to deceive the nations which are in the four corners of the earth, Gog and Magog, to gather them together for the war; the number of them is like the sand of the seashore.
>
> 9 And they came up on the broad plain of the earth and surrounded the camp of the saints and the beloved city, and fire came down from heaven and devoured them.
>
> 10 And the devil who deceived them was thrown into the lake of fire and brimstone, where the beast and the false prophet are also; and they will be tormented day and night forever and ever.
>
> 11 And I saw a great white throne and Him who sat upon it, from whose presence earth and heaven fled away, and no place was found for them.
>
> 12 And I saw the dead, the great and the small, standing before the throne, and books were opened; and another book was opened, which is *the book* of life; and the dead were judged from the things which were written in the books, according to their deeds.
>
> 13 And the sea gave up the dead which were in it, and death and Hades gave up the dead which were in them; and they were judged, every one *of them* according to their deeds.
>
> 14 And death and Hades were thrown into the lake of fire. This is the second death, the lake of fire.
>
> 15 And if anyone's name was not found written in the book of life, he was thrown into the lake of fire.

We also see in this passage the great judgment of God. He will sit on a white throne and judge all of the dead. After this judgment, death, hell, the devil, and everyone whose name was not written in the book of life will be thrown into the lake of fire. Remember that *God* is in charge of the lake of fire—not Satan. Satan will simply be one of the beings thrown into it.

I have heard many preachers say that everyone will spend eternity either in "heaven or hell." The truth is that no one will spend eternity in *either* heaven *or* hell. We just read that the unsaved will spend eternity in the lake of fire, not in hell. Now let's see where the Christians will spend eternity.

ETERNITY ON A BRAND NEW EARTH

Verse 11 of Revelation 20 tells us that at the time of this "great white throne judgment," the earth and heaven will flee away from the presence of God. This means that the existing heaven and the existing earth will be destroyed. This is more clearly detailed in 2 Peter 3:

> 10 But the day of the Lord will come like a thief, in which the heavens will pass away with a roar and the elements will be destroyed with intense heat, and the earth and its works will be burned up.
>
> 11 Since all these things are to be destroyed in this way, what sort of people ought you to be in holy conduct and godliness,
>
> 12 looking for and hastening the coming of the day of God, on account of which the heavens will be destroyed by burning, and the elements will melt with intense heat!
>
> 13 But according to His promise we are looking for new heavens and a new earth, in which righteousness dwells.

This tells us *how* the existing heavens and earth will be destroyed in the day of the Lord. It will be with intense heat, and the elements will essentially be dissolved. I am so glad that the Bible does not end at this point! God is going to create something fantastically new and wonderful, just for those whose names are written in the Lamb's book of life.

God is going to create a *brand new earth*—one without a sea. Will this earth be desolate and void of vegetation and animals? According to Scriptures, it will be as one giant garden. Imagine the most beautiful possible earth: there would be vegetables, fruit and flowers growing all over, it would eternally be spring, there would be no nighttime, nothing poisonous, and nothing harmful, and there would likely be beautiful, gentle animals to play with. Imagine that *kind* of an earth. Go on, imagine it. Got it? Well that is junk! What God is going to create is infinitely better than anything we can imagine. ". . . eye hath not seen nor ear heard, neither have entered into the heart of man, the things which God hath prepared for them that love him" (1 Corinthians 2:9 *KJV*). Revelation 21 tells us of God's new creation:

1 And I saw a new heaven and a new earth; for the first heaven and the first earth passed away, and there is no longer *any* sea.

2 And I saw the holy city, new Jerusalem, coming down out of heaven from God, made ready as bride adorned for her husband.

3 And I heard a loud voice from the throne, saying, "Behold, the tabernacle of God is among men, and He shall dwell among them, and they shall be His people, and God Himself shall be among them,

4 and He shall wipe away every tear from their eyes; and there shall no longer be *any* death; there shall no longer be *any* mourning, or crying, or pain; the first things have passed away."

I do not think that the new heaven and the new earth, and all that is within them, will be physical in the same sense as we know physical things today. They will be of a higher level of reality, just like Christ's resurrected body was real, but of a higher realm of reality than that which we presently experience.

Revelation 22 has more to say about life on this new earth where we will spend eternity:

1 And he showed me a river of the water of life, clear as crystal, coming from the throne of God and of the Lamb,

2 in the middle of its street. And on either side of the river was the tree of life, bearing twelve *kinds of* fruit, yielding its fruit every month; and the leaves of the tree were for the healing of the nations.

3 And there shall no longer be any curse; and the throne of God and of the Lamb shall be in it, and His bond-servants shall serve Him;

4 and they shall see His face, and His name *shall be* on their foreheads.

5 And there shall no longer be *any* night; and they shall not have need of the light of a lamp nor the light of the sun, because the Lord God shall illumine them; and they shall reign forever and ever.

Isn't that exciting! We will spend eternity, not in heaven, but on a new earth, created just for us so that we can be with the Lord forever! Halleluia! Praise the Lord!

Revelation 22:5 says that we shall reign with Him "forever and ever." I recently heard an interesting definition of eternity: If a bird from outer space were to come to the earth once every thousand years and carry away one grain of sand, when the earth was completely gone, eternity would be no closer to an end than when the bird first started. This wonderful, joyful life—

our blessed hope—in which we shall see Christ face to face and know Him as our Bridegroom, will go on for time without end.

THE HAPPY UN-ENDING . . .

.

"For as many as are led by the Spirit of God, they are the sons of God." (KJV)

—Paul

APPENDICES

TABLE OF CONTENTS

APPENDIXES

APPENDIX A

HOW TO BECOME A CHRISTIAN

If you are reading this I am assuming that you are not sure that you have received Jesus Christ as your personal Savior. Not only is it possible to know this for sure, but God *wants* you to know. This is what 1 John 5:11-13 has to say:

11 And the witness is this, that God has given us eternal life, and this life is in His Son.

12 He who has the Son has the life; he who does not have the Son does not have the life.

13 These things I have written to you who believe in the name of the Son of God, in order that you may know that you have eternal life.

These things are written to us who believe in the name of the Son of God, so that we can *know* that we have eternal life. It is not a "guess so," or "hope so" or "maybe so" situation. It is so that we can *know* for certain that we have eternal life. If you do not have this confidence, please read on.

In order to get to the point of knowing that we have eternal life, we need to first go back and review some basic principles. First, it is important to note that all things that God created (the stars, trees, animals, and so on) are doing exactly what they were created to do, except man. Isaiah 43 indicates why God created us:

7 Every one who is called by My name,
And whom I have created for My glory,
Whom I have formed even whom I have made.

Here it says that humans were created to glorify God. I am sure that neither you nor I have glorified God all of our lives in everything that we have done. This gives us our first clue as to what "sin" is. We find more about it in Romans 3:

23   for all have sinned and fall short of the glory of God.

This says that we have all sinned and that we all fall short of the purpose for which we were created—that of glorifying God. I have an even simpler definition of sin. I believe that sin is "living independent of God." A young person out of high school can choose which college to attend. If he makes this decision apart from God, it is "sin." This was the basic problem in the garden of Eden. Satan tempted Eve to eat the fruit of the tree of "the knowledge of good and evil." He said that if she would do this, she would know good from evil and would be wise like God. This would mean that she could make her own decisions and would not have to rely on God's wisdom and guidance. Since you and I fit in the category of living independent of God and not glorifying Him in everything we do, we need to look at what the results of this sin are.

First let me ask you what "wages" are. After thinking about it, because you probably receive wages from your job, you will probably come up with a definition something like "wages are what you get paid for what you do." That is a good answer. Now let's see what the Bible has to say concerning this, in Romans 6:

23   For the wages of sin is death, but the free gift of God is eternal life in Christ Jesus our Lord.

Here we see that the wages of sin is death—spiritual, eternal death. Death is what we get paid for the sin that we do. Yet this passage also gives us the other side of the coin: that is, that through Jesus Christ we can freely have eternal life, instead of eternal death. Isn't that wonderful?!

But let's return for a moment to this death penalty that the people without Christ have hanging over their heads, because of the sin that they live in. In the Old Testament God made a rule: "The soul who sins will die" (Ezekiel 18:4). If we were able to live a perfect, sinless life, we could make it to heaven on our own. If we live anything less than a perfect life, according to God's rule, we will not make it to heaven, but instead will be sentenced to death. All through the Bible we find no one living a good enough life to make it to heaven.

This brings us to the place where Jesus Christ fits into this whole picture. His place was beautifully illustrated to me when I was considering receiving Christ as my Savior, by a story about a judge in a small town.

In this small town, the newspapermen were against the judge and wanted to get him out of office. A case was coming up before the judge, concerning a vagrant—a drunken bum—who happened to have been a fraternity brother of the judge when they were at college. The newspapermen thought that this was their chance. If the judge let the vagrant off easy, the headlines would read, "Judge Shows Favoritism to Old Fraternity Brother." If the judge gave the vagrant the maximum penalty, the headlines would read, "Hardhearted Judge Shows No Mercy to Old Fraternity Brother." Either way they had him. The judge heard the case and gave the vagrant the maximum penalty of thirty days or $300 fine.

The judge then stood up, took off his robe, laid it down on his chair, walked down in front of the bench and put his arm around the shoulders of his old fraternity brother. He told him that as judge, in order to uphold the law, he had to give him the maximum penalty, because he was guilty. But because he cared about him, he wanted to pay the fine for him. So the judge took out his wallet and handed his old fraternity brother $300.

For God to be "just," He has to uphold the law that says "the soul who sins will die." On the other hand, because He loves us He wants to pay that death penalty for us. I cannot pay the death penalty for you because I have a death penalty of my own that I have to worry about, since I, too, have sinned. If I were sinless, I could die in your place. I guess God could have sent down millions of sinless beings to die for us. But what God chose to do was to send down *one* Person, who was equal in value, in God's eyes, to all of the people who will ever live, and yet who would remain sinless. Jesus Christ died physically and spiritually in order to pay the death penalty for you and me. The blood of Christ washes away all of our sins, and with it the death penalty that resulted from our sin.

The judge's old fraternity brother could have taken the $300 and said thank you, or he could have told the judge to keep his money and that he would do it on his own. Similarly, each person can thank God for allowing Christ to die in his place and receive Christ as his own Savior, or he can tell God to keep His payment and that he will make it on his own. What you do with that question determines where you will spend eternity.

Referring to Christ, John 1:12 says:

12 But as many as received Him, to them He gave the right to become children of God, *even* **to those who believe in His name,**

John 3:16 says:

16 "For God so loved the world, that He gave His only begotten Son, that whoever believes in Him should not perish but have eternal life.

Here we see that if we believe in Christ we won't perish, but we will have everlasting life and the right to become children of God. Right now you can tell God that you believe in Christ as the Son of God, that you are sorry for your sins and that you want to turn from them. You can tell Him that you want to accept Christ's payment for your sins, and yield your life to be controlled by Christ and the Holy Spirit. (You must accept Christ as your Savior *and your MASTER.)*

If you pray such a prayer, Christ will come and dwell within your heart and you will *know for sure* that you have *eternal life.*

If you have any questions about what you have just read, I would encourage you to go to someone that you know, who really knows Jesus Christ as his Savior, and ask him for help and guidance. After you receive Christ, I would encourage you to become part of a group of believers in Christ who study the Scriptures together, worship God together and have a real love relationship with each other. This group (body of believers) can help nurture you and build you up in your new faith in Jesus Christ.

If you have received Christ, as a result of reading these pages, I would love to hear from you. My address is at the end of this book.

Welcome to the family of God.

Jim McKeever

APPENDIX B

POINTS FOR THE

PRE-TRIBULATION

RAPTURE THEORY

The pre-Tribulation Rapture theory is not without any basis; otherwise, intelligent men of God would not have subscribed to it. There are three passages of Scripture that might tend to lead one to conclude that the Rapture will occur at the beginning of the Tribulation. These are:

2 Thessalonians 2:1-10

Revelation 3:10

Matthew 24:42-44

Even though these are the most difficult passages to reconcile to a post-Tribulation Rapture, I believe that the Holy Spirit has given me some insights that might be helpful. I should also add that to build a belief that one will escape the Tribulation on these three passages, none of which are direct and explicit, I believe is building on shaky or sandy ground. Without further ado, let's look at each of these passages.

2 THESSALONIANS 2:1-10 —
THE RESTRAINER REMOVED

Those who hold to the pre-Tribulation theory believe that this passage implies that the Holy Spirit will be removed from the earth before the Antichrist appears. They reason that if the Holy Spirit is removed, the Christians must also be removed. As you read this passage, you will notice that the Holy Spirit is not mentioned directly. Before commenting further, let's read these verses in 2 Thessalonians 2:

> 1 Now we request you, brethren, with regard to the coming of our Lord Jesus Christ, and our gathering together to Him,
>
> 2 that you may not be quickly shaken from your composure or be disturbed either by a spirit or a message or a letter as if from us, to the effect that the day of the Lord has come.
>
> 3 Let no one in any way deceive you for *it will not come* unless the apostasy comes first, and the man of lawlessness is revealed, the son of destruction,
>
> 4 who opposes and exalts himself above every so-called god or object of worship, so that he takes his seat in the temple of God, displaying himself as being God.
>
> 5 Do you not remember that while I was still with you, I was telling you these things?
>
> 6 And you know what restrains him now, so that in his time he may be revealed.
>
> 7 For the mystery of lawlessness is already at work; only he who now restrains *will do so* until he is taken out of the way.
>
> 8 And then that lawless one will be revealed whom the Lord will slay with the breath of His mouth and bring to an end by the appearance of His coming;
>
> 9 *that is,* the one whose coming is in accord with the activity of Satan, with all power and signs and false wonders,
>
> 10 and with all the deception of wickedness for those who perish, because they did not receive the love of the truth so as to be saved.

To begin with, the Coming of our Lord mentioned in verse 1 here is the same Second Coming of Christ referred to in 2 Thessalonians 1:6-10. It says here clearly that when Jesus Christ returns from heaven, it will be in flaming fire, dealing out retribution to those who do not know God. Thus, we are talking about His return at the end of the Tribulation. Verse 3 above says that this will not occur before two things happen:

1.   Apostasy comes

2.   The man of lawlessness is revealed

Verse 7 is the key. It says that the mystery of lawlessness is already at work, only he who restrains will do so until he is taken out of the way. I do not believe that the restrainer is the Holy Spirit nor that He will be taken during the Tribulation. One reason for this is that there will be people who become Christians *during* the Tribulation. The Bible clearly says that no one can come to Christ unless the Spirit draws him. We also see the Holy Spirit empowering the two witnesses *during* the Tribulation. Thus we must conclude that the Holy Spirit is alive and well here on planet earth during that time.

In his book, *The Church and The Tribulation* (published by Zondervan Publishing House), Gundry devotes an entire chapter (8) to this passage. He points out that various writers have felt the restrainer was God, the Antichrist or Satan. Some believe that what is now restrained is the appearance of the Antichrist, or the mystery of lawlessness. What Gundry is pointing out is that God's power is today restraining the Antichrist or possibly Satan is doing the restraining. In Revelation 7:2-3 we see God acting as a restrainer. Someday the restraint will be lifted and lawlessness and the lawless one will come forth in full force upon the earth. There is little reason to think that the restrainer is the Holy Spirit. I certainly could not subscribe to a theological system that "guesses" that the restrainer is the Holy Spirit and that someday He will be removed from the earth.

REVELATION 3:10 –
KEPT FROM THE HOUR OF TRIAL

Revelation 3:10 is part of Christ's letter to the church of Philadelphia. Much of this letter was written specifically to the Christians at Philadelphia and may or may not be applicable to all Christians of all time. Christ says this in Revelation 3:

> **10** "**Because you have kept the word of My perseverance, I also will keep you from the hour of testing, that** *hour* **which is about to come upon the whole world, to test those who dwell upon the earth.**

The problem here is that it says that He will keep us from the "hour" of testing (or temptation). Ladd, on pages 85 and

86 of his book, *The Blessed Hope,* (mentioned in Chapter 2) comments so beautisley on these verses that I would like to present his thoughts:

"The language of this verse, taken by itself, could be interpreted to teach complete escape from the coming hour of Tribulation. The language is, 'I will keep thee *out of* the hour of trial' *(tereso ek).*

"This language, however, neither asserts nor demands the idea of bodily removal from the midst of the coming trial. This is proven by the fact that precisley the same words are used by our Lord in His prayer that God would keep His disciples 'out of the evil' *(tereses ek tou ponerou,* Jn. 17:15). In our Lord's prayer, there is no idea of bodily removal of the disciples from the evil world but of preservation from the power of evil even when they are in its very presence. A similar thought occurs in Galatians 1:4, where we read that Christ gave Himself for our sins to deliver us from (literally, 'out of,' *ek)* this present evil age. This does not refer to a physical removal from the age but to deliverance from its power and control. 'This age' will not pass away until the return of Christ.

"In the same way, the promise of Revelation 3:10 of being kept *ek* the hour of trial need not be a promise of a removal from the very physical presence of tribulation. It is a promise of preservation and deliverance in and through it. This verse neither asserts that the Rapture is to occur before the Tribulation, nor does its interpretation require us to think that such a removal is intended."

Therefore, I conclude that either these verses applied just to the church at Philadelphia, and not to us, or as Ladd points out, they do not imply our removal from the scene.

MATTHEW 24:42-44 —
THE LORD'S COMING WILL BE A SURPRISE

The suddenness of the return of Jesus Christ, or its surprise aspect, is mentioned in several places in the Scriptures. I have simply chosen the one in Matthew 24 as an example of this:

42 "Therefore be on the alert, for you do not know which day your Lord is coming.
43 "But be sure of this, that if the head of the house had known at what time of the night the thief was coming, he would have been on the alert and would not have allowed his house to be broken into.

44 "For this reason you be ready too; for the Son of Man is coming at an hour when you do not think *He will.*

The thrust of this admonition in Matthew 24 is that we should always be on the alert, watchful and ready for the return of Jesus Christ. I believe that this applies more to us today than to any Christians who have ever lived.

However, the problem in reconciling this to a post-Tribulation Rapture is that we would know that Christ was coming back seven years after the Tribulation began, and therefore it wouldn't be sudden or take us by surprise. This could possibly be true if we were to know exactly when the Tribulation started and if we knew for sure that it was going to be exactly seven years in length. However, I do not think that we will know exactly when the Tribulation begins. Christians should be able to discern the times and seasons and possibly get a rough idea as to when Christ might return. Remember, Noah wasn't surprised by the flood and Lot wasn't surprised by the destruction of Sodom, although they did not know exactly when these things were coming. However, to the vast masses of people on the earth, His return at the end of the Tribulation will be like a "bolt out of the blue."

We Christians will be like the virgins with oil in their lamps waiting for the bridegroom. They did not know exactly the hour when he was coming. They did know the season and they had to be ready continuously. I believe that this is a beautiful example of what we should be like as we await Christ's return.

Summary and Conclusion

I have dealt with these three passages very briefly. If you wish to pursue the matter, I would recommend purchasing and reading the two books that I have referred to in this appendix.

Let me conclude by saying that the three passages that we have dealt with here at best might very *obliquely suggest* that there *might* be a Rapture at the beginning of the Tribulation. However, weighting this against the clear and explicit statements that we will be transformed at the last trumpet and that the resurrection in Revelation 20 is the first resurrection, leads me to very comfortably conclude that the Rapture will take place at the end of the Tribulation.

To rest your future, and that of your loved ones, on these three passages, hoping that they indicate that you will be "snatched away" and not go through the Tribulation, I believe is unwise. I do not see the support in the Scriptures for such a position.

APPENDIX C

MEET THE AUTHOR

Jim McKeever is an international consulting economist, lecturer, author, world traveler, and Bible teacher. His financial consultations are utilized by scores of individuals from all over the world who seek his advice on investments, international affairs, and physical survival. He has spoken at monetary, gold and tax haven conferences in London, Zurich, and Hong Kong, as well as all over the North American continent.

Mr. McKeever is the editor and major contributing writer of *McKeever's Individual Strategy Letter (MISL)*. He was formerly editor of *Inflation Survival Letter*. In addition to his extensive economic and financial background, he has "lived off the land" for a year on Catalina, hunting, fishing, raising his own food and building his own cabin. He is one of the few men who has an in-depth knowledge and actual experience in both financial and physical survival.

For five years after completing his academic work, Mr. McKeever was with a consulting firm which specialized in financial investments in petroleum. Those who were following his counsel back in 1954 heavily invested in oil.

For more than ten years he was with IBM, where he held several key management positions. With IBM, he consulted with top executives of many major corporations in America, helping them solve financial, control and information problems. He has received many awards from IBM, including the "Key Man Award." He is widely known in the computer field for his books and articles on management, management control and information sciences.

After leaving IBM, Mr. McKeever founded and was president of his own consulting firm. In addition to directing the activities of more than 100 employees, he personally gave consultation to the executives of client organizations. In this capacity, he was a consultant to, and provided computer processing for such organizations as Campus Crusade for Christ, World Vision, Gospel Broadcasting Association, and Nicky Cruz Outreach. His counsel was sought by the executives of these and many other Christian organizations.

In 1972, Mr. McKeever sold his interest in this consulting firm and resigned as president in order to devote his "business" time to writing, speaking and consulting in the economic and survival field.

In addition to this outstanding business background, Mr. McKeever is an ordained minister. He has been a Baptist evangelist, pastor of Catalina Bible Church for three and a half years (while still with IBM) and a frequent speaker at Christian conferences. He has the gift of teaching and an in-depth knowledge of the Bible.

Mr. McKeever is founder and president of Ministries of Vision, which is a nonprofit organization established under the leading of the Holy Spirit to minister to the body of Christ, by the traveling ministry of many anointed men of God, through books, cassettes, seminars and conferences. The various ministries of Ministries of Vision are supported by the joyous gifts of those who are ministered to.

CHRISTIANS WILL GO THROUGH THE TRIBULATION
And how to prepare for it

by Jim McKeever

Now that you have read this thought-provoking book, why not send copies to your loved ones? You could be doing them a lifesaving favor by giving them a copy of this book.

If you would like to give away some copies, we could mail them directly to your friends, with a card saying that the book is a gift from you, or we could send them all to you to distribute personally.

- -

Omega Publications
P. O. Box 4130
Medford, OR 97501

I am enclosing the amount shown below for additional copies of *CHRISTIANS WILL GO THROUGH THE TRIBULATION:*

( ) _____ Copies of hardback at $10.95 each = $ _____

( ) _____ Copies of softback at $5.95 each = $ _____

Please add $.50 per book for postage and handling. $ _____

Send these copies to: TOTAL $ _____

My Name _____

My Address _____

City, State _____ Zip _____

Gift to: _____

Address _____

City, State _____ Zip _____

Gift to: _____

Address _____

City, State _____ Zip _____

Gift to: _____

Address _____

City, State _____ Zip _____

Gift to: _____

Address _____

City, State _____ Zip _____

SPEAKING ENGAGEMENTS BY MR. McKEEVER

As a minister, Mr. McKeever, president of Ministries of Vision, is available to speak at churches, Christian conferences, and other Christian gatherings, about the things contained in this book and many other significant Christian topics. The Holy Spirit has blessed his ministry and has anointed him as a gifted teacher and speaker.

As an international consulting economist, Mr. McKeever is in demand as a speaker in economic, monetary, investment, and tax conferences all over the world. He has spoken at conferences in London, Zurich, and Hong Kong, as well as all over the North American continent. He is also available to conduct one- or two-day private seminars for small groups of investors.

Jim McKeever
Ministries of Vision
P. O. Box 4130
Medford, OR 97501

Please send me information about:

( ) Having Mr. McKeever speak at our church or Christian conference.

( ) Having Mr. McKeever speak at an economic or investment conference.

( ) Having Mr. McKeever conduct a private seminar for our group.

Name _____

Address _____

City, State _____ Zip _____

THE ALMIGHTY
AND THE
DOLLAR

This is the title of a one-day seminar sponsored by Ministries of Vision that Mr. McKeever and some of his Christian associates conduct for churches and Christian organizations. In it are discussed such vital topics for the Christian as:

* Stewardship of your assets as well as your income.
* How to protect your investments from inflation.
* Estate planning and making a will.
* Insurance.
* Family budgeting and banking.
* Investments in stocks and bonds.
* Gold and silver investments.
* Real estate investments.
* Personal investment strategy.
* Physical preparation for troubled times.
* Planning and goal setting for Christian families.
* Developing a plan of action to achieve these goals.
* A Christian's attitude toward all of this.

This seminar can be of personal benefit to many members of the body of Christ, and can collectively benefit the local body of believers. Since a limited number of these seminars can be conducted each year, please give prayerful consideration to it before requesting one.

- -

Jim McKeever
Ministries of Vision
P. O. Box 4130
Medford, OR 97501

Please send me information about conducting the seminar "THE ALMIGHTY and the DOLLAR" for my church or Christian organization.

Name_____

Address _____

City, State _____ Zip _____

Organization _____

NOW YOU CAN UNDERSTAND
THE BOOK OF REVELATION

By Jim McKeever

At last, a book to help you study through Revelation! You will want to get a copy and read it thoroughly.

In both the first and last chapters of Revelation there is a blessing promised to those who read and *heed* the words contained in Revelation. Jim's book concentrates on the "heed" aspect. How do you *heed*—incorporate into your daily life—the things found in the book of Revelation? God commanded us to do this, so there must be some things in there that we need to be practicing daily.

CONTENTS OF THE BOOK

1. An Encounter With Jesus (Revelation 1)
2. The Letters to the Churches (Revelation 2 & 3)
3. How They Praise in Heaven (Revelation 4 & 5)
4. The Rapture and the Tribulation
5. The Seven Seals and the 144,000 (Revelation 6 & 7)
6. The First Six Trumpets (Revelation 8 & 9)
7. The Little Scroll, the Two Witnesses and the Seventh Trumpet (Revelation 10 & 11)
8. The Woman, the Man Child and the Two Beasts (Revelation 12 & 13)
9. The Second 144,000, the Three Angels, and the Two Harvests (Revelation 14)
10. The Seven Angels and the Seven Bowls of Wrath (Revelation 15 & 16)
11. Mystery Babylon (Revelation 17 & 18)
12. The Return of Christ and the Millennium (Revelation 19 & 20)
13. The New Heaven and New Earth (Revelation 21 & 22)
14. How to "Heed" this Revelation

In times past, understanding and heeding the book of Revelation was almost optional for a Christian. We believe now that the book of Revelation has become critical and essential to our understanding of what is happening in the world today, where we are going, and what we should do.

Get your copy of this exciting new book now!

- -

Omega Publications
P.O. Box 4130
Medford, OR 97501

( ) _____ Copies of hardback at $10.95 each = $ _____

( ) _____ Copies of softback at $5.95 each = $ _____

Please add $.50 per book for postage and handling. $ _____

Please send to: TOTAL $ _____

Name _____

Address _____

City _____ State _____ Zip _____

ONLY ONE WORD
by Jim McKeever

BOOKLET

"If you picked up a hitchhiker and led him to Christ, and in parting company you only had time to give him one piece of advice to encourage a good start in his Christian life . . . what would that one word be?"

This booklet by Jim McKeever answers this vital question. Read what Bob Munger (producer of such movies as "Born Again") had to say about it:

"Only One Word was one of the most helpful insights I have ever gotten from Christian literature in 25 years as a Christian. This article is must reading for every Christian leader in the world."

— —

Ministries of Vision
P.O. Box 4130
Medford, OR 97501

Please send me:

_____	Copies of *Only One Word* (for a contribution of $1 each)	= $_____
	Additional gift for Ministries of Vision	$_____
	Please add $.25 postage and handling per booklet.	$_____
	Total Contribution	$_____

Name _____

Address _____

City _____ State _____ Zip _____

CLOSE ENCOUNTERS OF THE HIGHEST KIND
by Jim McKeever

This is another book by Jim McKeever. Every believer will want to read this book and give copies to his non-Christian friends. After getting their attention with UFO's, this book introduces them to the spiritual world and encounters with God in the Old Testament. It then shows them step by step how they, today, can have an encounter with God by receiving Jesus Christ as Savior and Master.

You owe it to your non-Christian friends and relatives to provide them with a copy of this exciting book. (It would make an excellent Christmas gift.) They will not be able to put it down and yet, at the same time, they will have a clear presentation of the Gospel of Jesus Christ.

CONTENTS OF THE BOOK

Please read the titles of the exciting chapters and you will see why both believers and nonbelievers will be interested:

Chapter Titles

1. Man's Desire for Close Encounters
2. Close Encounters with Terrestrial Beings
3. Close Encounters of the First Kind—Sightings of UFO's
4. Close Encounters of the Second Kind—Evidence of UFO's
5. Close Encounters with Extraterrestrial Beings
6. Close Encounters with the Spirit World
7. Close Encounters with Satan
8. Close Encounters with God
9. How You Can Experience a Miracle
10. How You Can Have Supernatural Power
11. The Close Encounter of the Highest Kind
12. There are Close Encounters in Your Future

Chapter 9, "How You Can Experience a Miracle," discusses the miracle of the new birth, and how one can experience it. In Chapter 10, "How You Can Have Supernatural Power," the author discusses the filling by the Holy Spirit and the power that comes from this to live an abundant life today.

If you want to know what the "Close Encounter of the Highest Kind" is, which is discussed in Chapter 11, you will have to read the book to find out.

THE SEVEN KINDS OF CLOSE ENCOUNTERS

CE 1 — Sighting
CE 2 — Evidence
CE 3 — Contact
CE 4 — Communication

CE 5 — Commitment
CE 6 — Transformation
CE 7 — Union

The author then discusses these seven levels of close encounters in their relationship between two human beings, between a human and extraterrestrial beings (if they exist), spiritual beings, Satan and finally, God through His Son, Jesus Christ.

There is much about UFO's and the demonic world in this book that Christians *need to know*.

- -

Omega Publications
P.O. Box 4130, Medford, OR 97501

Please send me information on Jim McKeever's book CLOSE ENCOUNTERS OF THE HIGHEST KIND.

Name _____

Address _____

City _____ State _____ Zip _____